PRAISE FOR *NAVIGATING SUSTAINABILITY DATA*

'Sherry Madera poses the simple questions that many directors are too nervous to ask. *Navigating Sustainability Data* proceeds to answer them in plain English without condescension. A remarkable achievement in a complex area.'
Sir Douglas Flint CBE, Chairman, abrdn, and former Group Chairman, HSBC Holdings

'By demonstrating the potential for ESG data to improve organizational performance, *Navigating Sustainability Data* will help companies become more resilient in an era pregnant with a plethora of cascading and non-linear risks. Sherry Madera takes the reader systematically and critically through the key challenges and opportunities associated with ESG data and where it will go next.'
Ben Caldecott, Founder Director of the Oxford Sustainable Finance Group at the University of Oxford Smith School of Enterprise and the Environment

'The future of our planet is under threat, yet too often business leaders do not know how to respond. *Navigating Sustainability Data* explores the urgency of this dilemma and why sustainability and responsibility go hand in hand. Sherry Madera makes a compelling case for the benefits of understanding the complex sustainability-data landscape and why it matters, offering practical steps through which leaders can demonstrate stewardship of our precious planet today, while also building relevant organizations for tomorrow'.
Katherine Garrett-Cox CBE, Chair of Board of Trustees, CDP

'Highly recommended: an enlightening work written by an expert practitioner and entrepreneur. Data outlining sustainability should be simple, clear and actionable. This book is.'
Paul Dickinson, Founder, CDP, and Chair of the Trustees of ShareAction

T0293310

Navigating Sustainability Data

How organizations can use ESG data
to secure their future

Sherry Madera

KoganPage

Publisher's note
Every possible effort has been made to ensure that the information contained in this book is accurate at the time of going to press, and the publishers and author cannot accept responsibility for any errors or omissions, however caused. No responsibility for loss or damage occasioned to any person acting, or refraining from action, as a result of the material in this publication can be accepted by the editor, the publisher or the author.

First published in Great Britain and the United States in 2024 by Kogan Page Limited

2nd Floor, 45 Gee Street
London
EC1V 3RS
United Kingdom

8 W 38th Street, Suite 902
New York, NY 10018
USA

4737/23 Ansari Road
Daryaganj
New Delhi 110002
India

www.koganpage.com

Kogan Page books are printed on paper from sustainable forests.

ISBNs
Hardback   978 1 3986 1226 6
Paperback 978 1 3986 1224 2
Ebook   978 1 3986 1225 9

British Library Cataloguing-in-Publication Data
A CIP record for this book is available from the British Library.

Library of Congress Cataloging-in-Publication Data
Names: Madera, Sherry, author.
Title: Navigating sustainability data : how organizations can use ESG data
   to secure their future / Sherry Madera.
Description: London ; New York, NY : Kogan Page, 2024. | Includes
   bibliographical references and index.
Identifiers: LCCN 2023045606 (print) | LCCN 2023045607 (ebook) | ISBN
   9781398612242 (paperback) | ISBN 9781398612266 (hardback) | ISBN
   9781398612259 (ebook)
Subjects: LCSH: Sustainable development–Management. |
   Management–Environmental aspects. | Environmental auditing.
Classification: LCC HD75.6 .M334 2024 (print) | LCC HD75.6 (ebook) | DDC
   658.4/083–dc23/eng/20231004
LC record available at https://lccn.loc.gov/2023045606
LC ebook record available at https://lccn.loc.gov/2023045607

Typeset by Integra Software Services, Pondicherry
Print production managed by Jellyfish
Printed and bound by CPI Group (UK) Ltd, Croydon, CR0 4YY

To where I came from and where I'm going to.
With love to my mom and my daughter.

CONTENTS

LIST OF FIGURES AND TABLES

Figures

Tables

ACKNOWLEDGEMENTS

When I got a call suggesting I should write a book about ESG data for organizational leaders, I thought the idea of adding more to my plate was insane. Instead of the reaction I expected ('You want to do WHAT??'), my family were the first to nod and say that it made sense. As we all sat around the dinner table, they were the only ones who were sure I could do it.

Thank you to my supportive husband, Andy, and my inspiring daughter, Katya, for believing in me from the start and for giving up so many hours of family time while I beavered away on this book. Your wise editing revived me many times.

Thank you to my sister, Laura, who shared her own creative journeys and advice with me during some of the darker moments of authorship. There was a lot going on in our lives and I found great joy in amongst it by hearing your thoughts. Thank you to you and Alex and Ewan.

I believe in the family you choose. In the lifetime of this book, a few special friends need some individual thanks. To Heather Smith Nunez, for being my cheerleader and 'table of contents master' from the beginning. To Adrienne Down Coulson, for never telling me I was crazy to try to do it all. To Celeste Chiasson, for ensuring I never took myself too seriously.

I would never have been able to keep up with the breakneck speed of change in the global sustainability ecosystem without my partners in FoSDA. A specific call-out to my vice chairs and sense-checkers Richard Mattison and Pietro Bertazzi. To our long-suffering secretariat Kat Atkins and Emma McGarthy. To Sean Kidney for unfailing reminders of the 'So what?' To Patricia Torres, Leon Saunders-Calvert, Martina Macpherson, Nick Miller, Gavin Starks, Christopher Percival, Thomas Willman and David Harris for being dedicated, expert and uncompromising partners devoted to making the world a better place through data.

By writing this book, I hope to encourage others to learn more about what they can do to bring sustainability to the core of their organization. This has already been done so well by so many, and I took great inspiration when writing from my experiences with leaders such as Dr Ma Jun, Paul Dickinson, David Craig, Katherine Garratt-Cox, Sonja Gibbs, Simon Zadek, Annemarie Durbin, Bill Winters, Douglas Flint, Ann Cairns, Michael

Mainelli, Ben Caldecott and many others in business, non-profits and academia. I hope you are all aware of the positive impacts you make. You have my appreciation for what you do.

Last but not least, a big thank you to those who started this book on its journey: the wonderful team at Kogan Page. Thank you to Isabelle Cheng for finding me and your patience with me, together with Nick Hoar, as these pages came together. Better late than never. A fitting reminder for us all.

Why sustainability data matters to organizational leaders

1

REFLECTIVE QUESTIONS

- What is the right balance between sustainable activities and building corporate value?
- How can leaders of global organizations – small and large – steer decisions to reflect that balance?
- How can ESG data become a powerful management tool?

I have a great friend who is the COO of a large, global technology company based out of the USA. He told me that he had 'just inherited an ESG team' from another part of the business and wasn't sure what to do with it. He wasn't sure what data the team should produce, whether it was useful, or what he, as a senior executive in the company, should expect from them or should receive from them on a regular basis – if indeed anything.

He admitted he wasn't even sure what data really mattered to him and his board of directors, or why. He even declared (boldly, considering his audience) that he wondered whether he should cut the team entirely to save costs. All of his questions around the team and sustainability data were absolutely the right ones to ask.

I asked him a few questions in return. Questions not about sustainability, but about core business priorities:

- Did his business intend to raise money from banks, equity investors, public markets or others in the future?

- Did they want to attract and retain the very best talent – especially younger parts of the workforce and new graduates?
- Did the business operate in Europe, and intend to continue to do so and grow its footprint?
- Were they producing products that they sold on to others in a supply chain before reaching the end user?

As we sat and sipped some wine at a restaurant in London, he answered yes to all of the above questions. I suggested that perhaps he consider the possibility that without certain data his organization compiles on the ESG aspects of their business, his core business priorities may be difficult or even impossible to meet. That may be true today and, increasingly, tomorrow.

The next day, my friend was on his way to Paris and Frankfurt to meet with other colleagues who help drive growth in their European business. His meetings also included teams responsible for finance, HR, compliance, product delivery and facilities. I suggested he add a question or two to his agenda about the sustainability demands and challenges these colleagues were seeing in their day-to-day jobs. Asking these questions and many more would begin to scope the sustainability data needs for him and his leadership colleagues.

He said that he would, and that he would love to have a better understanding of how senior leaders should be engaging with sustainability and ESG data points more regularly. I told him to read this book!

I also explained that I believed it was time for organizations to focus on the data that matters most to promote sustainability. Based on worrying climate change projections and on the rapid maturing of the global data disclosure landscape, I am confident the time is now to make sustainability data an essential part of a global leader's decision-making toolkit.

Decision-useful data takes many forms, such as:

- data to track and trace where an organization contributes to a sustainable economy
- data that can improve practices for resource usage and production efficiency
- data that allows leaders to judge their organization's climate and social contributions – standalone and compared to their peers
- data that instils faith in any net zero commitments – by organizations, governments and countries

- data to help business leaders navigate the noisy and complex world of sustainable data and ESG
- data to ensure leaders do not misstep on industry-, country- or financial-level regulations

Whatever it might be, sustainability data is the starting point.

I also work closely with the CEO of a high growth business listed on a public stock exchange. The business is based in the UK and has operations and customers across Europe, Asia and the Americas. The offices and employee base of this company are much smaller than those of my global COO friend mentioned earlier. However, even with a workforce of hundreds, not thousands, and a revenue line of tens of millions, not billions, sustainability data is on this CEO's mind as well. Already the pressures from employees to understand the company's carbon footprint and sustainability principles were putting meaningful pressure on talent retention.

After the company's initial public offering (IPO) on the stock exchange, the visibility of the business increased across the investor community. While the company was encouraged to put out a sustainability statement as part of its annual report, that statement was neither mandatory nor did it require any specific content.

As we reviewed the business priorities and future plans, this CEO asked me which ESG metrics we should be tracking. What were the basic KPIs (key performance indicators) for sustainability she should be putting to her board? What was the minimum required? What were others in the industry, including her competitors, doing? How did her business disclosures compare to their sustainability statements and what mattered? What data gave her the most bang for her buck? Externally or internally?

The listed company CEO – a master in her industry and an inspiring leader – was very candid about her lack of knowledge about sustainability data. She is a busy woman. Her focus is on achieving her financial forecasts, ensuring her products are excellent, keeping customers happy and running an effective team. Her job is also to keep a close handle on costs and drive efficiency wherever she can in order to add strength to the bottom line of her financial statements. The thought of adding more data to gather and, together with her board of directors, analyse or at least consider... well, that was neither appealing nor top of her to-do list. Data sourcing, production, verification and amalgamation can be time-consuming and expensive.

Nonetheless, she felt she had to ask about sustainability and how to track it. Even if the insinuation embedded in the question was 'How little can I get away with?', questioning is a great start and – at the bare minimum – may be where it ends up.

I sit on the board (note that the university 'board' is actually its governing council) of a university. Universities are usually run as not-for-profit institutions delivering post-secondary education – seemingly a very different organization with very different priorities to the large global corporate run by my COO friend and the growth business led by the ambitious CEO.

However, on the topic of sustainability data, a university has more similarities than differences to profit-driven organizations. Perhaps due to the proximity to leading research on the environment and social impacts on our planet, universities have had an earlier focus on the broad topic of environmental impact compared to other organizations. Sustainability and achieving a net zero target are embedded in universities' strategy documents and published proudly on their websites.

Many universities have produced sustainability reports for many years under many different titles, including energy reports, environmental reports and sustainability reports. They also have many programmes promoting sustainability that they can be justifiably proud of – from teaching to sustainable procurement, from facilities management through to waste and recycling programmes.

This may make it sound as though universities are ahead of the game on ESG. That is an assumption too far. Speaking with university leadership teams, the challenges in sourcing, disclosing and monitoring sustainability data are just as exacting in a not-for-profit environment. Perhaps universities have many years' experience producing sustainability reports, but it may not be the case that those reports are full of data.

Not that piles of data is the goal! Far from it! Vast quantities of data that aren't used for monitoring of goals and targets or improving the business of education or student or staff experience add questionable value. On the other hand, if data on sustainability is not being regularly reviewed at the board and executive team level, how can progress towards net zero commitments and reduction targets in water, waste or methane gases be tracked? Is the university on target? Does it need some course correction? Are resources being used effectively to run the university sustainably?

Hopefully my not-so-subtle message is clear. Whether we lead a large, global multinational, or a smaller enterprise with big growth ambitions, or even a not-for-profit or charitable organization, as organizational leaders, it is our responsibility to be the stewards of the future. Our role includes maintaining good governance to embrace opportunities and mitigate risks. This role includes our obligation to deliver on sustainability targets, pledges, and plans as part of our role as organizational leaders. It is our responsibility to navigate our organization through ever more complex regulations and market pressures.

How can you be sure you and your colleagues are fulfilling their role to adequately oversee risks and opportunities related to sustainability? This question is relevant if you are a board director, a C-suite executive, a divisional leader or a responsible manager. The question is relevant if you are part of a publicly listed company, a private business, a global corporate, a domestic player, a profit- or non-profit-driven organization. It is relevant to all leaders because sustainability obligations are part of the new world in which we work.

Leadership responsibility is one thing, but what about data?

Great leaders make decisions based on the data available to them. This is a fundamental thread that runs through this book. It has served me well in my career and will serve you well too. It applies to making all types of business decisions. So, in order to make decisions about your organization's sustainability, you need sustainability data. But, what is sustainability data? Are we talking about ESG data? Well, yes… and no.

This book will take you through what data you should consider in order to lead your organization, inclusive of sustainability-driven considerations. You are unique and the organizations you work with are unique. It logically follows that the sustainability data you will need to be a great leader will also be unique. This book will help you map out what data is most important, based on how you will use that data (the use cases in Chapter 2), where you are on the ESG Data Maturity Journey (Chapter 4) and where you would like to be (adding in your organization's ambitions in Chapter 6).

I have been working in the area of sustainable finance since 2014. At the time of writing that's almost a decade. Many others in the market have been deeply embedded in sustainability and its intersection with finance for a lot longer. I applaud their vision and dedication.

My experience started in a strange way. I joined the UK Foreign Office and became a diplomat based in Beijing, China. China is the world's largest emitter of greenhouse gases (GHGs). This puts China firmly on the climate naughty step. However, this is not to say that Chinese citizens are not as worried as any other global citizens about their country's emissions status. Actually, the opposite is true. Chinese city dwellers are very concerned about carbon emissions. Overall, environmental concerns are a big deal in China.

Since 2010, in upmarket Beijing it is commonplace for people to have air purifiers scattered in most rooms of their homes. A Beijinger's morning reflex is to reach for their mobile phone and check their PM2.5 app to determine pollution levels, which will govern what their agenda is for the day. The measurement 'PM2.5' refers to particulate matter in the air with a diameter below 2.5 micrometres, and is often used as a measure of air pollution levels (Environment Protection Authority Victoria, 2021). These tiny particles can negatively affect your health.

As a Beijinger, how long you spent outdoors would be dictated by the level of pollution. It was a critical measure to determine what you would allow yourself and your children to do that day. When PM2.5 was 150 parts per million (ppm), the sky would be murky; at 200ppm the schools would not allow children to go outside for breaks. At 400ppm a red alert system was enacted (not reliably, but it was put into action a number of times during my tenure in Beijing), which instructed citizens to not go outdoors. A 700/800/900ppm reading or one that went off the scale was not unheard of. By way of comparison, New York or London would register 50ppm on a bad pollution day.

This very visceral understanding of the environment's impact on day-to-day life has made Chinese residents some of the most pollution-aware in the world. This has knock-on effects on topics prioritized in the wider economy.

Green finance was a topic I spoke about daily while I was living in China. Sustainability and the role finance could and should play in mitigating climate change took prime position on the diplomatic and economic agenda during the period (2014–17) when I was based in China. This spurred action on the part of Chinese policymakers, regulators and industry groups to sketch out ways to define, support and monitor sustainable finance in China's financial markets. This action produced the world's first sustainable finance taxonomy in the form of the Green Bond Endorsed Product Catalogue in 2015.

China may be the world's biggest emitter of GHGs, but it is also working on policies and frameworks to channel finance into more sustainable directions. We will consider how trends in sustainable finance affect your business and how this early work from China has now been eclipsed by action in the EU and elsewhere. My experience with sustainable finance and ESG data began in China. It was an excellent place to understand how the topic developed at the coalface... literally. China's economy was then and continues to be heavily reliant on coal for energy.

As a Canadian, my home country is renowned for its vast areas of natural habitats. Often Canada is depicted in marketing literature with clear, clean lakes and many more trees and forests than people and cities. Canada and

Canadians are rightly proud of our beautiful environment. Canada ranks as the country with the third largest forest area in the world (Government of Canada, 2023). However, Canada is not necessarily the lowest GHG emitter in the world, and implements practices such as fracking that damage the beautiful environment it shouts about. Canada is ranked 10th in the world for total GHG emissions and has the highest GHG emissions per capita from those top 10 countries (Environment and Climate Change Canada, 2022). Canada has a great reputation for environmentalism, but still needs work getting in line with required changes to achieve the Paris Agreement targets.

Globally there are a lot of preconceptions about country- and company-level sustainability that we need data to prove or debunk.

Before we dive into the rest of this book, I'd like to set out my position on sustainability data as the author. As this book has developed, ESG has taken a prominent role in the global debate on climate change action. ESG has been challenged as exemplifying woke-ism. Some voices question the relevance of disclosing environmental, social and governance data by corporates and entities. The premise that ESG data is material and should be disclosed based on the same logic that demands financial data disclosure is not universally supported.

In this context, here is my sustainability data philosophy:

1　Data is the solution, not the problem. ESG is on a journey to completeness. Blaming 'the data' for inaction on sustainability is not ok.

2　Without data we don't know how we are progressing and can't course-correct. What we can measure, we can manage.

3　**Some** data is better than **no** data. Ensuring full transparency on any uncertainties around data should be a priority, and if this is adhered to even incomplete data should be applauded, not derided.

4　Now is the right time to start to measure sustainability metrics. Your future organization will thank you for the historical data and ability to plot a trend. You need a baseline to work from.

5　An organization's sustainability agenda needs to be agreed at the board level and reviewed regularly to account for rapidly changing times.

We will dig deeper into all things data as we progress through this book. The fact that you have picked it up at all means you are at least curious. Curious about how sustainability data can be powerful for you and your organization. That's a good start.

Is sustainability really that important to my organization?

For many years, the debate about an organization's sustainability priorities has been linked to the organization's image and not to its core business priorities. If we reflect on the past decade, climate impact, governance of the business to support diversity and inclusion and the effects the organization has on the planet and its people have not been central to board- and executive-level strategic discussions. This is changing. Increasingly, questions about a company's impact are also being asked in the boardroom and around investor tables. This is driving an organization's sustainability impact right to the top of the leadership agenda, and requires all leaders to be more aware of what role they play in the overall sustainability agenda.

Moreover, what is an organization's role in the world? At the risk of getting incredibly philosophical, the reality is that the organizations we work with are linked to the economies we live in and the countries we call home. Organizations provide us with the fundamental needs of existence (food, water, shelter, etc) and more (entertainment, travel, transportation, knowledge, tools, etc). So when we talk about sustainability and the climate crisis and the need for a just transition to a sustainable future… who and what do you think makes that talk a reality?

In my view, it is down to you and to me and to the organizations we interact with to build a sustainable future for humans and the Earth we live on and in and with. When you are in a leadership role – be that as the CEO, regional president or division head, board director or manager – you have a little bit of power to shape that sustainable future. Sometimes you have a lot of power. It is important for us all to know how we can use it.

I can hear some of you shouting, 'But what about the government? They have the power! They need to do something! It is up to them!' I sincerely hope you were using your inside voice because not only would you draw some worrying attention if you are reading this in public, but you would also be wrong. While governments play an important role in setting policy, influencing regulation and making sustainable choices for the slice of the economy it directly manages (i.e. government buildings, public sector services, etc), it does not have the right to directly make choices for the private sector. It can certainly encourage – with both a carrot and stick – behaviour in line with its own commitments to sustainability. But that isn't the same as having direct power over what (in most countries) accounts for the majority of emissions: those that come from the private sector and independent organizations.

If you think deeply about it, what exactly are our governments committing to when they make country-level net zero pledges? They are standing up on the world stage and agreeing that their countries will lower the emissions coming from their jurisdiction. Other than the control they have over public entities, how are they going to achieve that pledge? When governments set targets to lower the methane emissions or to reduce waste or landfill within their borders, how are they able to do it?

The reality is that government commitments cannot be achieved unless the private sector makes and meets its own commitments to sustainability. We are all in this together. Our role as organizational leaders has never been more important to the common goal of combating climate change and creating a positive societal transition for the world we live in. Politicians can make commitments. We all will need to fulfil them.

Sustainability and climate change have been on the global political agenda for decades. Have you heard of the Paris Agreement? The agreement was signed at COP15, which was hosted by the French in Paris. It is often referenced when organizations discuss their commitments to climate change. It is also very relevant to reinforce the need for sustainability data.

Let's remind ourselves what the Paris Agreement is all about.

To understand the Paris Agreement, we need to understand what the Conference of the Parties (COP) annual meetings and the United Nations Framework Convention on Climate Change (UNFCCC) are all about.

The history of the COP dates back to the adoption of the UNFCCC in 1992 during the Earth Summit held in Rio de Janeiro, Brazil. The UNFCCC is an international environmental treaty that acknowledges the existence of climate change and commits signatory countries to work towards stabilizing GHG concentration in the atmosphere. The treaty came into force in 1994 and has been ratified by almost all countries in the world.

The COP is the ultimate decision-making body of the UNFCCC and holds annual meetings. They are a great global jamboree of policymakers who come in delegations from each of their countries to negotiate words that they can all agree on that seek to address the global challenge of climate change. Specifically, these words and agreements aim to further the UNFCCC treaty.

This may seem simple: we all want to have a habitable planet and so we surely can all work together to agree actions to secure that goal. However, it turns out it is far from simple. Actions to limit temperature rises that directly affect climate change require countries to agree to changes in the behaviour of their economies. Some countries are rapidly developing and gaining prosperity for their populations off the back of using fossil fuels to drive commerce. It is easy for a more developed nation (that has already leveraged fossil fuels to power their own economies in the past) to lecture developing nations about the evils of fossil fuels. But this preaching is not always welcomed or heeded. Why should developing nations limit their opportunities for prosperity when nations that came before did not?

In addition, island nations and low-lying countries have unique issues with negotiating country-level agreements at COP. These countries are on the front lines of climate change, with rising sea levels putting their populations at direct risk of flooding and famine. These countries, unfortunately, are also often the poorest nations and the ones with the lowest emissions. They are vocal about experiencing the worst effects of global warming and not having the financial capacity to either mitigate the effects or adapt. Nor do they have the market size to move the dial on global emissions by changing their own behaviours. The seemingly simple communal goal of limiting temperature rises to minimize climate disasters is achingly complex.

The first COP, COP1, took place in Berlin, Germany, in 1995, and since then subsequent COP meetings have been held annually in different host countries to review progress, negotiate agreements, and set future goals and targets related to climate change mitigation, adaptation, finance and technology transfer.

The COP meetings gained significant attention and momentum following the adoption of the Kyoto Protocol in 1997 during COP3. The Kyoto Protocol established legally binding emission reduction targets for developed countries and created mechanisms for international cooperation and emissions trading.

The historic Paris Agreement was adopted at COP21 in 2015. The agreement aims to limit global warming to well below 2° Celsius above pre-industrial levels, and encourages efforts to limit it further, to 1.5°C. It is a legally binding international treaty that sets out a framework for countries to take action on climate change, including submitting nationally determined contributions (NDCs) and regularly reporting on their progress.

Since Paris in 2015, there has been a special version of the COP meeting every five years to reset goals and NDCs. The last of these occurred in Glasgow in 2021.

In addition to the special sessions every five years, there are certain years designated by the UNFCCC to periodically assess the progress being made against the Paris Agreement. These sessions are known as the Global Stocktakes. These are like a poorly managed standardized test for Paris Agreement signatories. The stocktake process aims to enhance transparency, accountability, and ambition in global climate action. The first formal stocktake is scheduled to take place in 2023, during COP28, hosted in Dubai. Subsequent stocktakes will occur every five years thereafter.

At the time of writing, COP28 has yet to happen. What we do know in the lead-up to the first Global Stocktake is that it is shamefully late in coming (seven years after the Paris Agreement officially came into effect), and it includes woefully few agreed standard data points. The challenge of measuring and managing climate data is evident at this high level too. Countries and governments struggle to create comparable, coherent and comprehensive data for review. It is no wonder that private entities find this a challenge as well. So, that's the Paris Agreement backstory.

The Paris Agreement and the COP structure continue to guide climate emissions discussions. But what data sits behind them?

Arguably, one of the most important data points is a country's or entity's GHG emissions over a specific period of time, usually per year. Let's unpack that acronym: GHG. GHGs are gases in the Earth's atmosphere that trap heat. They act as a barrier, blocking heat radiated off the Earth's surface from escaping into space. Instead, heat builds up close to the planet's surface. This in turn raises temperatures.

GHGs include a number of gases – the largest by far by volume is carbon dioxide (CO_2). CO_2 made up 74 per cent of GHG emissions in 2019, with methane making up 17 per cent (World Resources Institute Climate Watch, 2023). This is why GHG emissions are often measured in tonnes of CO_2 or CO_2 equivalent (CO_2e).

When we start to measure GHG emissions by calculating CO_2, carbon truly becomes central to the data discussion. GHG emissions are a vital data point for all entities to disclose as part of their reporting on sustainability. This is because they reflect the carbon they are responsible for putting into the atmosphere. You may have heard the term 'carbon footprint' – this refers to the total GHG emissions both directly and indirectly caused by an individual, organization, event or product (Carbon Trust, 2018).

Calculating GHG emissions is at the heart of measuring and managing your impact on the environment. But it is tricky to do accurately and completely. Measuring your carbon footprint through your emissions data is a way to keep track of your impacts on rising global temperatures.

Does that sound too dramatic? It shouldn't – your emissions are a direct contributor to trapped heat in the atmosphere. That heat is making the climate crisis urgent.

Need proof?

The United Nations Intergovernmental Panel on Climate Change (IPCC) produces regular reports which assess scientific, technical and socio-economic information concerning climate change. In its synthesis report released in March 2023, the IPCC found that there is a more than 50 per cent chance that global temperature rise will reach or surpass 1.5° Celsius between 2021 and 2040 across all the studied scenarios (IPCC, 2023). This trajectory of rising global temperatures affects all life on earth – increasing the likelihood of droughts and therefore food insecurity, increasing the chances of extreme heat making parts of the Earth uninhabitable, and driving sea level rises, floods and further decline in sea life and coral reefs. All of this ultimately drives biodiversity loss and has knock-on effects on human survival. This is all pretty grim reading.

It also illustrates how data is being used to predict future scenarios that indicate the urgent need to act now to limit further rises in the Earth's temperature. The mantra coined at COP26 in 2021 in Glasgow was 'keep 1.5 alive' – a reference to the Paris Agreement's goal of limiting global warming to 1.5°C above pre-industrial levels . Pre-industrial levels align with the second half of the 19th century, before fossil fuel emissions from industrialization started to build up.

Two years on from Glasgow, at the time of writing, limiting temperature rises to 1.5°C is still the hope. But it is getting increasingly more difficult to keep that hope alive. In May 2023, the World Meteorological Organization reported there was a 66 per cent likelihood of exceeding the 1.5°C threshold in at least one year between 2023 and 2027. This doesn't mean it will stay above the 1.5°C threshold. But it will be the first time the Paris Agreement goal will be breached.

The window to address the climate crisis is widely understood to be rapidly closing, but there is time to secure a safe, liveable future according to the IPCC so long as we prioritize action today. Part of that action must be in scrupulously capturing, analysing and interpreting data that can measure our impact on the environment and society. It is the only way for us to determine if we are on track to meet our commitments made during the COP meetings or during our board meetings. If we're not on track, we need the data to help us course-correct. Otherwise, what is the value of climate pledges?

The read-across from COP to organizational management is very real. The international urgency and focus on sustainability does not exist in a bubble. It permeates all our activities, including those that we as leaders discuss around boardroom tables. The last several years have proven that sustainability is not a 'nice to have' – rather, it has become a fundamental strategic pillar for any best-in-class organization. Even with the simultaneous global crises in recent times, including a global pandemic, energy crises, a war in Europe, geopolitical tensions and soaring inflation, sustainability remains a priority topic for business and financial leaders.

Some market participants, including Mark Carney, the globally recognized UN Climate Envoy, have conceded there will need to be continued investment in fossil fuels to facilitate the eventual transition to renewable energy (Carney, 2022). Blackrock CEO Larry Fink, who has been a vocal champion of ESG integration, has also reframed his support of environmental and social shareholder proposals (Clifford, 2022), while reiterating that sustainability stewardship rests not only with management but definitively in the boardroom (Pagitsas, 2022). These leaders and many others recognize the complexity of the climate crisis and the centrality of finance in terms of making capital available to companies that are on a positive sustainability trajectory – and limiting funds to those that are not.

Allocating capital to sustainable investments has been a growing trend. Why does this matter to you? As your organization grows and needs to access capital, investors' criteria will become ever more important to your business. There has been an explosion in funds flowing to sustainable investment in the past decade. We will dig deeper into the detail behind these capital flows in Chapter 2. This volume of investments in sustainability has created the need to become more specific about what we are referring to when we talk about sustainability. The definitions of 'sustainable' and 'ESG' funds and how the underlying portfolio investments adhere to the fund criteria are being actively debated.

Later in this book we will review the progress of these definitions in the form of taxonomies, reporting frameworks, disclosure requirements and principles-based definitions. Spoiler alert: there is not yet one definition to rule them all. This makes your job as a leader even more difficult. However, the broad and deep pool of definitional work on sustainability has some common threads. What has emerged is a common grouping of datasets that fit into the hat trick of environmental, social and governance concerns that are generally used to frame sustainability.

The term 'ESG' has become very familiar in recent years, but its familiarity has also brought confusion about what it is – and what it is not.

Where did the term 'ESG' come from?

The acronym first came into use in 2004 when Kofi Annan, the then-UN Secretary General, asked the world's financial institutions to incorporate environmental, social and governance concerns into capital markets. However, predating Annan's speech in 2004, Adolf Berle, a professor at Columbia Law School, is often credited as being the true father of ESG thought. His work in 1932 produced a seminal text on corporate governance.

Berle continued to develop his thesis that regulations should be put in place to enforce 'business statesmanship' – the concept that businesses and their leaders had already begun to take on social responsibilities alongside their profit motives, and that corporate law should catch up to reflect this.

Work by the UN and the UN Environment Program Finance Initiative in the lead-up to Kofi Annan's 2004 speech pulled Berle's academic thinking into a future-facing measurable application to climate change. ESG is an old concept with new urgency that has caught hold globally and has developed strong roots in the financial ecosystem.

What is ESG?

ESG has become shorthand for sustainability – for example 'ESG funds', 'ESG scores' or 'reporting our ESG' as a business. What we may be forgetting by using this shorthand is that ESG more accurately describes the three top-level categories of data, under which many other more granular datasets reside.

The term is based on the sharing of information – data – on these top-level categories to help those inside and outside the organization take decisions. They may be investment decisions (Should I put my money into this company by buying their stock?), or business strategy decisions (Our carbon emissions in Europe are higher than our competitors, is this exposing us to increased risks?) or other decisions (Am I comfortable accepting a job at this company that has no women or ethnic minorities represented in their top leadership?). ESG is all about data, and which elements of ESG are important or necessary depends entirely on the use case and decisions being taken. These use cases will be unpicked in more detail in later chapters.

The essential point here is that ESG isn't a universal synonym for sustainability. The term sums up the data that is needed to form a view on sustainability-related topics in order to make business decisions. The granularity of the data that is needed depends on the decision and the use case. What is absolutely clear is that without strong and reliable data on environmental, social and governance topics, sustainability will be impossible to track and ultimately to achieve.

Datasets are the building blocks of information upon which sustainable finance and sustainable business can be built. As with the home you live in – be it a house, an apartment, a castle or a shed – you would make building your dwelling on strong foundations a priority. So too should we prioritize strong data building blocks upon which to build our business decisions (Figure 1.1). We need to ensure ESG data is robust and that we are not building our future on shaky foundations. How we define 'robust' is in itself an important consideration. We will look at the three Cs and three Es of data in Chapter 3 to give you more framing.

Unfortunately, we are not living in a world of perfect data. It is very true that we do not have all the data we would like in order to compare all opportunities

Figure 1.1 Strong ESG foundations

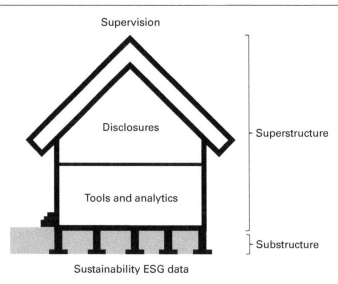

to deploy capital and resources sustainably. This data imperfection is nothing new to the world of finance and the financial community. Nonetheless, finance has been able to navigate valuations and risk and deploy capital for decades in this incomplete and imperfect world of data. We are rapidly adding an increasing density and variety of sustainability data, and ESG data's availability is increasing year on year. This is a positive direction of travel.

We need to embrace the attitude that data is the solution to sustainable finance – not the problem that will restrict it. This makes it increasingly urgent for leaders to understand the sustainable data ecosystem, and how it intersects with an organization's strategy and decisions. Leaders need to be inquisitive about ESG data. How is data essential to accessing capital? Where is it necessary for regulatory and compliance purposes – now and in the future? What ESG data is sought out by your supply chain, your employee base and your customers? What affects their decision to engage with your organization? These are the questions we will navigate in the chapters to follow.

Is sustainability data a topic for the board of directors?

Paul Polman, former CEO of Unilever, said: 'Today's boards are just not equipped to deal with today's challenges,' in particular with ESG and climate knowledge. In PWC's 2021 Annual Corporate Directors Survey, only 25 per cent of directors reported that their board understands ESG risks very well. Similarly, the NYU Stern Center for Sustainable Business reviewed the credentials of 1,188 Fortune 100 board directors and found that only about 1 per cent possessed expertise in any environmental field, including energy, conservation, climate and sustainable development (Whelan, 2021).

Many boards are adding this expertise through new board appointments. However, all senior leaders should understand how to measure and manage sustainability issues. This skill enables them to identify risks and opportunities that others may miss. This requires an understanding of what data is needed, available and comparable. This knowledge is essential for any organization to aid the C-suite, board of directors, shareholders and employees to take sustainable actions in their industries.

As a non-executive board member and adviser on both public and private company boards, I agree with Paul Polman's assessment. Excellent, seasoned board directors unparalleled in their business strategy and financial acumen do not have the tools or experience to assess sustainability factors or navigate ESG data. It is still rare to find these skills at the board level which are needed to challenge the management team to produce, improve and track ESG KPIs.

If we look at the pool of senior leaders in the C-suites of businesses located anywhere around the globe, sustainability data skills are generally less well developed than other business critical skills. Knowledge about ESG datasets and expertise in understanding what ESG data is needed to assess risks require development.

To build the skills needed within the leadership of an organization, it is important to first ask why these skills are needed. All skill development and acquisition takes time, energy and money. Let's find out why this is an investment you and your organization should make.

Why is sustainability data important to an organization?

This is the million-dollar question. If you can't answer it, you can't commit resources to building sustainability data skills or content. There are a number of areas to explore to answer this question. To make it relevant for your purposes, you need to explore how sustainability data is needed for your core business. You need to believe ESG data is fundamental to your organization's success. It can't be a secondary consideration or somewhere far down your list of requirements. It needs to drive essential business needs such as your organization's access to capital, business growth and efficiencies and compliance with regulatory demands.

To establish sustainability data's importance to your organization, consider three essential business use cases – I call these the ABCs of sustainability data. They can be found in more detail in Figure 1.2.

These use cases explain how ESG data needs to be central to you as a business leader. In Chapter 2 we'll dig deep into each of these use cases. They should provide you as a leader with compelling reasons why you need to navigate sustainability data to secure your organization's future.

I believe strongly that sustainability cannot be considered as an add-on, or as a separate objective to the success of the organization. Neither can ESG data be considered separate to data used to drive core business objectives. By understanding sustainability's importance to your core business objectives you are starting your journey towards deciding what ESG data you and your organization need for your overall success.

Figure 1.2   The ABCs of sustainability data use cases

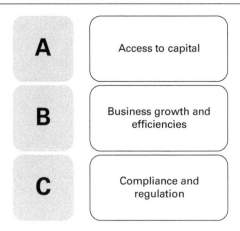

It is not too bold to aspire for your ESG data to become a competitive advantage. As we can see from the narrative above, sustainability affects critical areas of an organization's success. ESG data exists at all levels of the economy – from your organization through its immediate value chain to its wider industry and further still to the country level. With data, sustainability can be an accelerator for your organization's future success and make you and your team a contributor to the wider goals of mitigating climate change.

The direction of travel is for your market and regulatory landscape to change beyond recognition on the topic of sustainable data disclosures. You can address that proactively or reactively. You can lead or follow. There is no judgement in this book on the choices you make on this score. However, all the choices you make will need data for you to make them well and clearly. This book explores how to use the right data for the appropriate use case to drive efficient decisions for organizations and the planet.

It is high time for data to empower material debates on sustainability at the world's top tables. And you are on your way to being well equipped to do that.

References

Carbon Trust (2018) A guide: Carbon footprinting for businesses, www.carbon trust.com/our-work-and-impact/guides-reports-and-tools/a-guide-carbon-footprinting-for-businesses (archived at https://perma.cc/VD3D-5PHK)

Carney, M (2022) Financing the net zero revolution, Bloomberg, https://assets. bbhub.io/company/sites/63/2022/05/Financing-the-Net-Zero-Revolution_ NZDS-Speech-by-Mark-Carney.pdf (archived at https://perma.cc/6HRD-WD84)

Clifford, C (2022) Blackrock to vote for fewer climate shareholder provisions in 2022 than 2021, CNBC, www.cnbc.com/2022/05/11/blackrock-to-vote-for-fewer-climate-provisions-in-2022-than-2021.html (archived at https://perma.cc/7T6A-9AJU)

Environment and Climate Change Canada (2022) Global greenhouse gas emissions: Canadian environmental sustainability indicators, www.canada.ca/en/environment-climate-change/services/environmental-indicators/global-green house-gas-emissions.html (archived at https://perma.cc/N8AN-DVYG)

Environment Protection Authority Victoria (2021) PM2.5 particles in the air, www.epa.vic.gov.au/for-community/environmental-information/air-quality/pm25-particles-in-the-air (archived at https://perma.cc/EC6P-K66A)

Government of Canada (2023) How much forest does Canada have? https://natural-resources.canada.ca/our-natural-resources/forests/state-canadas-forests-report/how-much-forest-does-canada-have/17601 (archived at https://perma.cc/AAX7-YRH9)

IPCC (2023) *Climate Change 2023: AR6 synthesis report*, www.ipcc.ch/report/ar6/syr/ (archived at https://perma.cc/UM36-R5S5)

Pagitsas, C (2022) *Chief Sustainability Officers at Work: How CSOs build successful sustainability and ESG strategies,* Apress, New York, NY

Whelan, T (2021) *US Corporate Boards Suffer from Inadequate Expertise in Financially Material ESG Matters,* NYU Stern Center for Sustainable Business, www.stern.nyu.edu/sites/default/files/assets/documents/U.S.%20Corporate%20Boards%20Suffer%20From%20Inadequate%20%20Expertise%20in%20Financially%20Material%20ESG%20Matters.docx%20%282.13.21%29.pdf (archived at https://perma.cc/8LF8-E4PZ)

World Resources Institute Climate Watch (2023) Historical GHG emissions (1990–2020), www.climatewatchdata.org/ghg-emissions (archived at https://perma.cc/GXY3-9AUF)

The ABCs of sustainability data use cases

In order to understand which data points are most necessary to your business, you need to know what it is you are using the data for. Much noise is made about putting sustainability 'at the heart of the business', but what this actually means is much less obvious. A good way of grounding this idea of centralizing sustainability is to explore the use cases for acting sustainably – and the data that drives those actions. We briefly touched on three use cases in Chapter 1: the ABCs of sustainability data. In this chapter, we will dive more deeply into each of these.

Your job as a business leader is to consider which of these use cases resonates most clearly with your organization's objectives and priorities. This will help clarify why ESG data is important for you to engage with.

Let's start with a reminder of the ABCs of sustainable data:

A Access to capital

B Business growth and efficiencies

C Compliance and regulation

We will look at each of these in turn in this chapter.

Before we jump in, remember that all of these use cases have an umbrella rationale that drives an organization: building value. What 'value' means varies – some define this purely through financial metrics, others through achieving their mission statements. It can be argued that all organizations are in the business of building value. We should not lose sight of this macro-objective as we dive into these sustainability data use cases, because they themselves symbiotically support the organization's overarching goal of building value.

You may not agree with this yet. You may believe that sourcing ESG data from your organization is a make-work project that you have neither the time nor resources to pursue. Less emphatically, you may consider sustainability data valuable so your organization can play its part in tackling the global challenge of climate change, but of little value outside this silo. I hope as we dive into the ABCs of sustainability data use cases, you will consider the value of this data to the ultimate use case: building value in your organization.

Use case one: Access to capital

One would hope the reason for the increased interest in sustainability is due to a growing consciousness of the precarious position the planet finds itself in. In reality, the reason sustainability may need a leader's attention could be much closer to home than this big-picture rationale. Leaders may be interested in sustainability in order to protect their organization and those that govern it. A much more local and personal motivation. Either way, driven by external or internal factors, or some other pressure, understanding the relationship between an organization's sustainability and access to capital is critical for leaders.

All organizations – be they public, private, not-for-profit, governmental or non-governmental organizations (NGOs) – need resources to run. In most cases, 'resources' is shorthand for money. Money that organizations can use to hire people, to pay for inputs, to develop and improve their offering, to promote and market their products and services and to build value. Some businesses are able to grow and thrive without the need for external funds in the form of loans or equity investment or grants. But most do need external sources of capital to grow or to manage cash flows or to invest in the future – at least from time to time.

This need for capital applies to all organizations at some point in their life cycle. Even in the scenario where a company is self-funded, most businesses will have shareholders that take an interest in the business who need to be informed. This information influences the shareholder's decision to buy, hold or sell its shares.

The most robust and obvious forums for shareholders are the public capital markets which host shares of publicly traded companies. However, private shareholders across the investment cycle are also consuming information provided by the business they own a stake in to take decisions on their holdings. Investors represent the pool of stakeholders that have the ability to participate in a company's financing – they become shareholders when they transition that ability into action and take a position in the stock (equity), or debtholders when they participate in loan offerings (debt or bonds, etc) by committing capital.

Increasingly, investors, shareholders and debtholders are demanding more ESG data before they commit that capital. They are also looking for regular sustainability data updates after they have capital allocated to decide if they will retain, sell or increase their holdings. For simplicity we will use the term 'investor' for financial participants of all forms including equity or debt, and the term 'shareholder' for those holding a stake in the organization, in whatever form the organization's governance dictates.

The need for capital extends further to include NGOs and not-for-profit groups who also require access to capital markets or private financing to grow, expand or manage their day-to-day expenses. These groups have external stakeholders who require information from the organization. So, to keep it simple, ALL organizations should care about access to capital. ALL organizations – including yours – should care about how investors and shareholders are engaging with ESG data. Your job is to consider what data they need and why. Their needs will be your needs if you want their money.

You may be a financial expert or you may not. Let's first give every reader a financial industry baseline to work from. It may be worth reviewing a simplistic stakeholder map to remind ourselves of all the players in the financial chain when an organization raises funds or accesses credit. Figure 2.1 helps trace the flow of information needed by stakeholders in the chain.

Looking at Figure 2.1 from the bottom up, the bottom boxes represent the executive functions of your organization. The executive functions depicted by the Finance, Operations, Sales and HR boxes feed up into the executive management team. You may play a role in one or many of these functions or sit at the executive leadership table.

Figure 2.1   An organization's access to capital stakeholders

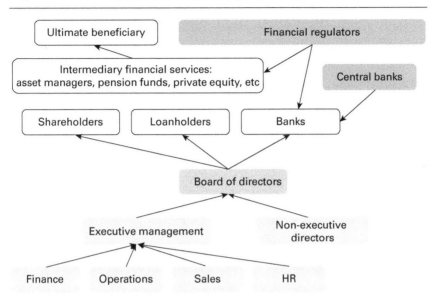

The executive management (or a subset thereof) plays a critical role as executive directors. Together with the non-executive directors, the two groups make up the organization's board of directors. Non-executive directors are generally there to be independent, to challenge and support the executive team, and have a duty of care to the shareholders to protect the value of the organization.

From the board of directors downwards, these boxes represent the entity seeking capital.

Sitting above the entity are the boxes marked shareholders, loanholders and banks. Again, simplifying for the purposes of this book, these three groups represent an entity's channels to securing funds. Shareholders will offer funds for stock in the company (equity investment). Loanholders will offer funds for a promise by the entity to pay it back according to terms of a financing agreement (this can be a bond, a loan, or other interest-bearing instrument). The concept of a bank is very familiar to us as individuals. Banks offer similar services to entities in the form of interest for deposits, loan or overdraft facilities or a myriad of other products to help entities manage their cash flow and balance sheet.

In some instances, shareholders or loanholders are represented by an intermediary. A common example of this is where an asset manager (also called fund managers or portfolio managers in certain cases and geographies)

or a pension fund buys stock on behalf of its investors or policyholders. In this scenario the entity raises its money from the intermediary financial institution: the asset manager or pension fund or other financial firm (venture capital, private equity, etc). The investor (be that a company or individual) sits behind the financial intermediary, one step removed from holding the stock of the entity directly. The investor is the ultimate beneficiary, but their name does not show up on the entity's shareholder or bondholder list. Their investment relies on the financial intermediary acting on their behalf.

The top right boxes in the diagram above represent the regulators in the financial value chain. Financial regulators are notoriously intense. In every jurisdiction there is a unique set of regulators, with variations in which financial institutions and banks fall under their oversight. While this may seem vague, in mature financial markets with deep pools of capital, it is crystal clear which regulators oversee which firms and which regulations these financial actors need to comply with.

It is worth calling out specifically the role of central banks in this ecosystem. Central banks generally play two roles in a country's economy. They act as the banker for the government, issue bonds and loans and participate in the currency markets and other financial markets in a similar way to commercial banks (a vast simplification, but useful for this purpose). Central banks also often play the role of prudential regulator and oversee the banks within their jurisdiction. These powers of supervision increasingly include giving guidance to banks on sustainability factors.

When it comes to sustainability data, these relationships are important to consider as you decide what data your organization needs to supply to unlock capital from various sources. Shareholders acting alone may have certain requests for information, but financial institutions acting on behalf of the ultimate beneficiary may have significantly more requirements for data. This may be because financial intermediaries not only have a duty of care to their own investors, but need to consider their direct regulatory obligations. Both of these reasons are increasingly focused on monitoring sustainability and demanding ESG data.

The same goes for banks. Banks have both financial and prudential regulators to consider when offering services and products to a company. As sustainability rises up the global agenda, risks associated with sustainability are becoming increasingly important to banks. This drives ESG data disclosure from their clients – the entities you lead and manage.

You may ask why financial regulators care about sustainability when their real job is to monitor the financial system. A great question that different regulators answer differently. Regulators that support adding sustainability monitoring to their mandate look at it from a risk perspective: financing unsustainable businesses creates medium- to long-term instability in the capital markets. Funding something today that has the potential to lose value due to its sustainability practices creates the potential for stranded assets and the need to restate portfolio values in the future.

Regulators that reject the requirement to police sustainability often quote 'caveat emptor' – buyer beware. Alternatively, they refer back to their purpose statements that do not include sustainability in their remits.

The counter-argument to the caveat emptor view is that regulators play a role in consumer protection. As ESG funds have grown in assets under management and funds continue to flow into these vehicles, there is a strong argument that regulators do have a role in making clear to the consumer (the ultimate beneficiary in our diagram above) what an ESG fund is and what it is not. Most regulators embrace at least the need for increased transparency. Much is being built from that foundational viewpoint.

So, the point is that disclosing sustainable information is rapidly becoming a requirement for organizations to access capital. Gone are the days when it was a rare occasion for investors to inquire after sustainability data. Investors are increasingly considering sustainability track record and metrics in assessing risk and value before deploying capital. Once money is deployed, they are continually reviewing their portfolios for sustainability metrics. This is driving intense demand for ESG data from organizations seeking investment or already part of an investor's portfolio.

Data requests are becoming increasingly codified through the activity of standards-setters and regulatory bodies such as the International Sustainability Standards Board (ISSB), the European Financial Reporting Advisory Group (EFRAG), the Securities and Exchange Commission (SEC) and the International Standards Organization (ISO), operating in all corners of the globe. Not only are traditional metrics such as greenhouse gas (GHG) emissions required, but additional granularity and variety of climate, environmental, social and governance data points are being included in requests from both the investment community and regulatory supervisors. We will call out regulation in more detail in this chapter. We will also review standards development later in this book.

With this overview in place, let's review the perspective of the investor community and then consider the interests of shareholders.

The investor perspective on ESG data

In order to make investments, investors need information from the company in which they are considering investing. Behind that simple statement is significant detail and nuance to unpack. There are some very standard financial information sets that investors require (including financial accounts, projections, detailed breakdown of costs and revenues, profit and loss accounts and balance sheet notes and details) as well as non-financial information. This non-financial information may include market and industry data, benchmarks and averages, personnel data on experience, organization charts, responsibilities, etc, data on macroeconomic or geopolitical risks, regulatory requirements and more.

For decades the analysis of these financial and non-financial inputs has been used by the investor community to make decisions on whether to invest – or not. Investors' primary requirement for non-financial information is materiality. Does the information matter to the business? Does it affect its success? Does it impact its valuation?

Materiality and the triple bottom line

> Information is *material* if omitting, misstating or obscuring it could reasonably be expected to influence decisions that the primary users of general purpose financial statements make on the basis of those financial statements, which provide financial information about a specific reporting entity (IFRS, 2018).

A material risk can threaten targets or goals – something of keen interest to investors. In the context of ESG, this is known as single materiality and includes factors that may pose a threat or opportunity to a business and its bottom line. An example is the threat of extreme weather, which may materially affect some firms. For example, businesses reliant on agricultural output (e.g. bananas) may have their production disrupted by extreme weather.

Take the case of a fruit smoothie manufacturer in Greece. Let's call it Smoothnana. In the case of Smoothnana, disclosing the direct relationship smoothie production has with extreme weather is material for investors. If extreme weather is predicted to increase, the risk that Smoothnana will not achieve its production targets increase. This climate-related (E in ESG) information is material for investors. It would be wise for Smoothnana to provide data on its governance of these risks (i.e. a G data point in ESG) and its plans to mitigate these risks (which should sit with the company's strategy). For example, replacing low-yielding bananas with wheatgrass (yuck).

As this example shows, a material piece of climate-related information doesn't tell investors anything about how 'green' a company's business practices are. Instead, it is intended to be transparent about how vulnerable its earnings may be to climate risks.

The Smoothnana example was illustrative of the concept of materiality. With the increasing interest in sustainability, the concept of double materiality has materialized.

> While materiality covers the effect of climate change on finance and corporate activities, double materiality includes the effect of finance and corporate activities on climate change.

How things such as double materiality should be accounted for in corporate reports remains the subject of intense debate. At the highest level, this concept suggests that financial data points are no longer enough for investors to make an informed decision on whether to invest in a company or not. This is a game-changer for companies seeking capital. Traditionally, investors were using data provided by the company to assess the veracity and strength of a company's bottom line today – and tomorrow. That ability to assess a company's tomorrow is a critical input when projecting the future value of the business.

Materiality has always been a guiding principle of financial disclosure. Now we are migrating beyond materiality bringing the business's financial performance and bottom line into new territory.

Even the concept of the bottom line is being challenged. What is the 'bottom line'? The bottom line primarily refers to a company's net income, which appears as the final line on the income statement. It's the total amount of profit a business has remaining after paying expenses. This seemingly fundamental economic and financial concept is in itself facing challenges in light of sustainability. Some practitioners believe there should be a triple bottom line rather than just a single bottom line to consider.

> The *triple bottom line* (TBL, or sometimes 3BL) is a business concept that posits firms should commit to measuring their social and environmental impact – in addition to their financial performance – rather than solely focusing on generating profit, or the standard 'bottom line'. It can be broken down into 'three Ps': profit, people and the planet (HBR Business Insights Blog, 2020).

Where did the concept of the TBL come from? Back in 1994, John Elkington, a British management consultant and early sustainability authority, coined the phrase 'triple bottom line' as his way of measuring performance in corporate America. His position was that a company can be managed in a way that focuses not only on making profit, but equally on social and environmental positives to protect and enhance people's lives and the planet's resilience (Elkington, 2018).

According to TBL theory, companies should be working simultaneously on these three concerns:

- Profit: This is the traditional profitability measure in the company's profit and loss (P&L) account.
- People: This measures how socially responsible an organization is and has been.
- Planet: This measures how environmentally responsible a firm is and has been.

TBL thinking is increasingly being applied by investors (perhaps not always using that term!) when they analyse companies. However, as in many areas of sustainability, measuring the TBL can be problematic. In reality, adopting a TBL approach for your organization is primarily high-level signposting of your commitment to social and environmental issues as well as profitability.

Once you decide to embrace a TBL strategy, a strategy for sustainable measurement and data collection needs to follow. Saying you prioritize a TBL strategy will definitely result in questions about how you are standing behind that statement. These questions will come from all manner of stakeholders: investors, shareholders, employees, partners, financiers, etc. Therefore, understanding what a TBL is and whether your firm wants to prioritize this concept is a good first step. Understanding it fully and planning for the data needed to back it up will help to ensure you are not called out for 'greenwashing'. Greenwashing is the process of conveying a false impression or misleading information about how a company or its products are environmentally sound. Greenwashing is a big topic, and one we will review in detail in Chapter 9.

Profitability vs TBL

Table 2.1 shows an example of TBL and the three Ps in a well-known global brand – IKEA.

So, if a big brand such as IKEA is using TBL, does it mean profitability isn't as important as it was before?

After looking at the idea of the TBL, questioning the priority of profit is a natural question. It is a good time to put ourselves in the shoes of the investor to consider this question from their perspective.

Investors are driven by return on investment. They are looking to get more money out of an investment than they put in. The investor's view of the probability of a positive return depends on the information the investor has at any given point along the lifetime of their investment. It is influenced by what they consider to be the risks associated with the investment, and what they predict the returns from it will be. Overall, the rule of thumb is that higher risk yields higher potential returns, albeit with a strong alternative possibility of a low (or no) return. Welcome to the concept of volatility. If this wasn't the case, there would be no incentive to invest in riskier investment cases.

Avoidance of volatility and the potential downside of higher risks is the reason why investors don't all choose riskier assets in the hopes of higher returns. How an investor creates a balance between risk and return will depend on the investor's own criteria and risk tolerance.

In an age of sustainability, you may ask if the fundamental principle that investors are driven by returns is being upended. Here are two ways to mull this over.

First, if we retain the view that an investor's primary purpose is to seek a return, we should remind ourselves how this is achieved. The investor makes a return when the business it is investing in increases in value between the time the investment is made and the time the investment is sold. If we add to traditional financial data the information about a company's sustainability, usually through its ESG data disclosures, this can provide insight into risks and opportunities for growing that company's value. In particular, ESG data that shows high carbon emissions may expose the business to sales headwinds as the global supply chain starts to make decisions on the basis of

Table 2.1 TBL and the three Ps in IKEA

Company	Description	Profit	People	Planet
IKEA	This Swedish retailer is a global household name in furniture and furnishings. www.ikea.com	IKEA's annual retail sales were €44.6 billion in 2022. While revenue has previously been the top priority for IKEA, shifts in its investments and use of the company profits are starting to show its commitment to the other two bottom lines of People and Planet. As an example, IKEA reinvested its profits into waste materials recycling in 2016, increased its investment in R&D to find more sustainable materials and boosted investment into renewable energy and fleet management.	IKEA aims to inspire 1 billion people to live healthier, sustainable lives within the boundaries of the planet, which they aim to do via the product range they offer. The company ensures international labour standards are met for all its workers throughout its supply chain through implementing the IWAY standard 6, an initiative it began in September 2020.	In 2016 IKEA started to recycle waste material using old materials to make new top-selling products. To date the business has calculated it uses 60 per cent renewable materials and 10 per cent recycled materials in its product offering (IKEA, nd). IKEA pledged to use 100 per cent renewable or recyclable materials by 2030. To help them reach this goal, in 2017 the company invested in Morssinkhof Rymoplast, a Netherlands-based plastic recycling plant (Waste360, 2017). To support their commitment to the circular economy and building a circular business that eliminates waste, IKEA launched a buy-back scheme for their old products. Regarding use of fossil fuels for energy usage, IKEA has set a goal to be powered by 100 per cent clean energy and has started to invest in renewable energy sources such as solar panels on its warehouses, with operations across Australia announced. IKEA also aims to transition their delivery fleet to 100 per cent zero emissions by 2025, and have made good headway on rolling out electric vehicles throughout their network.

carbon emissions (companies are starting to take this data point into account as they consider their Scope 3 emissions – more on this in later chapters).

Other data points, including workforce diversity, waste management statistics or governance gaps, may increase the firm's risk of achieving its business goals. All of these data points contribute to an investor's perception of the risks the company is facing. Positive ESG data lowers certain risks. Poor ESG data increases certain risks. No ESG data also increases certain risks – predominantly the risk associated with lack of transparency. Saying nothing may not work in a investee's favour.

In all of these cases, ESG data provides insight into a company's risk profile. This influences the company's valuation. Therefore, ESG data influences an investor's ability to achieve its primary purpose: to seek a return on its investment. In this line of thinking, ESG data is a new contributor to an old concept. It is data affecting risk versus return and therefore important to an investor.

There is a second way to consider if an investor's primary purpose remains seeking a return. Consider the idea that the investor is seeking a return, but not at any cost. This is an evolution of the basic principle. In this scenario, the investor may be retaining risk versus return as their 'true north' and adding *additional* purpose. Note that this is an 'and' not an 'or' situation. Investors still invest to make a gain and they also wish to protect societal and/or environmental value; in this view, investors are adding the need to be environmentally and socially positive to their top line investment criteria. How this is defined varies between investors.

The concept of being environmentally and socially positive is subjective. It may only include an investment's impact on the planet and climate (the E in ESG) or be driven by excluding companies that have a poor workforce diversity policy (the S). It is difficult to unpick the myriad reasons for these choices by investors – most certainly reasons include personal beliefs (at the individual investor level), demand from the ultimate beneficiary (at the asset manager level) or prudential oversight requiring limiting exposures (at the bank level).

This second way to consider if investors are ditching the financial risk vs return decision matrix favours a decision to invest that does not rest solely on financial factors. It limits the universe for investment to companies meeting relevant ESG criteria.

Let's remind ourselves of the investment value chain. Financial markets are often considered complicated, and our simplistic view of an investor and an investee is rarely this simple. As we see in Figure 2.1, there can be a number of layers to the flow of funds. Investors are often aggregators of capital that need to adhere to criteria set by others in the investment value chain. This magnifies the need for transparency so that the ultimate beneficiary (be that an individual or an entity) is fully aware of what they are investing in. This principle is what fundamentally guides the need for disclosures by a company seeking to access capital, and has created the demand for financial statements as a tool to disclose fundamental financial information to investors. These financial statements have evolved to reflect global accounting standards that have been in place for decades.

Financial statements – the myth of standardization

So, financial statements are well defined and completely comparable, right? Think again.

Finding harmony across jurisdictions is not a new challenge: The case of GAAP

Financial statements are formulaic, accurate, specific and comparable. Or are they? Financial statements are not immediately globally like for like. They can require restating to be comparable. This is something we have accepted and navigated in the world of finance. It would be wise to keep this in mind as we look at challenges for ESG reporting statements. There is hope yet!

So what are the current rules for financial statements? And how can we learn from their development and apply lessons for sustainability disclosures?

The Generally Accepted Accounting Principles (GAAP) are a set of accounting standards, rules and procedures that companies in the United States follow to prepare their financial statements. The history of GAAP accounting dates back to the 1930s, when the SEC was created in response to the stock market crash of 1929. The SEC was tasked with regulating securities markets and improving the accuracy and transparency of financial reporting.

In the 1930s and 1940s, the American Institute of Certified Public Accountants (AICPA) established the Committee on Accounting Procedure (CAP) to develop accounting principles and standards. In 1959, the CAP was replaced by the Accounting Principles Board (APB), which further refined and updated GAAP. In 1973, the Financial Accounting Standards Board (FASB) was established as an independent organization to develop and update GAAP standards.

This evolution and baton-passing between organizations of accounting standards feels familiar to today's ESG disclosure rule-makers. There are many batons in play in many lanes in the global ESG disclosures standards race right now too.

Today, GAAP is used by companies in the United States to prepare their financial statements, such as balance sheets, income statements and cash flow statements. The SEC requires public companies to follow GAAP accounting standards when preparing their financial statements, and failure to do so can result in fines or legal action.

While GAAP is specific to the United States, many other countries have developed their own accounting standards based on GAAP or have adopted similar principles. Notably, these other countries' versions are not a carbon copy of GAAP. Wouldn't it have been easier to just harmonize and use one globally agreed set of standards?

The question is: easier for *who*? Certainly easier for those interested in comparing financial statements from different global sources. However, is a single GAAP easier for jurisdictions who would like to prioritize certain local methodologies or disclosures over others? The variety in the world's jurisdictions reflects the variety in the world's priorities.

The closest that countries have come to adopting exactly the same accounting standards is via the International Financial Reporting Standards (IFRS). These have been developed by the International Accounting Standards Board (IASB) and are used in many countries around the world. The adoption of IFRS has been driven by the globalization of financial markets and the need for consistent accounting standards across borders. However, some countries, such as the United States, still primarily use GAAP.

When comparing accounting standards, there are several key differences to consider. US GAAP is highly prescriptive and rule-based, whereas IFRS is more principles-based and allows for more professional judgement. In Australia, Canada and Japan, standards include variations in accounting treatment or disclosure requirements, as well as differences in the specific industries or contexts in which the accounting standards are used.

While there is no single 'European GAAP' accounting standard, many countries in Europe have developed their own accounting standards, some of which are based on or similar to IFRS. Still, accounting standards used in Europe can vary widely depending on the country and the specific regulatory environment. The European Union has been working to establish a common set of accounting standards through the adoption of IFRS, so there may be less variation in accounting practices across Europe in the future.

So, how on earth can we accurately compare financial statements built using different standards? The world has become adept at restating statements to follow different standards in order to compare apples to apples. Companies may restate their financial statements into other countries' accounting standards for a variety of reasons. Here are some common situations when companies may choose to do so:

- Cross-border transactions: When companies engage in cross-border transactions, such as mergers and acquisitions or joint ventures, they may need to prepare financial statements that conform to the accounting standards of the countries involved.

- Listing on foreign stock exchanges: If a company decides to list its shares on a foreign stock exchange, it may need to prepare financial statements that comply with the accounting standards of that country.

- Compliance with local regulations: Some countries require foreign companies to prepare financial statements that comply with their local accounting standards as part of their regulatory requirements.

- International reporting: Companies with global operations may choose to prepare financial statements that conform to a common set of accounting standards, such as IFRS, for international reporting purposes.

In general, companies restate their accounts into other countries' accounting systems or to different recognized GAAPs to ensure compliance with local regulations, facilitate cross-border transactions or improve transparency and comparability for international investors.

The accounting standards journey may indicate a path that ESG disclosure standards may take. The situations where companies restate their financial statement as listed above may also be cases where organizations may need to restate their ESG disclosures. That may be the case for many years to come. Or forever. It may never be that one standard will rule them all.

Back to the investment value chain and the access to capital use case.

At all stages of the investment ecosystem, data and transparency are essential. This is why understanding what ESG data is needed by the participants in the investment value chain is essential for any organization seeking to access capital. Let's take the example of a company wishing to raise funds from an asset manager.

Cleverclogs, a management consulting firm based in Amsterdam with operations across Europe, wishes to raise €25 million from ClimateBux, an asset manager whose fund is domiciled in Luxembourg. ClimateBux has a successful generalist equity fund and an ESG-focused equity fund. ClimateBux is regulated by the Luxembourg financial regulator, which has adopted the European Commission's regulatory guidance on mandatory disclosures on sustainability for all its funds.

Cleverclogs pitches its investment case to ClimateBux, who asks Cleverclogs' management for ESG data before they are willing to invest in the business. Unfortunately, Cleverclogs does not collect or disclose data on its GHG emissions, carbon footprint, sustainability impact on water or waste... none of the data points ClimateBux requests.

Without the data from Cleverclogs, ClimateBux cannot consider Cleverclogs as an investment for the ESG fund. This is because ClimateBux is required to show the portfolio-level data to its regulator to confirm it is complying with the criteria to be called an 'ESG fund'. ClimateBux is also not comfortable investing through its general fund. This is because ClimateBux discloses its emissions data and that of its entire portfolio as part of its own disclosure governance policy. The risk of Cleverclogs being an unsustainable business is too high – and the transparency on this data which is important to ClimateBux is too low.

Being a consulting business, Cleverclogs has little in the way of fossil fuel emissions associated with its services and has a company philosophy to travel by train instead of by air to minimize GHG emissions. This seems to reflect positive sustainability efforts by Cleverclogs. Without collecting the data and disclosing it to ClimateBux (or any other funding source who would likely ask the same questions!), Cleverclogs could not secure the funds they needed to grow. Not very clever.

The onus is on the organization seeking capital to meet the needs of investors through its disclosures. Simply put, without ESG data your organization is at risk of not being able to access capital in the future. This not only relates to equity investments; it is true across the board. Loans from banks require ESG data. Private equity investors ask for ESG data. Stock exchanges require ESG disclosures. This is not something that may happen. It is already happening.

Use case two: Business growth and efficiencies

It is said that companies that have integrated sustainability into the core of their business have a significant competitive advantage, benefiting from improved brand equity, greater share of customer spend, attracting and retaining next generation talent, future-proofing their supply chain, and complying with ever more stringent regulatory requirements. As Jamie Dimon, CEO of financial behemoth JP Morgan Chase, and several other enlightened CEOs have stated, sustainability and ESG are not the enemy of the shareholder, but a tool for value creation of all types – financial, social and environmental.

How does an organization harness this value? Certainly the first step is to convince the group's leaders this value is real – and set up a plan to unlock it. While CEO support is crucial, the ultimate responsibility for ensuring that companies reap these benefits lies squarely within the purview of a company's most senior decision-makers.

Research from Grant Thornton's International Business Report (IBR) survey shows that sustainability is now a major priority, with more than six in 10 businesses (62 per cent) believing sustainability to be as important or more important than financial success. The survey draws on the views of around 5,000 business leaders across 29 economies, with research conducted between May and June 2021.

This isn't just for big companies. Mid-market companies (defined here as companies with $50 million–$500 million in annual revenues) are also noting the importance of sustainability. Since the start of the Covid-19 pandemic, 41 per cent shared that sustainability has become 'much more' important and another 30 per cent a 'little more' important (Grant Thornton International Ltd, 2021).

Capturing hearts and minds is a first step to prioritizing sustainability. The next steps are to be clear on how to implement a sustainability plan. This must be based on understanding how running a sustainable business benefits growth and drives efficiencies. There are a number of ways this value can be realized.

Let's now make the case for some of the most significant drivers: supply chain pressures, supporting the circular economy, business model evolution and talent engagement. There are more. But we have to start somewhere.

Supply chain pressures

Increasingly, supply chains – from raw materials all the way through to the consumer – are factoring sustainability into their buying decisions. In order to accurately reflect your own carbon emissions, collecting data from your supply chain is necessary. We do not work or produce in a vacuum. All organizations have relationships for physical or intangible inputs into their products and services. These inputs and outputs build up the supply and value chains in which our organizations function.

We could not produce our products and services without our supply chain. Neither can we reflect our sustainability impacts without considering our supply chain. We need to factor in the entire chain to reflect an organization's complete impact on people and planet.

Different logic needs to be applied to assessing the benefits of sustainability reporting if you are looking upstream versus downstream in your supply chain. The upstream supply chain is the flow of materials along a production process. Upstream processes include raw materials – such as plastics, woods, metals, and other more specific and intricate products. These inputs are necessary to create the goods and services you sell. If you are a company confident and transparent in your ESG reporting, this can be welcome news for your customers who are looking to manage their upstream supply chain's sustainability impacts. It may win you business against competitors who are less able or willing to share data.

Downstream supply chain operations involve the movement of finished goods from a business to its customers. These operations include distribution, order fulfilment and delivery. Again, if you are a part of another company's downstream supply chain, disclosing sustainability data brings clarity to their supply chain. Your disclosures can win you business and strengthen relationships with your customers.

Together, upstream and downstream supply chain management adds to an organization's ability to optimize their activities and accurately represent their sustainability profile to the market.

Figure 2.2 gives you the general idea of how ESG data can flow through a value chain. ESG data gathered from upstream and downstream must be added to a company's own data from their manufacturing/delivery processes

Figure 2.2 Data along the supply chain

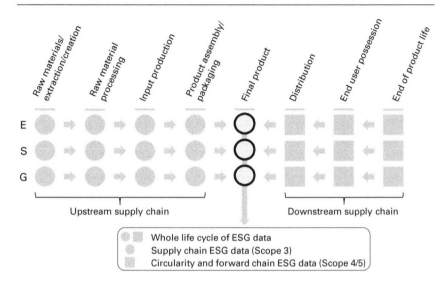

E   S   G

Upstream supply chain   Downstream supply chain

Whole life cycle of ESG data
Supply chain ESG data (Scope 3)
Circularity and forward chain ESG data (Scope 4/5)

to accurately reflect a 'whole of life cycle' sustainability metric. The whole of life cycle ESG data is represented in Figure 2.2 as the addition of all of the circles from the upstream supply chain to all of the squares in the downstream supply chain.

This may seem complicated. That is because it is. Getting an entire value chain to reliably disclose ESG data so that it can be amalgamated and reflected at each company's level – and at a product level – is still a work in progress. Thinking about the entire value chain makes sustainability everyone's job. ESG data disclosure is therefore an increasingly important part of the procurement process – not only to tick a box, but to use as a basis for buying decisions.

You may have heard of the concepts of 'Scope 1/2/3' emissions. (If not, you soon will in Chapter 3.) For now, be aware that supply chain data sits squarely with Scope 3 emissions reporting. Be confident that if ESG data is unavailable from your organization, the risk of losing new business or existing customers is very real.

To allow some of the practical elements of a supply chain to come alive for you, let's consider the distribution element of the simple supply chain outlined in Figure 2.2. The end user of your product or service often gets hold of it through a delivery mechanism. For example, that new kitchen gadget you bought online that was assembled in Germany with Hungarian-made parts, clever Taiwanese-produced silicon chips and Californian design which promises to turn you into the next winner of *MasterChef* arrives at your doorstep just in time for you to host the neighbourhood dinner party.

The delivery of your gadget required physical transportation to your door. Transportation as an industry sector has the highest reliance on fossil fuels of any sector and accounted for 37 per cent of CO_2 emissions from end-use sectors in 2021. Even taking into account the Covid-19 pandemic in 2020 and 2021, when we were all limited in our abilities to use transport and borders were less permeable to trade traffic, transportation remained a significant portion of global emissions. Perhaps this was due to the increased number of Amazon and TaoBao and Rakuten and Flipkart deliveries made while we were all locked down. Many of us grew meaningful relationships with the delivery teams knocking on our doors during those years. Even when most of us were able to leave our houses without restrictions, in 2022, emissions attributable to the transportation sector increased further. According to the International Energy Association (IEA), total transport emissions increased in 2022 by 2.1 per cent year on year.

Of course, not all of these emissions can be attributed to the delivery of your kitchen gadget referenced above. On the other hand, neither can the transportation and delivery elements of the downstream supply chain be discounted or ignored. Interest in the supply chain is climbing as climate change and natural capital impacts move up the agenda.

At the very end of many supply chains is the consumer. This vast number of yous and mes is also increasingly adding sustainability considerations alongside longstanding variables such as price, colour, size, etc when making buying choices. Consumption is changing. What people are buying is changing. According to the European Parliamentary Research Service, more than two-thirds of Europeans would buy environmentally friendly products regardless of an increase in cost (European Parliament, 2022). This trend towards buying sustainably includes buying products from socially responsible companies that demonstrate prioritizing workers' rights and other policies to support local and international communities.

Paired with the increase in digitization and ecommerce, the consumer now wields more power than ever before in supporting a sustainable economy. Researching products and the companies that provide them in advance of making a purchasing decision is easy online. Toggling from your full ecommerce cart to a search for 'company X carbon footprint' or 'product Y vs Product Z – which is more sustainable?' takes only a few moments and a few clicks. But we are only able to do this research when sustainability data is disclosed by companies.

There is big business in providing information on company and product sustainability to the end consumer. This business is set to grow. If your business is not disclosing sustainability data, you may be excluded from consumption choices going forward and left out of consumer-focused apps geared to consumers. Increasingly there is nowhere to hide.

Beyond product delivery – enter the circular economy

The end user may not actually be the end of your supply chain. In a sustainable world, the supply chain includes the ultimate destination of the raw materials in your product. This stretches the life of your product beyond the end user. In Figure 2.2, this is the 'End of Product Life' phase. The questions for you as an organization continue well after your product or service has been sold. What happens to your product when it is no longer fit for purpose? Is it a contributor to landfill? Does it leech toxins into the soil or become unstable or dangerous? Could its components or raw materials be reused?

The theory that sustainability helps make businesses more efficient is linked to the megatrend of the circular economy. The principles of the circular economy promote reusing and recycling materials. Circularity also seeks to minimize the amount of resources and raw materials used in product creation. According to McKinsey, a sustainability strategy can reduce costs substantially and can affect operating profits by as much as 60 per cent (Koller and Nuttall, 2020). This results when measuring input usage uncovers opportunities to minimize the volumes of inputs used in production such as water intake and energy consumption. These inputs cost money, and while they are sometimes dismissed as commodities with sticky prices, measuring usage with a goal to minimize inputs can also lower costs.

Changing processes after accurately measuring inputs and outputs can drive efficiencies. By decreasing the inputs needed at the front end and limiting the amount that goes to landfill, an organization can both protect the environment and create efficiencies for the business itself.

A great example comes from the exhibition display market. Companies in this sector have been renowned for single use construction produced for clients that require a physical display that is used for a finite period of time. This period of time could be as little as hours, while the materials that go into the display have significant impact on landfill volumes for decades. This does not seem logical in a sustainable world. A new approach adopted by some companies in this sector is to create plastic display stands – including plastics that have been beachcombed or recycled from consumer packaging – that could be reused rather than thrown away when the exhibition is over.

You can create business efficiencies driven by sustainable objectives by also considering changes to your business model. For example, the exhibition display company keen on improving their sustainability and business efficiency could pivot to a service-based business model that rented out their display stands rather than offering them for sale. This change in strategy could not only drive sustainability but also offer lower supply chain costs and the opportunity for speed in delivery, ultimately delivering bottom-line benefits.

Again, circularity and waste management (and the data behind these actions!) are important to monitor and manage to uphold sustainability and mitigate reputational risks. Sustainability is tangibly affecting buying decisions as ESG data points and disclosures influence buying choices all along any organization's value chain. That affects a company's growth. That affects its future potential. That's important because without future potential, your organization's value plummets – and with it your effectiveness as its leader.

CASE STUDY   McDonald's' transition to paper packaging

In 1990, McDonald's, the global fast-food giant, started to work with the Environmental Defense Fund (EDF) to review its use of plastics – starting with the iconic and ubiquitous polystyrene clamshells that most of their burgers were served in. McDonald's made a groundbreaking decision to shift from plastic to paper packaging for its products as part of its commitment to environmental sustainability. This case study delves into McDonald's' strategic move to adopt paper packaging, and the pivotal role played by the EDF in providing data and research into business efficiencies.

As the world's largest fast-food chain, McDonald's has always been under scrutiny for its environmental impact, particularly concerning single-use plastics. The company recognized the growing global concern about plastic pollution and decided to proactively address the issue. By transitioning to more sustainable paper-based packaging, McDonald's aimed to reduce its carbon footprint and set a positive example for the fast-food industry as a whole.

In partnership with McDonald's, the EDF played a crucial role in guiding the transition to paper packaging. Their mission to find solutions to environmental challenges through collaboration with businesses made them an ideal partner for McDonald's ambitious sustainability goals.

EDF conducted research and gathered data from McDonald's processes to assess options for change. Beyond the environmental benefits of the transition, the EDF also researched business efficiencies that could be gained through the switch to paper packaging. This involved a thorough analysis of the McDonald's supply chain, packaging processes and distribution methods.

The EDF identified several key areas where efficiencies could be achieved, including:

- **Logistics and transportation**: By optimizing packaging dimensions and weight, McDonald's could enhance space utilization during transportation, reducing the number of shipments required and lowering fuel consumption. This led to significant cost savings and a reduced carbon footprint.

- **Supplier partnerships**: The EDF encouraged McDonald's to collaborate with suppliers committed to sustainable practices, which not only aligned with the company's environmental goals but also fostered stronger relationships within the supply chain.

- **Consumer and employee perception and loyalty**: The transition to paper packaging resonated with environmentally conscious consumers, bolstering McDonald's reputation as a responsible and forward-thinking brand. This positive perception translated into increased customer loyalty and a potential boost in sales.

The EDF's research demonstrated that McDonald's could achieve substantial cost savings by transitioning to paper packaging. Over the next decade, McDonald's eliminated more than 300 million pounds of packaging, including the polystyrene clamshells, recycled 1 million tonnes of corrugated boxes and reduced restaurant waste by 30 per cent.

As a result of these and other changes, McDonald's saves an estimated $6 million per year (EDF, 2018).

In 2022, McDonald's officially completed the transition to paper packaging across its global outlets. The shift was met with widespread acclaim from consumers, environmental advocates and industry peers. By taking this bold step towards sustainability, McDonald's not only reduced its plastic waste but also inspired other businesses to re-evaluate their packaging practices.

What about the people? Talent wants to know

As we consider growth and efficiency as factors in sustainability data's importance, we can't forget about the people in our organizations who make things happen. Organizations at their centre are driven by talented individuals who play all sorts of roles in the business – from executive offices to the shop floors. Increasingly, this talent cares about sustainability and chooses workplaces that reflect their standards and ethos.

It is expensive to replace talented employees. In general, retaining strong contributors to the company is an advantage for a business. Retention mitigates the need to train up new hires on company best practices, content and specific processes or skills. It can also positively contribute to a sense of team and belonging that adds value to a wider group of employees. So, how can ESG data help to retain employees? Here are four ways of looking at it:

1 **Aligning with employee values:** When an organization has strong positive ESG data, it demonstrates to employees that the company is committed to being socially responsible, which aligns with the values of many employees. Employees are more likely to be engaged and committed to a company that they believe is making a positive impact in the world.

2 **Enhancing company reputation:** Everyone likes to be proud of the company they work for. We all spend a huge amount of time at work, so it makes sense to feel good about being there. Companies with good ESG scores are often perceived as more reputable and trustworthy. This can help to retain employees and attract new employees who want to work for a company that is aligned to a positive sustainability priority.

3 **Increasing employee satisfaction:** Employees who feel that their company is committed to doing the right thing for society and the environment are often more satisfied in their jobs. When employees are satisfied, they are more likely to stay with a company for the long-term, reducing employee turnover.

4 **Demonstrating good management practices:** Strong ESG data can reflect strong management and governance practices in place. This can be attractive to employees who value good governance and seek out transparency.

Overall, disclosing ESG data – even if that disclosure is initially only internal to the organization – can help to both retain and attract top talent by aligning with their values, enhancing company reputation, increasing employee satisfaction and demonstrating good governance. This is borne out by the numbers. A study published in 2018 shows that companies with an inclusive culture have 27 per cent higher profitability and 22 per cent greater productivity (Deloitte, 2018).

Sustainability in all its forms can create bottom-line benefits for an organization and lower HR costs in the short, medium and long term.

Use case three: Compliance and regulation

Stay awake. This is an important one. And no – you can't get your lawyer to deal with this for you. As a business leader you need to understand your obligations for compliance today and tomorrow. They are changing quickly, so let's get started by convincing you that compliance and regulations make sustainability data important to your organization. And to you.

Increasingly, organizations need to consider what their obligations are to uphold positive sustainability and explain how their activities have an impact on people and planet. These obligations may be driven by regulation and the need for organizations to comply with specific legislated limits, governance rules, actions or inactions, etc. Regulations may require strict compliance and provision of information to an overseeing board or institution that can be national, regional, local, industry-specific, based on a capital market or financial requirement, or another body that oversees the activities that an organization participates in.

Requirements to comply with regulation may sit at the sector or industry level. Standards and compliance requirements may vary across geographies. Many times, there is no globally unifying set of requirements. It can be tricky for you as a leader to get your arms around regulatory requirements depending on your business complexities and reach. You (or your colleagues) will be the experts on the regulations on certifications, testing, labelling, etc that are unique to your products, services and industry. You may be less familiar with sustainability standards – all of which continue to evolve.

A good way to get a handle on how sectoral obligations for sustainability compliance break down is to map them to the sectors comprising the S&P 500 index. The S&P 500 divides the global economy up into 11 sectors. These all have different regulations that affect their sustainability compliance. Some examples are presented in Table 2.2.

Table 2.2 is not intended to be globally and universally comprehensive. Its goal is to remind you that alongside financial regulations that will impose

Table 2.2 S&P 500: 11 sectors and examples of sustainability compliance

Sector	Sector descriptions	ESG data examples
Energy	The sector includes companies involved in oil and gas exploration, production and distribution. The Environmental Protection Agency (EPA) regulates emissions from energy production and consumption in the United States through programmes such as the Clean Air Act and the Clean Power Plan.	Ratio of renewable energy use/produced Emissions (CO_2, methane, etc)
Materials	This sector includes companies involved in mining, metals and other raw materials. The USA's Consumer Product Safety Improvement Act (CPSIA) regulates the use of certain chemicals in products, while the Toxic Substances Control Act (TSCA) requires manufacturers to report and manage the risks associated with chemicals used in their products. The EU has regulations on the use of chemicals in products, including the REACH (Registration, Evaluation, Authorization, and Restriction of Chemicals) regulation, which requires companies to register and evaluate the safety of chemicals used in products. The UK Waste Electrical and Electronic Equipment (WEEE) Regulations require companies to ensure that their electrical and electronic products are recycled or disposed of in an environmentally friendly way. The Australian Packaging Covenant (APC) is a voluntary agreement between government and industry to reduce the environmental impact of packaging. Companies in the materials sector can join the APC and commit to sustainability targets for packaging.	Waste management governance Impacts on nature and biodiversity Volume of waste sent to landfill Human rights protection

(continued)

Table 2.2 (Continued)

Sector	Sector descriptions	ESG data examples
Industrial	This sector includes companies involved in manufacturing, transportation and other industrial activities. In the US, the EPA's Resource Conservation and Recovery Act (RCRA) regulates the management of hazardous waste generated by industrial activities. The EU has regulations on emissions of air pollutants from industrial activities, including the Industrial Emissions Directive. The Directive sets standards for emissions of pollutants such as nitrogen oxides, sulphur dioxide, and dust. The UK Climate Change Act sets legally binding targets for reducing greenhouse gas emissions, including emissions from the industrial sector. Companies in the industrial sector must report on their emissions and set targets for reducing them.	Emissions Power usage
Consumer discretionary	This sector includes companies that provide non-essential goods and services to consumers. The Consumer Product Safety Commission (CPSC) regulates safety standards for products sold in the US market, while the Federal Trade Commission (FTC) regulates advertising and marketing practices. The Fair Labor Standards Act (FLSA) establishes minimum wage and overtime requirements for most workers, while the Foreign Corrupt Practices Act (FCPA) prohibits companies from bribing foreign officials to obtain business. The EU has regulations on the labelling and marketing of textiles, including requirements for environmental and social responsibility. The EU Ecolabel certifies products that meet these standards. Global jurisdictions have varying local requirements for consumer discretionary producers – these can cover specific goods and need to be reviewed based on where the company is headquartered, whether it has production facilities, or whether it has end users in the jurisdictions.	Waste management Human rights protection

Sector	Description	Topics
Consumer staples	The sector includes companies that provide essential goods and services to consumers. The Food and Drug Administration (FDA) regulates the safety and labelling of food and personal care products, while the Occupational Safety and Health Administration (OSHA) regulates workplace safety in the USA. The Japanese government has established the Food Sanitation Act, which sets safety standards for food and beverages, including maximum levels for pesticide residues, additives and other substances. The Brazilian government has established the National Programme for the Reduction of Agrochemicals (PRONARA), which aims to reduce the use of agrochemicals in agriculture and promote the use of alternative, more sustainable practices.	Hazardous substance disposal policies Land use policies
Healthcare	The sector includes companies that provide healthcare products and services. The Affordable Care Act (ACA) regulates health insurance and healthcare delivery in the United States, while the FDA regulates the safety and efficacy of drugs and medical devices. The EU has regulations on medical devices, including requirements for environmental performance and the reduction of hazardous substances. The National Health Service (NHS) in the UK has developed a Sustainable Development Unit, which promotes sustainable healthcare practices and sets standards for reducing carbon emissions and waste in the sector. The Japanese Ministry of Health, Labour and Welfare has developed guidelines for reducing the environmental impact of healthcare facilities, which includes measures to reduce energy use and waste.	Energy usage Labelling governance Water usage
Financial	This sector includes companies that provide financial services, such as banking, insurance and investment management. The Dodd–Frank Wall Street Reform and Consumer Protection Act regulates the financial industry and requires public companies to disclose their executive compensation practices. There are increasingly more regulations for disclosure in the financial sector worldwide. (We will deep dive into these regulations related to the access to capital use case later in the book.)	Emissions Power usage Fossil-fuel exposure

(continued)

Table 2.2 (Continued)

Sector	Sector descriptions	ESG data examples
Information technology	The sector includes companies involved in technology and information services. The European Union's General Data Protection Regulation (GDPR) regulates the collection, use, and storage of personal data by companies operating in the EU. In the US, the Federal Trade Commission (FTC) regulates privacy and data security practices, while the National Institute of Standards and Technology (NIST) sets standards for cybersecurity. Governance requirements feature heavily in the sustainability goals of this sector. In addition, production of IT equipment has sustainability-related regulatory requirements. For example, the Chinese government has established the China RoHS (Restriction of Hazardous Substances) regulation, which requires electronic and electrical products sold in China to comply with certain hazardous substance restrictions. The South Korean government has established the Act on Resource Circulation of Electrical and Electronic Equipment and Vehicles, which requires manufacturers of IT products and other electronic devices to take responsibility for recycling and disposal of their products.	Rare earths and mineral procurement governance Impacts on nature and biodiversity Data governance
Communication services	The sector includes companies engaged in communication and media-related services. The Federal Communications Commission (FCC) regulates the use of the public airwaves for communication services such as radio, television and wireless telephony in the USA. This includes data privacy and content moderation and accessibility. This all contributes to positive social impact and influences the sector's S in ESG.	Workforce diversity Data governance
Utilities	The sector includes companies that provide electricity, gas and water services. In the US, Environmental Protection Agency (EPA) regulates air and water quality, while the Federal Energy Regulatory Commission (FERC) sets standards for energy delivery and pricing. The North American Electric Reliability Corporation (NERC) regulates the reliability and security of the electric grid in North America.	Water usage Land usage

Real estate	The sector includes companies involved in real estate development, management and investment. The Leadership in Energy and Environmental Design (LEED) certification programme provides standards for sustainable building design and construction and has wide global adoption. The EU has established the Energy Performance of Buildings Directive (EPBD), which requires member states to establish minimum energy performance standards for new and existing buildings, and to regularly inspect and assess the energy performance of buildings. The Chinese government has established the Three-Star Rating System for Green Buildings, which provides certification for buildings that meet certain environmental standards in terms of energy and resource efficiency, indoor environmental quality, and other sustainability factors. The Australian government has established the National Australian Built Environment Rating System (NABERS), which provides a rating system for the environmental performance of buildings, including energy efficiency, water usage and indoor environmental quality.	Energy usage Land usage Emissions Water usage

compliance criteria on your ability to access capital, sector-specific regulations exist as well which will require ESG data. Knowing what data needs to be used to comply can help you as a leader guide your business's data prioritization plans.

It's worth noting that this is not an exhaustive list, and that there are many more regulations and standards that apply to specific industries or companies. The regulatory landscape is constantly evolving, and companies should stay up to date on any changes that may affect their operations.

The other area of regulation your organization may be subject to is financial regulation. Specifically, financial disclosure regulation which includes ESG data reporting.

Data use cases are often interrelated. Investigating why sustainability data is essential to the access to capital use case is a good precursor to considering how sustainability data is essential to compliance and regulation. The use cases have some overlap where the regulation directly applicable to your organization comes from financial regulators. Even if you are not a financial services firm, these regulations can put you in scope of regulation if you want to access capital from the financial services markets. You may even fall into scope if you do sizeable business within the regulator's jurisdiction.

The financial sector is engaged in sustainable finance disclosure regulation that stretches beyond firms in the finance sector itself. Financiers are considering their role as change agents. Many of us know the quote 'Follow the money', meaning to follow a trail of money transfers to track down the source of political corruption – a idiom made famous by the 1976 docudrama *All the President's Men*. However, we can tweak the phrase to say 'Follow the *path* to the money'. This can help us understand the power of the financial system in driving behaviours in an economy.

If accessing investment – money! – were to require that you improve your sustainability profile, and that improvement was proven by disclosing ESG data on your activities, it is likely that companies would both disclose that data and seek to improve their sustainability profile. Logically, in this scenario, it is the stewards of money (the financial institutions) that would demand sustainability disclosures for companies. These disclosures, once analysed, would govern what was acceptable to fund at what price.

Moving up the chain, to drive the behaviour of the financial institutions, the financial regulators play the role of rule-setters for the financial institutions. When these rules on how to lend or deploy money include sustainability data requirements, financial institutions not wanting to fall foul of the rules will drive the requirements down the chain into investment criteria. So when we 'Follow the path to the money', we see the regulations and compliance requirements of the financial system definitively make ESG data important to secure money. Compliance with financial regulations is required directly and indirectly.

Let's get a little more detailed on how ESG data can help you 'follow the path to the money' by complying with regulations.

Financial regulatory obligations

Financial auditors are required to adhere to high standards and quality in line with outlined and agreed principles, usually monitored by an industry association such as the Financial Reporting Council (FRC) in the UK, the National Association of State Boards of Accountancy together with the Public Company Accounting Oversight Board (PCAOB) in the USA, or the Public Accountants Oversight Committee of ACRA in Singapore. Audited financial accounts in line with accounting standards have been a longstanding regulatory requirement for a public company to maintain its access to the public markets.

So, for regulatory purposes, financial information needs to be set out in accounts, those accounts need to adhere to the accountancy standards stated by the regulator, and the accounts need to be audited by an independent firm that upholds quality codes.

How does this 'accounting' transparency translate into a company's 'sustainability data' transparency?

First, let's get some language translated from the financial world to the sustainability world. Table 2.3 helps compare the two terminologies.

Table 2.3 Translation of financial terminology to the sustainability world

Accounting language	Sustainability data language
Financial accounts	ESG datasets
Accounting standards (e.g. GAAP)	Disclosure standards (e.g. ISSB developments)
Audited	Assured or verified
Independent auditor (i.e. a Big Four accounting practice)	Sustainability verification/assurances providers (many)

Remember that financial accounts are simply a framework for providing data. A profit and loss (P&L) account or balance sheet contains data very familiar to those reviewing the data contained within them because they look very similar. This makes it easy to compare the data in a financial statement between one company and another – within the same industry or market segment, or across different business types.

It is important to note that while there are accounting standards that the majority of mature markets have adopted (i.e. GAAP, as we discussed earlier), even accounting standards are not global. There exists a range of standards which makes comparability across geographical markets more challenging (as previously noted). However, the range of standards overall have tried and tested ways of being restated to make the data they contain comparable. The financial markets have found a way to bridge the differences and create robustly comparable data to allow global companies across markets to be assessed against each other.

If you are in scope of financial sustainability disclosure regulation, you have other questions to consider. As you see in Table 2.3, accountancy language offers an independent auditor as part of the disclosure process to verify the information you provide to the public. Should you do the same for sustianability data? The process of independent verification is much less mature in the world of sustainability disclosures. Many regulatory regimes allow for self-reporting. This allows firms to disclose ESG data without an external 'auditor' or verification team. Some regulatory requirements include the need for external verification (or sometimes the word 'assurances' is used for ESG data).

So, not only is ESG data non-negotiable for you to have available in these regulatory circumstances, it is non-negotiable for you to pay for an external firm to review how you collected and calculated that data. The direction of travel is towards increased verification and assurances on ESG data reporting. You need your data to be clear and traceable to get this right. We will review how to ensure data is as valuable as possible in Chapter 3. The point is clear: you need data for financial regulation, and you need that data to be robust.

Regulation is rapidly evolving to include more ESG data disclosure requirements in more jurisdictions around the world. We will deep dive into this in Chapter 8. Be it either sector-specific or financially driven regulation, being compliant is definitively an essential ESG data use case.

All the ESG data use cases all the time

No matter what business you run, one or more of the use cases in the ABCs of sustainability data will apply to you. It may be that all three of these use cases are compelling reasons for you to read on and understand more about the significance of ESG data for your business. By considering these ESG data use cases, you are already well on the way to successfully navigating sustainability data for your organization. Framing the way you will use the data is an excellent grounding for what is to come.

Now that you know why you need sustainability data, we are ready to ask an even more philosophical question: what *is* data?

In the next chapter, we will explain what we mean when we use the term 'data'. We will also consider a few more ways to use data specifically for sustainability purposes.

References

Deloitte (2018) *Inclusive Mobility: How mobilizing a diverse workforce can drive business performance*, www2.deloitte.com/content/dam/Deloitte/us/Documents/Tax/us-tax-inclusive-mobility-mobilize-diverse-workforce-drive-business-performance.pdf (archived at https://perma.cc/QJ74-VQHU)

EDF (2018) McDonald's saves billions cutting waste, www.edf.org/partnerships/mcdonalds (archived at https://perma.cc/PU3H-SMUT)

Elkington, J (2018) 25 years ago I coined the phrase 'triple bottom line.' Here's why it's time to rethink it, *Harvard Business Review*, https://hbr.org/2018/06/25-years-ago-i-coined-the-phrase-triple-bottom-line-heres-why-im-giving-up-on-it (archived at https://perma.cc/VY7L-WK9R)

European Parliament (2022) Empowering consumers for the green transition, www.europarl.europa.eu/RegData/etudes/BRIE/2022/733543/EPRS_BRI(2022)733543_EN.pdf (archived at https://perma.cc/2479-ECGS)

Grant Thornton International Ltd (2021) Creating competitive advantage through sustainability, www.grantthornton.global/en/insights/articles/creating-competitive-advantage-through-sustainability/ (archived at https://perma.cc/M772-KYEX)

HBR Business Insights Blog (2020) The triple bottom line: What it is and why it's important, https://online.hbs.edu/blog/post/what-is-the-triple-bottom-line (archived at https://perma.cc/9S9N-3W54)

IFRS (2018) Definition of material, www.ifrs.org/content/dam/ifrs/project/definition-of-materiality/definition-of-material-feedback-statement.pdf?la=en (archived at https://perma.cc/7MZM-XQJY)

IKEA (nd) Towards using only renewable and recycled materials, https://about.
    ikea.com/en/sustainability/a-world-without-waste/renewable-and-recycled-
    materials (archived at https://perma.cc/LC7P-4CS3)

Koller, T and Nuttall, R (2020) How the E in ESG creates business value,
    McKinsey, www.mckinsey.com/capabilities/sustainability/our-insights/
    sustainability-blog/how-the-e-in-esg-creates-business-value (archived at
    https://perma.cc/CYS3-GNQW)

Waste360 (2017) IKEA to invest in plastics recycling plant, www.waste360.com/
    plastics/ikea-invest-plastics-recycling-plant (archived at https://perma.cc/
    VFR9-AD2G)

What is ESG data?

3

REFLECTIVE QUESTIONS

- When we talk about ESG data – what type of data are we actually talking about?
- Where do you find and measure sustainability data? What is the source?
- What data do you need to put the data you have in perspective?

Data. We speak of it as though it's one thing.

But it's not.

It is many different things. In some ways, this concept is exemplified by the word itself: data. There is an active grammatical debate raging over if the word 'data' is singular or plural. I know I've struggled with using it uniformly in this book. I hope that all of you grammar nerds will forgive my inconsistancy. *The Economist* reviewed the use of the word, and decided it was singular. They even wrote an article about it in August 2022 (The Economist, 2022).

Other experts have taken a different view. Data's ambiguity extends from the grammatical into the practical, and can edge into the philosophical. Let it be known here that sustainability data is not immune to differing definitions. That should not stop us from striving to be as clear as possible about data and why it matters.

This chapter outlines how data types are defined, what data may be considered 'sustainability' data, where that data comes from and some general health warnings including how to ensure data is as valuable as possible.

Defining 'data'

Data is a shortcut term for an often fragmented collection of information defined by varying degrees of quality, relevance and usefulness. According to the Oxford English Dictionary, data can be thought of as 'facts and statistics collected together for reference or analysis', while Merriam-Webster defines it as 'factual information (such as measurements or statistics) used as a basis for reasoning, discussion, or calculation'.

In other words, data is information we can analyse, interpret and use for decision-making. As management consultant W Edwards Deming, the architect of Japan's manufacturing revolution of the 1970s, put it: 'Without data, you're just another person with an opinion.'

Data comes in many forms and from many, many different sources. We are producing more data than ever before, and that trajectory is charting a course to higher volumes of data produced every year. Some estimates suggest that the total amount of data created, captured, copied and consumed globally will increase to 181 zettabytes by 2025 (International Data Corporation, 2022).

For some perspective on this, consider that one zettabyte is equal to the number of all the grains of sand lying on all the world's beaches added together. That's a lot of sand. And that's a lot of data.

If you drill down into this accumulation of facts and figures, you'll find a rich mix of numbers, text, images, audio and video. These bits of data were gathered because they were of importance or interest to someone or to some use case. We have all experienced the proliferation of data in our personal lives through our daily use of mobile technology. Technology has indeed accelerated the accumulation of data in our personal capacities – we no longer need to ration our photography skills on the basis of the availability or cost of developing physical film. We all now carry around an entire photography and video creation studio in our pocket via our smartphone. In November 2020, Google announced that more than 4 trillion photos are stored in Google Photos, and every week 28 billion new photos and videos are uploaded on Google Images. By 2030, there will be 382 billion images on Google Images. In the business world, data has also proliferated.

In this ever growing sea of data, this book is most interested in data that can be used to measure and manage sustainability impacts. This is the ESG data we have referenced before.

Data types

First, let's look at data types so that we understand the universe of ESG data more accurately. One of the most obvious distinctions is between 'quantitative' data, which can be measured in numbers and analysed using mathematical and statistical methods, and 'qualitative' data, which can't be expressed in terms of numbers. Instead, qualitative data describes qualities and characteristics such as attitudes, beliefs, opinions and emotions collected through free text questionnaires, interviews, focus groups and surveys to which thematic and content analysis and similar methods are then applied. ESG data includes both types of data: quantitative and qualitative.

We also distinguish between 'structured' data that is in a specific format, such as a spreadsheet, and 'unstructured' data that has no specific format at all, like a text file. Both structured and unstructured data can be equally valuable. The difference between the two can add complexity to amalgamating, analysing and comparing the data. This is especially true when data pertaining to the same underlying item takes two different formats – or has no format at all. It is logical that formatted data is easier to pull together and compare, but as sustainable data evolves, some data you would like to compare across your own business units may take different formats. This requires some level of transposing data into a common format to make it useful.

The challenges posed by structured and unstructured data have longer tail implications. When regulations and compliance come into play, as in in the C use case we described in Chapter 2, accuracy and comparability become essential. This introduces the benefits of standardizing data – be that structured or unstructured. The more standardization, the better the comparability. Accuracy can also be improved if standards clearly state the desired structure of the data. It leaves less room for interpretation. This can drive clarity and be helpful to those who gather the data.

We can understand the impacts of using structured versus unstructured data combined with quantitative versus qualitative data through an example. Remember: quantitative and qualitative data can exist about the same underlying subject. For example, we can have 'quantitative' data that can be represented numerically, such as CO_2 emission levels reported specifically in tonnes. A related 'qualitative' data example may include consumers' opinions about CO_2 emissions. This data will be presented as words, and is unstructured. Both of these datasets have value, but they are difficult to combine, compare or contrast.

At university I attained a chemistry degree. I enjoyed the solidity that came from experiments that resulted in numbers. Numbers I could use to derive outcomes, and numbers I could analyse and decide what they told me. Where my friends (the ones who irritatingly had no lab time and therefore many fewer weekly scheduled hours) turned out qualitative analysis in essays and wordy surveys, I cranked out hard numbers from my experiments. I took comfort in my numbers.

But even (way) back then, I needed to include qualitative elements in recording my outcomes – especially to put perspective on data that was odd or data that was difficult to explain. For example, a dirty beaker needed to be qualitatively documented to explain an inconsistent measurement. The subtlety of colour gradients in a solution often required words, not numbers, to record the results.

I have to admit that I am inclined to try to make as much data as quantitative as possible, and it is often possible to do so. Even a consumer's opinion on climate can be quantified by surveying an appropriate sample size and attributing a percentage of respondents with a certain opinion. Bingo! You have a numerical data point. However, this example illustrates an opportunity to introduce bias into the data. Answers to questions inherently contain influences from the creator of the questions. This is bias.

Bias is also demonstrated though decisions taken when structuring the survey and reflecting the results. What sample group size and attributes truly reflect a uniform opinion in a given scenario? Are the qualitative questions asked with neutrality, or phrased to introduce preference for a certain answer? If the unstructured results come in the form of words or descriptions, who determines which words reflect an equivalent point of view? We will dig further into data dangers in both qualitative and quantitative ESG data, including the dangers of the three Es of data, later in this chapter.

There are a number of other data-related terms that provide data on the data. For example, 'time-series' data, such as ongoing global temperature readings, is collected over months and years, while 'cross-sectional' data is gathered at a specific moment, during a one-off survey, for instance. Both of these data types result in a numerical data point. If you are unaware of how the data was collected, you could make assumptions when reviewing the data or comparing it inside or outside your organization. This can lead to false assumptions.

'Raw' data (also called source data, unprocessed data, original data or primary data) refers to data collected first-hand from something like an academic study, or, in the case of ESG data, from disclosures by a corporate or government. 'Derived' data builds on raw data and is created based on a combination of datasets and factors. 'Static' data doesn't change much, while 'dynamic' data does. So, a company's legal name, address and registration number are static data, while stock prices and weather information fall very much under the heading of dynamic data.

Disclosure data vs macro data

The demand for sustainability data – including ESG data – is growing. The data itself is also growing in volume. Interest in collecting, disseminating, analysing and selling ESG data is booming. It is predicted that the total addressable market for ESG data will exceed $5 billion by 2025, up from an estimated $2.2 billion in 2020 (Environmental Finance, 2020). Where does this data come from?

ESG data comes from two primary sources: 'disclosure' data and 'macro' data.

The first of these, disclosure data, is generated by an organization and contains information about its climate impact (E data), social impact (S data) and governance credentials (G data). Increasingly, data is being requested – and disclosed – on specific topics such as energy usage and efficiency, biodiversity and habitat protection measures, waste management and reduction policies, human rights and labour practices, the sustainability of supply chains, community engagement programmes and diversity, equity, and inclusion initiatives… among a growing list!

Since this data is specific to the organization's operations, it can be used to identify and track the sustainability performance of individual companies and can be used by customers, investors, analysts and regulators for comparison between firms and for better decision-making.

ESG data from disclosures (also termed 'reporting') sits in all corners of your organization. It can pour in from virtually every function and area of operation. That may seem daunting. However, it should also be comforting. As an organization you will be collecting data to run your business already. Some of this data may be ESG-useful data. You may or may not already be collecting it to use as a sustainability data point. It may be data you use in your normal course of business to grow, improve, monitor, tweak or pivot.

You may already be collecting more ESG data than you think. In Chapter 4 we will dig deeper into how data savvy your organization is. There is a wide range of data proficiency across organizations. Your organization will already be somewhere on that ESG Data Maturity Journey. You may be further ahead in this journey than you thought!

Let's break down ESG data to better understand where it comes from in your organization.

Climate data – the E

You may have the view that climate data is the most closely linked part of ESG data to sustainability objectives. E data describes how an organization manages its impact on the natural word. Some examples of data falling under E include greenhouse gas (GHG) emissions, electricity and water usage, waste and pollution, deforestation and land use.

These data points can come from various areas of your business. They could be collected as data from manufacturing processes, facilities management, IT or logistics. In many firms, much of this resides in the 'operations' department. The fact that what one company includes in operations differs from another (even in the same sector) means you may need to look harder for a complete view of E data points than a single division in your company.

Your E data may also need searching for outside your organization. Your supply chain and partners may be significant contributors to some of your E metrics. This is the case when you consider your GHG emissions – specifically when calculating Scope 3 emissions. See the following box for more detail on what we mean by scopes.

The scope for GHGs

How do you quantify GHG emissions? Here is where Scope 1, 2 and 3 fit in.

You may have heard of the terms Scope 1, 2 and 3 data when talking about sustainability. From an ESG perspective, Scope 1, 2 and 3 are terms used to classify GHG emissions based on their source as defined by the GHG Protocol. Here's how they are defined.

Scope 1

These are direct emissions from sources owned or controlled by an organization. So, these include emissions from:

- combustion of fossil fuels in boilers, generators and vehicles
- industrial processes such as those involved in the production of chemicals, cement and steel
- on-site transportation such as forklifts and company cars
- on-site landfills and waste treatment facilities

- on-site agricultural activities such as livestock production
- on-site stationary fuel-combustion equipment like gas engines, turbines or fuel cells

Scope 2

These are indirect emissions from the generation at a separate facility of the electricity, steam, heating and cooling purchased and consumed by the organization, as well as from the use of renewable energy and carbon emissions offsets.

Scopes 1 and 2 are usually grouped together, and an organization often discloses these two scopes as data listed both separately and combined. When combined, they are sometimes considered an organization's total value for GHG emissions if that company is not disclosing Scope 3 emissions.

The detail behind carbon emission offsets will be outlined in Chapter 5.

Scope 3

These are other indirect emissions occurring in an organization's value chain not covered by Scope 2. Examples include emissions from:

- the extraction and production of purchased goods and services
- employee commuting and business travel (car, air and sea)
- use of sold products and leased assets
- waste disposal and treatment that are not owned or controlled by the organization
- the generation of electricity, steam, heating and cooling from sources not covered by Scope 2
- the production of goods and services that are not owned or controlled by the organization
- the disposal and treatment of waste generated by operations not owned or controlled by the organization
- the use of water, land and other resources
- the extraction, production and transport of the fuel used for employee commuting and business travel

Scope 3 emissions collection and calculations are a lot more challenging than Scopes 1 and 2 because they rely on the organization's supply chain to supply their emissions data for inclusion. It is not uncommon at the time of writing for firms to still be working on calculating their Scope 3 emissions – even when they have disclosed Scope 1 and 2 for many years already.

Certainly, Scope 1, 2 and 3 emissions are by far the most commonly used scopes for disclosure. That is not to say they are the only defined scopes. Scopes 4 and 5 focus on the impacts of the organization's products as they continue their journey though the circular economy. They ask for carbon emissions resulting from an organization's product's usage and end of life. They are defined as follows.

Scope 4

These are emissions occurring outside of a product's life cycle or value chain, but as a result of the use of that product. Here we have emissions from:

- the production of raw materials used in the production of goods and services
- the use, disposal or end-of-life treatment of a company's products
- the entire life cycle of a product, including the entire supply chain and its disposal
- the use of products, infrastructure or services not owned or controlled by the organization
- the use of land, water and other resources throughout the product's life cycle

Scope 5

These are emissions from third-party operations that are neither owned nor controlled by an organization. They include emissions from:

- the disposal and treatment of waste generated by operations not owned or controlled by the organization
- the use of products, infrastructure or services not owned or controlled by the organization
- the combustion of biomass and biofuels

- the use of land, water and other resources throughout the product's life cycle
- the production of raw materials used in the production of goods and services
- the use, disposal or end-of-life treatment of a company's products
- the entire life cycle of a product, including the entire supply chain and its disposal

While Scopes 4 and 5 are not mainstream, guidance on how to collect and calculate this data is being developed. These are certainly ones to watch out for as the ESG disclosure journey continues.

Social data – the S

If we look for social (S) data, a major source within an organization will be the HR department. The HR team are responsible for collecting and analysing all sorts of data on the employee base and this can already include reporting on data related to gender, race, ethnicity and age. Typically, HR will also review data on employee turnover, promotion rates, and training and development opportunities. The business use case for this data is ultimately to retain and attract talent and to ensure that the organization's human capital is fit for purpose and future-proofed in line with business strategy.

Additionally, an organization's corporate social responsibility (CSR) function, if there is one, might offer input about community engagement activities, charitable giving and sustainability performance metrics. This adds to the organization's impact on the societies and communities it works in and with.

The PR and communications departments gather material from press coverage, social media and customer feedback, all things that affect an organization's reputation as well as stakeholder perceptions. Together with marketing and sales, all these functional areas might bring together data and insights on the social and ethical implications of a company's internal and external campaigns.

Your organization's supply chain plays a role in measuring your S data as well. Data about supplier diversity and compliance with labour and human rights standards would sit with supply chain managers in your organization.

Data on how well your organization meets its obligations related to labour practices, human rights and community engagement is likely to be generated by your legal and compliance departments. Adhering to laws and best practices for tracking data on human capital bleeds over into the final element of ESG data: governance.

Governance data – the G

Governance data throws light on a company's policies, structure and management practices. The ultimate custodians of your organization's governance are its board of directors, board of trustees or governing council (depending on the type of organization you are). All of these structures exist to protect stakeholders of the organization by ensuring laws made externally and policies agreed internally are fit for purpose, implemented and enforced.

The primary sources of governance data are the legal and compliance departments, which should reflect not only the policies, but also how compliance is policed. Examples of governance data may include data on the board's composition including the number and percentage of independent directors, the diversity of the board, and the level of engagement of the board in overseeing sustainability issues. Policies on elements including resource usage, employee protections, etc fall into the G category of ESG data.

Alongside the legal and compliance department, the risk management departments would be responsible for providing data on the company's approach to managing risks, such as climate change, cyber security, or supply chain disruptions. These data points can be used in sustainability reporting.

It may seem like G data is very straightforward. But – as always – the devil is in the detail. A G data point may be deceptive. For example, a data point may answer the question 'Do you have a board composition policy?'. This question needs to be answered 'yes' or 'no', and so the data point associated with this question is binary: yes or no. In this example, the data point gives no information on the suitability or relevance of the board composition policy. It may be a single written line such as: 'The board will be composed of tall people.' Alternatively, it may be a substantive policy that defines a diverse and inclusive board of directors in compliance with local regulations and details how the policy will be monitored, over what period, and how non-compliance will be dealt with by the company.

Both these board composition policies will result in a 'yes' data point to the question 'Do you have a board composition policy?' However, we can obviously see that they reflect different company profiles and risks.

Defining what good governance data looks like is more difficult than it may seem. In the example above, more questions need answering and more data needs gathering before the data point becomes useful. Is the policy best in class? Is it comprehensive? Is it enforceable? Without additional granularity, a G data point can have limited meaning and utility.

Macro data for sustainability

Large-scale 'macro' data, compared to disclosure data, provides a broad overview of the economy and environment rather than reflecting data related to a specific organization. It includes figures about a country's gross domestic product (GDP) and inflation and unemployment rates, as well as environmental indicators about GHG emissions and water use at a global, country, regional or local level. Typically, such data is collected and published by government agencies, think tanks, universities, research houses and central banks, and used by economists, policymakers and market participants to better understand what is happening in the wider economy.

Macro data can be used to assess the overall sustainability of an economy and the progress being made towards its sustainability goals. Figures, for instance, on energy consumption can provide insight into the overall energy mix being used in a region, while data on GDP can help track the growth of a country and be set against other data such as gender pay gap figures to draw out meaningful sustainability impacts.

Where is macro data sourced? Many places!

Here are a few of the places where you can frequently find macro data that can be useful on your company's sustainability journey. They are all from outside your organization, as opposed to the disclosure data from within your own firm:

- Government agencies at local, state or national levels collect sustainability data to inform policy decisions and measure progress towards sustainability goals. For example, the Environmental Protection

Agency (EPA) in the US, the Environment Agency (EA) in the UK and the European Environment Agency (EEA) in Europe all collect data on air and water quality, hazardous waste and other environmental factors.

- Non-governmental organizations (NGOs) and other non-profit organizations gather sustainability data as part of their advocacy or research efforts which they use to raise awareness about sustainability issues and drive action to address them.

- Researchers in universities and other academic institutions conduct studies on sustainability topics, such as climate change, renewable energy and sustainable agriculture. They may use environmental monitoring tools to generate real-time data about air quality, water quality and weather patterns that can then be used to inform policy decisions, alert people to potential hazards and track progress towards environmental goals.

- International organizations like the United Nations and the World Bank generate sustainability data that inform global policy decisions and measure progress towards sustainability goals.

- Utilities provide data about energy generation mix, renewable energy capacity and energy efficiency programmes, which is then used to assess progress towards reducing GHG emissions and increasing the share of renewable energy.

- Agricultural and food companies amass data on farming practices, water use and supply chain sustainability, information that can be used to understand the environmental and social impacts of food production and consumption.

- Consumer surveys indicate the public's sustainability preferences and behaviours. They can measure consumer demand for sustainable products and willingness to pay more for them, as well as wider attitudes towards sustainability issues such as climate change.

- Social media platforms offer insights into public opinions and discussions on sustainability issues. For example, analysing social media data can help identify emerging sustainability trends, understand public sentiment towards sustainability issues, and track the impact of sustainability campaigns and initiatives.

A very well respected and often-used source of macro data is the United Nations Intergovernmental Panel on Climate Change (IPCC), which we reference in earlier chapters and will again below. It frequently updates climate data that underpins climate scenarios and forward projections.

As a leader, understanding the type of data you are looking at and how it was collected helps you use the data effectively. This is particularly true for ESG data in order for you to challenge its comparability with other organizations' data and to ensure it is fit for purpose in applying it to your organization's intended use cases.

The power of combining disclosure data and macro data

By combining and analysing both disclosure and macro data, it is possible to gain a more complete understanding of the sustainability of an economy and the organizations that contribute to it.

It can also be useful for your own organization to track and understand trends from macro data sources to consider risks arising from sustainability issues that could affect your organization. Some of the key risks include economic and societal risks, security risks and physical risks. Physical risks of climate change can radically impact a business model over time and are worth reviewing specifically.

What are the physical risks of climate change?

Physical risks are those associated with the impacts of climate change and are categorized into two types:

1 Acute physical risks are event-driven and include extreme weather events such as heatwaves, floods, wildfires and storms.

2 Chronic physical risks are longer-term shifts in climate patterns, such as rising sea levels, increased temperatures or changing precipitation patterns.

Physical risks may have financial implications for organizations, such as direct damage to assets and indirect impacts from supply chain disruptions.

The power of combining disclosure data with macro data can be illustrated by the case of an organization that has physical fixed assets on its balance sheet. For example, a hypothetical medical product manufacturer, HealthGizmo Inc., has a dozen factories all logically located beside oceans for efficient use of salt water in their processes. The macro data on global temperature change affecting sea levels can be used to assess HealthGizmo's risk of increased flooding at these sites.

Macro data is only useful in this example when combined with HealthGizmo's internal data – in this case, the location of each of HealthGizmo's factories. An external stakeholder will also be interested in HealthGizmo's physical risks. They may use geospatial data to pinpoint assets on a map and analyse risks across HealthGizmo's portfolio and that of its competitors.

These external stakeholders are not only shareholders, customers and investors. Insurance companies are also keenly interested in assessing physical risks. They use both disclosure and macro data to help them make calculations to price insurance premiums. This affects HealthGizmo's costs for insurance and, potentially, the overall insurance costs for those in HealthGizmo's sector.

A combination of disclosure and macro data is the only way for interested parties to make informed decisions. Their decisions affect both HealthGizmo and its wider industry sector.

In terms of sustainability, both disclosure and macro data hold an even more specific purpose. Remember that the desire to produce, use and monitor sustainability data is not the ultimate goal. The urgent need for action to prevent continued climate change is our **actual** collective goal.

Understanding the data today is only half the battle. It is a means to an end. We are in fact looking to monitor our actions today as they stand on a trajectory towards tomorrow. Change we make today can alter the future. If we use data to act more sustainably, we can alter the pace and outcomes of global warming and societal sustainability. We can map a path through data to a better future. That is the ultimate goal.

From looking back to looking forwards

The period of time that data relates to is called its temporality, and, again, this can vary widely. The temporal element of a data type is particularly important to ensure the data is useful and relevant. There is a time element

Figure 3.1   The temporality of data

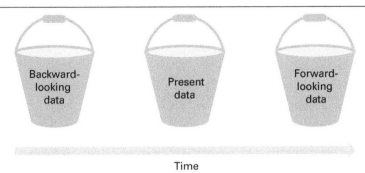

Time

to all data, including sustainability data, which can be grouped into three 'buckets': backward-looking data, present data and forward-looking data (Figure 3.1).

Data can only ever give us a snapshot of a moment in time. Having year-old data might not be a problem if circumstances aren't changing that fast or if you're looking at long-term trends. However, it's of little use and potentially highly misleading if your marketplace has been disrupted after the data has been captured and you are relying on it to make an investment decision.

Most sustainability data that is disclosed by organizations is backward-looking data. It is retrospective and gives us a historic view of what has happened up to a point in time when the data has been captured. As we touched on in Chapter 2, historical data can be audited. For sustainability data, there is a wide range of service providers that offer their third-party services to provide assurances and verification of this data. Sometimes this is required by regulators – sometimes it is not. Rapid change in the market makes mandatory verification of your historical ESG data something your organization needs to check to be sure you are factoring this cost and time in where it is necessary.

Not all data is historical. There is also 'present data' that is again linked to a point in time (the present), but also connected to a future outcome. An example of present data would be the status of planning permission granted today that gives a company permission to start building a power plant at a particular place in five years' time. Another example could be capital expenditure on new equipment that's signed off by a CFO but won't impact, for better or worse, an organization's sustainability metrics until a later date. Present data is useful as a data point today, and becomes even more powerful as a signpost to the future state of the business.

Finally, we have what is arguably the most critical of all three of the time-related data 'buckets' for the climate agenda: forward-looking data. Even though there is no official definition for this data, we can think of it as predictive data that is giving us insight into the future. Even though it's not verifiable or auditable (the future has yet to happen!), it does give us a sense of the direction of travel and so is useful for planning and target-setting. In terms of environmental data, the case for future data is both compelling and disturbing. In Chapter 1 we referenced some recent data from IPCC on climate change and projections for the planet's temperature rises in the future. This is forward-looking data at its most harrowing.

The IPCC provides well-respected, forward-looking data on climate, temperatures and biodiversity that feed into scenario planning and future objectives. These are important ESG macro datasets that sit alongside the data that organizations disclose. The IPCC reviews temperature data gathered from land-based weather stations, ships and buoys. It also monitors changes in ice sheets and glaciers using samples from ice cores, on-site observations and satellite-generated measurements to better understand why ice sheets are melting and how this might affect sea levels — a topic being monitored by tidal gauges and satellites.

Data about the temperature, salinity and circulation of oceans feeds into forward-looking climate data on water scarcity and pattern changes. Oceanic data provides fresh insights into reasons for ocean warming and how this may impact marine ecosystems. Hydrological data is collected about river flows, precipitation levels and soil moisture content. This data is not just important to our water system; all these water-related factors affect agricultural yields. They also impact a location's ability support human life. Pretty fundamental stuff.

Similarly, data is gathered and analysed about the composition of our atmosphere. This is crucial knowledge signposting how climate and weather patterns might change as global temperatures rise.

To provide a long-term perspective, the IPCC also looks at paleoclimate data. This comes from the analysis of tree rings and ice and sediment cores, and is a way to help reconstruct the natural variability of past conditions on our planet.

The IPCC and other institutions dedicated to collecting data on all these various planetary conditions are important data partners to drive sustainability. You do not need to become an environmental or climate data expert. Thankfully, those people already exist. Your job is to be aware that the data they produce may be useful to your organization. In turn it can help you to frame the trajectory of the wider world. This helps you align your forward-looking ESG data to future climate scenarios. We will scope out how this works later when we look at transition planning.

As we have outlined, forward-looking data can be disclosed data or macro data, and can be gathered from market research, customer insights, economic forecasting, environmental predictions and financial modelling. Forward-looking data is critically important to the sustainability agenda because it is the basis for scenario and transition planning.

Transition plans and pathways

First, let's be clear on the meaning of 'transition' in this context.

In the parlance of sustainability, transition refers to systemic changes and actions needed in response to the environmental crisis the world is facing. An organization's transition plan outlines the alterations it intends to make to its current 'business as usual' to achieve a lower carbon footprint. There is an inherent need to calculate an organization's baseline carbon emissions level before a transition plan makes sense. This baseline uses the organization's actual disclosed data associated with year one of its transition plan.

Logically, there needs to be a jumping-off point from which to compare future disclosures over the life of the plan. This will determine if the organization is successfully transitioning to a more sustainable model. ESG data is at the core of creating this baseline and monitoring changes from one period to the next.

Increasingly, there is a call for companies and countries to have a transition plan. A transition plan maps out the steps the organization or government intends to take to shift their emissions to a lower level. Critical to a transition plan are clear goals and timelines. Making these goals and timelines public and transparent allows external stakeholders to evaluate their robustness, ambition and progress.

We referred earlier to the Paris Agreement and the globally shared goals of limiting temperature change to 2°C (and ideally 1.5°C) above pre-industrial levels. Transition plans are usually linked to becoming 'Paris-aligned'. Let's be ambitious together and use 1.5°C as the target for Paris alignment for the rest of this book. Being Paris-aligned means that the organization will be contributing to keeping temperature change to below 1.5°C. This can be complicated maths, but there are frameworks both available and in development to help you align with this goal if you choose to use this target.

In recent years, dozens of guidance documents on transition planning have been created. Alongside these documents many initiatives, organizations and associations have pivoted their focus to addressing climate transition actions. Brace yourself for a number of names and acronyms of these groups to be thrown at you from here on.

How you and your organization can get involved in these initiatives, among many others in the sustainability space, is addressed further in Chapter 10. As we discuss transition here, be aware that these associations offer suggested methodologies for both corporates and governments on which to base their transition plans. The world is increasingly adopting a whole of economy approach to transition. In 2022, the UK government launched a Transition Plan Taskforce to develop a standard for transition plans. The first iteration of their framework launched in October 2023. In 2022, the Glasgow Financial Alliance for Net Zero (GFANZ) published their guidance, which builds on the various plans already in the market and describes detailed steps for a financial audience.

A potentially useful source for transition planning is the work being done by the Transition Pathway Initiative (TPI). The TPI is primarily intended to be used by the investment community, but the tool is powerful. It uses data on companies and their climate-related targets to track transition. The TPI was developed to enable investors to assess a company's performance against internationally agreed benchmarks and to track its progress towards a low-carbon economy.

You can go online to search corporate names to get the TPI's assessment of the success of their transition. Assessment is made using best-available data and publicly available company information and an academically rigorous approach, The tool can be used to help inform investment decisions and as a basis for engagement with companies on their progress towards specific targets (TPI, 2023).

In very simple terms, your transition plans should include the following actions and outputs:

1 Conduct an emissions inventory associated with a baseline date.

2 Set targets and timelines to align with limiting global temperature rises to 1.5°C.

3 Plan the steps your organization needs to take across its business to achieve your targets.

4 Publish your plan.

5 Assess progress against your plan regularly.

6 Consider external validation of your baseline data and progress review data.

Transition is the basis of the work of the Science Based Targets Initiative (SBTi). What is this phrase 'science-based targets'? Good question to ask, since you will hear it often in your sustainability journey.

Science-based targets and global targets

An organization's carbon emissions targets are considered to be 'science-based' when they track to the levels necessary to achieve reductions in line with the Paris Agreement goals. In order to achieve the levels necessary to meet these goals, we need to accept that each organization plays a part in the global whole. It is also necessary to accept the macro data that is published on the current and projected global carbon emissions, and their effects on global temperatures. This is why macro data and the work of IPCC and others are essential in the sustainability data ecosystem. Without the macro data, transition targets are useless.

Once you accept that we are all in this together, you can consider the idea of the global carbon budget and your organization's role within it.

There is a scientific equation that projects the impacts of carbon emissions on temperature change. This is the basis for carbon reduction targets and the bedrock of the Paris Agreement. This scientific equation allows us to estimate the maximum level of further emissions we can put into the environment before the possibility of keeping temperature rises below 1.5°C becomes impossible. Continuing to emit carbon at the same level we do today and expecting to limit temperature increases to 1.5°C – or even 2°C – is unrealistic. The stuff of fantasy. Unicorns frolicking in a field of candy canes. I think you get the picture.

A carbon budget sets the global maximum amount of carbon we can emit to stay on track to achieve the Paris Agreement goals. A science-based target divides that carbon budget amongst global emitters based on percentage reductions from baseline levels. This results in the carbon reductions your organization needs to make for you to do your part.

Calculating your reductions to create your science-based target needs a clear, agreed methodology. In 2015, the SBTi released the most commonly used and detailed methodology to date, the Sectoral Decarbonization Approach (SDA). This methodology enables companies to set a science-based target based on the required decarbonization trajectory of their sector, or the sectors in which they each operate.

The SDA takes into account the potential for sectors to reduce emissions through improved efficiency and new technology, factoring in future growth projections and market share for different geographies. (At present, the SDA can only be applied in certain sectors, but this is continually changing so that the methodology can be adopted by more and more organizations.) Companies can then calculate the level of emissions reductions that they themselves will need to achieve to put their sector on track for a below 2°C pathway. This is how science meets practical business actions.

Using climate scenarios

Climate scenarios are another area in which forward-looking data is needed to create a plan for the future. Scenarios are a derived dataset that use the data we have today to map out if/then outcomes for our climate in the future.

There are many climate-related scenarios created and mapped for a variety of purposes. The IPCC has created a number of scenarios based on their macro data that they call 'pathways'. The International Energy Agency (IEA) has created a global energy and climate model that provides scenario analysis of future energy trends (IEA, 2022). Scenarios play a role in developing targets, caps, regulations and plans.

To assess the impact of climate change on assets, for instance, central banks have developed a climate stress-test model that relies on forward-looking data fed to them by banks. This data comes from the projects and customers the banks are involved with. The Network of Central Banks and Supervisors for Greening the Financial System (NGFS) is an international group dedicated to building best practice in governing risks in the banking system.

The NGFS climate scenarios bring together a global, harmonized set of transition pathways, physical climate change impacts and economic indicators. The group has recommended for central banks to impose scenario stress tests on the portfolios of banks that they supervise to get a clearer picture of risks to the financial system from climate change.

The trickle-down effect of the development of these scenarios and subsequent mandatory stress-test data from banks to their central bank supervisors means that companies that banks lend to need to provide data up the chain. Banks lend to all sorts of companies in all sectors and geographies.

Through their own regulatory obligations, they require data from the companies they lend to on the risks of various future climate scenarios for their businesses. Adding up all the risks from all the loans from all the banks will give a country's central bank a good idea of how, when and if climate change will create systemic risks to the financial system and economy. All this is based on future climate-driven scenarios, which are based on data.

If you hold a loan or a line of credit or an overdraft facility, this trickle-down effect makes these scenarios very relevant to you and your ESG data requirements.

Garbage in, garbage out

Recalling the vast zettabytes of data we are generating globally, not all of it can be of great use to our sustainability agenda. I am sure you've heard the phrase 'garbage in, garbage out'. It usually refers to the idea that in any system, the quality of the output is determined by the quality of the input.

When applied to ESG data, when raw data that is not of high quality (i.e. garbage!) becomes an input into metrics, tools, transition plans and other datasets that build on these raw datasets, the derived outputs are questionable. Garbage raw data creates garbage derived data. In the house analogy from Figure 1.1, the garbage raw data creates very shaky foundations, and everything built on top becomes questionable.

Even if the data offers insight into E, S, or G topics, the data itself may not be fit for purpose. What characteristics do we need data to have to be considered useful? Being useful is good. So, to keep it simple, we're going to call useful data 'good' data and unhelpful data 'bad' data.

Fundamentally, inaccurate data is not good data. It needs to be true to be useful. This is the absolute minimum requirement for data to be of any use. To get more sophisticated, we can outline some guiding principles to define what makes data good beyond being accurate. I call these the 'three Cs'. On the other hand, there are some red flags that may indicate data is less good. I call these the 'three Es'.

The three Cs of data

To maximize the benefit of data, it needs to be comparable, coherent and comprehensive. These are the three Cs of data. Let's understand why this is important.

Comparability of data allows data to make sense. If data from one source is not able to be compared to another source, there is no context or relativity for the data. There is no way of knowing if the information the data is giving you is positive or negative. Comparability is important for disclosure data when the audience for the data wishes to compare one organization to another. The entities may be in the same industry, sector, product category or geography. Or they may not. If the data that they both produce are not in the same units of measurement, referring to the same time period, or reflecting the same scope, the data is impossible to compare and becomes of limited use.

You may think that some of the most well-known ESG datasets would have already moved past the challenges of comparability. Sadly, this is not the case. While the issue of poor comparability is recognized, it has not been solved even for GHG emissions – a very mainstream data point.

Challenges in ESG data comparability – the GHG emissions example

In order to be comparable, ESG data needs to be defined in detail. Even GHG emissions – a deeply important data point – can be interpreted in multiple ways. For example, your organization may define GHG emissions to include Scope 1, 2 and 3 data. You may only include Scopes 1 and 2 or just Scope 1 in your definition. All three interpretations result in a single figure for GHG emissions.

The gases that are covered in the full Kyoto protocol definition of GHG gases are carbon dioxide (CO_2), methane (CH_4), hydrofluorocarbons (HFCs), nitrous oxide (N_2O), perfluorocarbons (PFCs) and sulphur hexafluoride (SF_6). Your organization may only collect and disclose data on a subset of these six gases. Others in your industry may include a different mix of GHGs. This is inconsistent with comparability.

Measurement and calculation of GHG emissions – if you can believe it! – is still a challenge. For example, the unit of measurement used and details of energy consumption (including when the emissions were produced) may vary across units within your own organization, making it tricky to unify. Have a look at Table 3.1.

All of the lines in this table contribute to GHG emissions calculations. However, due to the differing units of measurement and the frequency with which the data is calculated, getting to a single emissions number requires

Table 3.1 GHG emissions: data sources and frequency examples

Activity	Unit of measurement	Data sourced from	Frequency calculated
Electricity use	Total kilowatt hours or joules	Electricity bill	Monthly or quarterly
Renewable energy use	Total kilowatt hours or joules	Multiple inputs: solar, wind, hydro, etc.	Monthly or quarterly
Gas use	Total kilowatt hours or joules	Gas bill	Monthly, quarterly or annually
Fuel usage – company vehicles	Gallons of fuel bought	Invoices/receipts	Weekly or monthly
Company travel	Miles flown, mileage covered by car, train and other transport	Distance calculations	Monthly or quarterly

calculations, estimations and assumptions. A common path to a comparable dataset is not straightforward. This results in data being reported differently by different companies. Comparability becomes difficult and it opens up the possibility for moral hazard: for companies to choose the most favourable definition to make them look good.

What if we just pick one methodology to use as the base case? Then we can restate other methodologies to be equivalent to the base case, and presto – we have unlocked comparability. I wish it were that simple. From an external perspective it may be impossible to do this restating and equalizing. Let me give you another example to explain why. If we narrow down the data we want to compare to just energy usage, and we focus on one set of published standards – the popular Global Reporting Initiative (GRI) standards – you would be forgiven for thinking this would yield a clear and comparable data disclosure.

Unfortunately not. Even within this narrow disclosure definition, there are ambiguities that can make comparison of data difficult. The GRI reporting guidance allows for company choice in:

- units of energy (i.e. joules, watt-hours or multiple)
- definition of renewable and non-renewable sources

- standards, methodologies and assumptions
- source of conversion factors
- calculation tools

Companies that make different choices on the list above will deliver different data outcomes. This results in data that is nearly impossible to unpick from outside the reporting company. Of course, this variability is known and undesirable, so the GRI includes detailed guidance to organizations to help be more specific about disclosures. Even so, there is room for continued ambiguity.

In summary, the guidance is helpful but remains open to interpretation. It leaves both reporting organizations and their audiences with some challenges in contextualizing the data and comparing it. Your job as a business leader is to encourage your disclosures to be as easy as possible for anyone looking at your data to use for decisions. That 'anyone' includes you and your wider leadership teams, the board of directors and your external stakeholders.

For example, if Company A chooses to define GHG emissions as including Scope 1, 2 and 3 emissions of all types of gases, and reports them in metric tonnes of CO_2 equivalent (tCO_2e), and Company B chooses to define GHG emissions to only include Scopes 1 and 2 and only CO_2 emissions and a broad definition of renewables, reporting them in tCO_2e, it is likely the results would be difficult to compare meaningfully. Without clarity on what goes into an emission disclosure, the data is difficult to understand in a wider context.

In addition, if the company is adhering to a strict definition governing their disclosures (i.e. the CDP Climate Change response framework or GRI standards), while another company is defining its data through a different framework (i.e. its own definition in its sustainability report), the ability to compare the data erodes further still.

The GHG Protocol supplies the world's most widely used GHG accounting standards at the time of writing. It provides a methodology to create a comparable GHG emissions dataset that investors and others can use to analyse data from across the universe of companies reporting. Not all companies disclosing GHG emissions numbers use this methodology so there remain some challenges in even what many believe to be the most common ESG metric: GHG emissions.

Data comparability is further challenged by the time element of data. Often organizations disclose their ESG data at the same time as their year end financial statements. The fact that companies have different year end dates, and their supply chains have different year end dates, makes this simple statement complicated. Are the dates for disclosing emissions and other data points aligned? Or are disclosure dates potentially up to 12–24 months out of date due to inconsistent data capture dates within the business or along the value chain? Problematic.

The second C is **coherence**. It refers to uniformity across shared resource data, as well as logical connections and completeness within a single dataset and across datasets. Coherence is a key factor in data transparency. It is also closely related to comparability, as outlined above. Coherence may be impaired by differences in calculations or definitions of a data disclosure.

An example of incoherent data is when there are two differing values reported for the same data point about the same entity. How might this happen?

Consider a glass manufacturer, Clearlythere Inc, which reports its water usage data to a global data provider, DataGoGo Ltd. DataGoGo proactively requests information from companies at the end of every calendar year. Through Clearlythere responding to DataGoGo, a number associated with Clearlythere's water usage has been made public. If, in June, Clearlythere also discloses its data to CDP during its annual disclosure process, there is a second data point publicly available on the water usage of Clearlythere. If it is not clear what timeframe the water usage data reflects, a market stakeholder who has access to both DataGoGo and CDP data on Clearlythere in October would be confused. There would be two differing numbers associated with the same data request on Clearlythere's water usage.

The final C is **comprehensive**. Comprehensive data can help ensure that all the data that an audience needs is available. For example, if a company listed on the Tokyo Stock Exchange chooses to disclose ESG data only on their water usage, and another company listed on the same exchange chooses to disclose data only on waste management, it would be impossible to assess either of the companies' total sustainability impacts from either of these data points.

Moreover, if an industry or sector produces only a very small number of data points from a few companies, it is again impossible to be confident that the data that is available can be meaningful. Data density and breadth is the goal, and being comprehensive allows for a better overall picture of economies, industries and geographies.

Threats to data quality: the three Es

Among the prominent threats to the quality of data are the 'three Es': estimations, extrapolations and errors.

Estimation is the process of making assumptions about data that is not available, often by using existing data. While this can be a useful tool, it can also lead to inaccurate results if the assumptions on which it is based are incorrect, or if contextual factors vary significantly.

In relation to ESG data, estimations are often not illustrative of reality. This is because even if the data points being used to create the estimation are from very similar companies in similar situations, each organization could be on a very different energy or sustainability transition plan.

Moreover, estimation is most robust when there are many data points available. ESG data is not yet as complete as we would like it to be. This can – and has – led to estimations based on insufficient amounts of verified raw data to be meaningful or illustrative. If there are 20 comparable companies in a portfolio, but only two companies have disclosed their methane emissions, an estimated data point for that portfolio group is not fit for purpose – no matter how similar their underlying businesses are.

Extrapolation involves using existing data to make predictions about data that has not yet been obtained to make predictions about future events or trends, based on existing data. For example, if your organization has already brought one operation online and is planning on developing another, similar one in the near future, likely trends for the future operations can be extrapolated from data on the one already initiated.

Extrapolation can be useful for predicting future trends, but it is necessarily hypothetical, and highly dependent on the assumptions that underpin it. In an environment where ESG disclosures are not universally mandated, extrapolation can also take the form of creating a data point for a later year based on data disclosed in an earlier period, but which was left out of disclosures in subsequent reporting windows. Again, this can yield inaccurate results. Making investment or strategic decisions on these extrapolated data points can be harmful or dangerous.

Finally, and most prosaically, the final E – **errors** – are mistakes in the data. Such mistakes can arise from a variety of sources: simple human error, conflicts or inconsistencies in data collection and reporting systems, disruptions to operations, and so on. Of course, erroneous data will provide erroneous representations of the phenomena in question. Some margin of error is inevitable, and reliable data-handling methods factor this in.

The primary means of reducing errors in data is putting a governance system in place. A governance system ensures that data collection and reporting systems are up to date and reliable, and reviewed regularly to guarantee that they are fit for purpose. Quality control is likely to be a function within some area of the business either formally or informally. The production of ESG data needs to employ the same level of rigour an organization applies to its business processes. Transparency of this process and governance adds trust and credibility while addressing the core need to produce reliable error-free data.

Increasing the quantity of data, and variety of data sources, is also a useful way of reducing the risks of estimation and extrapolation. The more data you have, the more confident you can be that the estimations and extrapolations based on it are reliably representative.

Similarly, collecting data from a variety of sources helps reduce the risk that a bias inherent in one source will skew your estimations and extrapolations systematically. This principle is called 'triangulation': by considering a given phenomenon via data from a variety of sources, you can compare the pictures each of these provides, and triangulate the findings to sharpen precision. Triangulation can also help identify potential problems. For example, if one source of data provides a very different picture from another, this indicates that at least one of them is wrong, and thereby flags up areas of concern.

We introduced the idea of raw data being the foundation of the ESG house we build to measure and manage sustainability. When the raw data is affected by the three Es, we are introducing potential cracks in the foundations of our ESG house. When we build on these shaky foundations, the decisions we make as stakeholders – as investors, board members, clients or regulators – become shaky as well. This is why the three Es of data are threats to watch for, or at the very least be aware of.

We can think of data demonstrating the three Cs as good data – the kind you can use to help make properly informed decisions, while data demonstrating the three Es – with the provisos of transparency as detailed above! – needs to be treated with caution. The data may potentially be inaccurate, unreliable and irrelevant and lead to ill-informed judgements.

Of course, things are never as black and white as 'good' and 'bad'. Just as with people, data can have a mix of good and bad features all muddled up together to create what we can call a 'data quality spectrum'. To create this data quality spectrum, we need to include the concepts of materiality and temporality as discussed above and previously in this book.

For example, you could have data that's comprehensive (good), but includes estimates from a poorly populated dataset (bad). Or data that is accurate in real time (good), but arrives too late for it to be of use (bad). Or data that is timely (good), but is riddled with errors (bad). It is important for leaders to challenge the good and bad elements of data being presented to them for decisions or review so that any decisions made are based on a solid data footing.

As we have said many times already, perfect data is often a unicorn. It may be that imperfect data with thorough transparency regarding its limitations and clear logic and disclosure behind any decisions derived from it is the best way to take diligent actions. In the case of sustainability planning, data is not yet perfect. It may be a very long time before it is. As the journey continues, awareness of the three Cs, three Es, temporality, materiality and transparency is essential.

Putting data into perspective

It's easy to fall into the trap of seeing sustainability data, particularly when it is quantitative, as an objective measurement. However, relativity is important. Where is that data point relative to others in the industry? How is that data reflecting a positive transition? As our global climate situation evolves, what constitutes a favourable ESG data value is also changing. As we are experiencing at the time of writing, worsening climate data (i.e. rising global temperatures) will drive more intense disclosure requirements and climate actions from companies. This becomes a constantly moving target as the global physical environment constantly changes.

The data you choose to present to the wider world can have a profound effect on how your organization is perceived. Without context, your data may lead your audience to wrong or incomplete conclusions. This can lead to confusion at best, and misrepresentation at worst.

As a one-time British Prime Minister Benjamin Disraeli supposedly said, there are 'lies, damned lies and statistics'.

Data needs context. How can we know if an ESG data point is sustainability positive or negative? Is the data you get as a business leader showing your organization to be an environmental leader or a laggard? The answer requires context. For example, a manufacturer's high level of carbon emissions might suggest that it is doing poorly in terms of sustainability when compared to an overall economic average. But look again at similar companies in the same industry, and it could be one of the 'cleanest' players in its sector.

In another example, data could show that a firm's water usage is falling year on year, something that's to be applauded because it suggests a commitment to protecting scarce resources and acting sustainably. But what if that drop is down to external factors like regional regulation limiting water usage? And what if the firm's water usage is not meeting these newly regulated limits? Should we still be applauding?

The same data can tell two very different stories.

It is sometimes difficult to know whether data is big or small, important or irrelevant, or showing a rising trend for a falling one until we compare it with something else. We can do this in several ways.

If we compare data historically, we can see trends in progress. For instance, are your carbon emissions higher or lower than they were last year? And how does that compare to the year before that? Data gives a sense of the direction of travel. As we learned earlier, this year-on-year context is the basis for transition work.

For a board director or senior leader, data showing a clear direction of travel is an excellent input to understand how the organization is progressing towards its sustainability goals (or not!). This is where it is useful to marry your data with your ambitions (we will work out your organization's ambitions in Chapter 6). KPIs can help leaders focus on an organization's progress against goals and track progress from one period (monthly? quarterly? annually?) to the next. KPIs are a tool for leaders to leverage as they manage and make decisions. KPIs are considered in more depth in Chapter 10.

KPIs are a good way to internally benchmark where an organization is trending. But no organization operates in a vacuum. The reality is that comparing your organization to others can be used to assess your relative sustainability. Understanding how you are doing against others in your industry, geography or value chain provides good context for the progress you may be making as a standalone business. This context and comparability is regularly used by financiers to add sustainability premiums or discounts to their valuation of an organization.

The demand for sustainability context has created a universe of tools. These tools seek to summarize and rank a company's sustainability or ESG strengths in comparison to others. They can provide a quick guide to where companies fall on a scale. Each tool provider has created their scales based on their own methodologies. These ESG ratings or scores are not raw data points, but they can be useful derived data used by a variety of external stakeholders to compare organizations.

Organizational leaders should be aware of ESG ratings and scores to understand their use and implications. These tools can be additional input in building a relative picture of your organization within the wider marketplace.

Benchmarks, ratings and scores

Benchmarking your own performance against others in your industry or sector is a strong tool to put things in context. The critical factor is selecting the right benchmark. Choose incorrectly, and you won't be making any meaningful like-for-like comparisons. If, for instance, you are in the energy sector, you would want to benchmark your carbon emissions against those of a company in the same industry, in the same region and of a similar size in order to derive value from the comparison.

Benchmarks are yours as a leader and an organization to set. There are targets and caps and limits set for various ESG metrics by various entities – industry- or geography-specific, or not. You can choose to make one of these externally set targets your benchmark. You could instead set your own benchmark or choose a peer's data to use as a benchmark. Alternatively, you could choose to use published ESG ratings or scores as your benchmark.

Who's rating who?

As the correlation between a company's ESG performance and its investment value becomes even more linked, the need for robust ESG data and the demand for tools to help make this data useful is increasing.

Environmental data is complex and requires expertise to make sense of it. This is beyond the capacity of some investors and stakeholders, especially as the information provided by each disclosing entity is often incomplete. Institutional investors frequently cite a lack of 'data robustness' as the main barrier to greater adoption of ESG strategies. It is a challenge for the investment and finance community to manage the data we have today – even if it is imperfect or incomplete. The lack of talent available to analyse ESG data also leaves stakeholders shorthanded in mining raw ESG data in-house. This has driven the creation of ESG and sustainability ratings and scores – a derived dataset.

While ESG scores or ratings may not act as the sole basis of engagement and investment decisions, these tools can serve as a foundational source of data, a convenient shortcut to a greater understanding of an organization's ESG performance and a starting point for further research.

But there is a dilemma.

At the time of writing, there is no standardization in the way ESG performance is defined or measured, and therefore scores and ratings can vary significantly based on the unique methodology of each provider. Depending on the metrics the provider uses and the different weightings given to each data point, the same company can be ranked highly by one provider and quite poorly by another.

Some providers collect publicly available data while others supplement publicly available data with their own generated by analysts through interviews, questionnaires and independent analysis to which they then apply their own methodology. There are also providers that specialize in specific ESG issues like carbon emissions, corporate governance, human rights or gender diversity. These providers offer valuable insights that address a particular issue.

Ratings overall are based on data points that may contain elements of the three Es we learned about earlier. Consistency of results is hard to achieve when some companies provide detailed current ESG data and others do not. Poor data density impacts the results of ESG ratings. The incorporation of estimation and extrapolation creates difficulty in correlating one score to another. Data collection timeframes for data can also differ, so recent ESG-related improvements may be reflected by one provider but not yet be included in another's disclosures.

With more than 600 ESG rating agencies said to be operating in the market today, this creates a wide variety of methodologies and focus areas for investors, regulators and companies to use. This can offer richness of insight as long as what exactly the ratings are ranking is clear. All of these ratings and scores are derived data. Remember our data 'house' with foundations? Ratings and scores are a level up from the raw data inputs that are the foundations of the data house. Ratings and scores rely on the accuracy and completeness of ESG data disclosed through the raw data.

CDP reviewed the relationship between raw data and ESG ratings and products. They categorized the challenges and shortcomings of ratings and derived data products into two categories: ex-ante challenges and ex-post challenges (Figure 3.2).

Figure 3.2   Ex-ante and ex-post challenges

ESG data

ESG ratings and
data products

Ex-ante

Ex-post

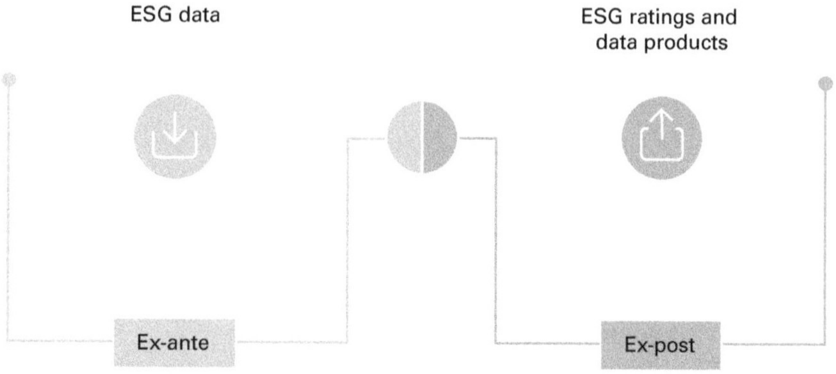

Reproduced with permission from CDP, © 2023

- **Ex-ante challenges:** These are challenges often related to an imperfect ESG data environment. They are considered ex-ante because even though they exist despite ESG ratings and data products, their existence directly impacts the construction of these tools. They include issues with the transparency, comparability and availability of ESG data.

- **Ex-post challenges:** These are challenges inherent in the construction and provision of ESG ratings and data products, such as the diversity of methodologies designed for these tools, the lack of transparency around these methodologies, conflicts of interest, coverage and costs, and interactions between providers and rated entities (CDP, 2023).

Ex-ante and ex-post challenges as outlined above apply to various tools and innovations that rely on ESG data. While there are immense benefits to you as a leader in these tools and ratings and derived datasets, an awareness of their limitations and shortcomings will help you to use them wisely.

Data uncovered

We have covered the various types of raw data you should be aware of (E, S and G) and picked out some important derived data (i.e. ratings and scores). In order to marry this knowledge up we need to pull back into the frame the 'why?' and the ABCs of sustainability data use cases: access to capital, business growth and efficiencies, and compliance and regulation. Which use case or cases are you trying to cover? For each of these, you need to cater to your audience and provide the data they need for their *own* use cases. This audience includes both internal and external stakeholders.

You now know why sustainability is important from Chapter 1, and the use cases for sustainability data from Chapter 2. From this chapter you should have a handle on data types. You should have a better understanding of the dangers of building the three Es into the foundations of your ESG data plans and the data you release to your internal and external audience. You should be more comfortable questioning your organization about the data you receive to base your decisions on. You may already be looking ahead to what data you'll need for your organization to play a role in the global transition.

It is time to turn our view inwards, into your own organization. Next, we will define where you are today on your ESG data journey. You will then be in a position to plan your ESG data future.

References

CDP (2023) Data for public good: Steering the role of ESG ratings and data product providers, www.cdp.net/en/reports/downloads/7242/ (archived at https://perma.cc/PZ7T-SBQJ)

Environmental Finance (2020) ESG data market to more than double, to $5bn, www.environmental-finance.com/content/news/esg-data-market-to-more-than-double-to-$5bn.html (archived at https://perma.cc/L5ZW-ZYKM)

IEA (2022) *Global Energy and Climate Model: Documentation*, https://iea.blob.core.windows.net/assets/2db1f4ab-85c0-4dd0-9a57-32e542556a49/GlobalEnergyandClimateModelDocumentation2022.pdf (archived at https://perma.cc/CP68-2YZ6)

International Data Corporation (2022) Worldwide IDC global datasphere forecast, 2022–2026: Enterprise organizations driving most of the data growth, www.idc.com/getdoc.jsp?containerId=US49018922 (archived at https://perma.cc/N2KL-S53G)

The Economist (2022) Should 'data' be singular or plural? www.economist.com/culture/2022/08/11/should-data-be-singular-or-plural (archived at https://perma.cc/A4D9-7PX7)

TPI (2023) FAQs, www.transitionpathwayinitiative.org/faq (archived at https://perma.cc/ESZ3-M98L)

How to map your organization's ESG maturity

4

REFLECTIVE QUESTIONS

- How can I plan for the sustainability data I need?
- What category of sustainability data organization am I today?
- Which stakeholders are influencing my organization?
- How data savvy (and how ESG data savvy) are we?

Now that we have convinced you of the centrality of data in the sustainability agenda of organizations, and reviewed what sort of data we're talking about, the question becomes: what data do I need to produce, disclose and monitor?

In other words, what data matters to MY organization?

Boards and organizational leaders have some choices to make to answer these questions. These choices are informed by your business's sustainability and data maturity today, and where you would like to be tomorrow. In addition, your choices are influenced by your organization's priorities and external requirements and influences.

To begin, you need to ask yourself questions to build up a picture of where your organization is on its sustainability journey – and on its business journey – at the present moment. That is what we're going to focus on in this chapter before we look ahead to the future. Consider this step as defining your sustainability data snapshot of today. Go through this process by answering questions with the mindset that none of the answers you will give are wrong. The most important guidance for you is that your answers need to be honest so that you can make good choices based on the reality of where your organization is on its journey. Mapping where you are today is a crucial first step.

After this exercise, you will be able to categorize your organization on the ESG Data Maturity Journey. To help with categorization, this book has defined five sustainability data maturity categories. It uses an approach that helps you and your teams to assess your organization's readiness to engage in sustainability data reporting. That reporting may be to an internal or external audience – the choice will be yours, and this book will help you decide.

You'll hear more about the Sustainability Data Categories, and how to determine which one you are in this chapter. By mapping your organization to a category, you can more easily consider the data you have and what data you need. Your category is a description of today's reality and will need considering against your organization's culture, ethos, priorities, capabilities and ambitions. This will require choices on where you plan to be on the ESG Data Maturity Journey over what period of time.

Only you and your colleagues will be able to make these choices in order to ensure the sustainability path you take will be as successful as possible and for you to reach your ESG disclosure goals. Where you are today paired with the choices you make for the future will deliver a data strategy underpinning your organization's sustainability plans.

Once you are clear on where you are today, where you want to be tomorrow and the sustainability data strategy you wish to employ, you can get down to the nitty gritty and make informed choices about your data priorities. Consider questions like:

- What data do you need that you don't have?
- What data do you not need to collect?
- What data do you need from outside your business to scenario plan accurately?
- What data is so new or scarce you should be finding ways to shape policy and regulation to help you find it?

Today's category + organizational ambitions = your data priorities

Change is the only constant in life.

HERACLITUS, GREEK PHILOSOPHER, 535 BC

It has been said many times and in many ways that the only reliable change is change itself. As per the quote from Heraclitus in Ancient Greece, this applies to life. I am also sure you agree it also applies in management and business. Change is particularly present when it comes to ESG data usage and disclosures.

ESG data usage continues to evolve. We will hear a lot more about this in Chapter 8. This flux can be frustrating to organizations that have signed off on an ESG data strategy, only to have to reconsider it in light of global changes to policy or industry requirements. The best advice is to breathe deeply and buckle up for the journey. It will be bumpy. This is rapidly changing territory, and your role as a business leader is to recognize where changes impact your plans and decide how to pivot your business to accommodate them – this is what you do already in other areas of decision-making. This is nothing new. You've got this.

In the next section, we will take you through three key steps to bring clarity to navigating your organization's sustainability data. The first step is to take you through the questions you need to answer to map to your

Figure 4.1   Steps to map your sustainability data journey

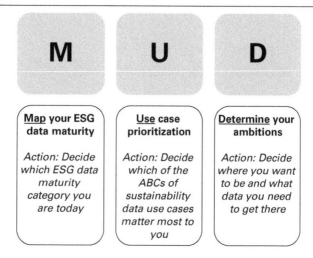

M	**U**	**D**
Map your ESG data maturity	**Use case prioritization**	**Determine your ambitions**
Action: Decide which ESG data maturity category you are today	*Action: Decide which of the ABCs of sustainability data use cases matter most to you*	*Action: Decide where you want to be and what data you need to get there*

Sustainability Data Category. The second step will consider your organization's priority use cases based on the ABCs from Chapter 2.

Finally, the third step will challenge you as a leader to determine your ambitions for the future.

These steps are outlined in Figure 4.1.

This may be clear as MUD to you at the moment, but it will all fall into place. In this chapter we will focus on the 'M' – mapping your ESG data maturity.

ESG data – how mature is your organization?

The ESG Data Maturity Journey is a representation of how mature an organization is at using ESG data for various business goals. Notice that this is not about how sustainable a business is. This journey is focused on the data, and how sophisticated a business is at using data for sustainable measurement and management. Of course, by analysing the data disclosures from a mature ESG data organization, conclusions can be drawn by those outside the organization on how sustainable that organization is, based on the outside analyst's criteria. However, you live within your organization. You have more data and insight than those looking in from the outside. This gives you the power to use data to make change.

In order to help shape your organization's impact and image to your stakeholders inside and outside the organization, you need to first get a handle on your data. That's what this book is about and is what the ESG Data Maturity Journey is designed to help you assess and plan.

The ESG Data Maturity Journey has five different Sustainability Data Categories, as depicted in Figure 4.2.

Five categories based on five indicators

Wedging all organizations of all sizes and types into only five classifications has its limits. Each organization is unique, and the reason why you as a business leader are reading this book will also be unique. However, a high-level classification is very useful before you determine your next steps and helps you plan for tomorrow.

Figure 4.2   An organization's ESG Data Maturity Journey

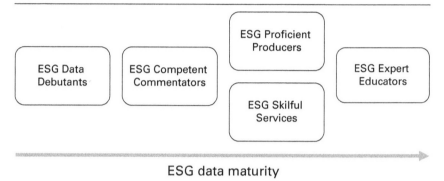

ESG data maturity

Naturally, where you are tomorrow may not be a choice fully in your control. The pressures of the market, regulation and your employee base can affect your plans. Nonetheless, in all cases – and this should be no surprise based on the thesis of this book – data will be essential to get you to where you would like to go.

The best way to start is to map your organization on the following indicators:

- data maturity
- ESG data disclosure
- regulatory pressures
- stakeholder engagement
- climate vs sustainability

This seemingly geeky first step will help in accurately mapping where your organization is today.

1: The Data Maturity Index

How data savvy is your organization?

Data maturity is a measurement that demonstrates the level at which a company utilizes data to conduct its business. To achieve a high level of data maturity, data must be firmly embedded throughout the business and fully integrated into all decision-making and activities. This index is about all kinds of data – not just sustainability data.

As you think this through, think about all the data that your organization uses, generates, considers, analyses and actions. This can come from finance, operations, HR, sales, product development, marketing or anywhere else that matters when running your specific business.

The 'maturity' part of the phrase 'data maturity' is designed to encompass the whole organization. If a company is mature with their data, it means that they utilize their data effectively to ensure that they are getting the most out of collecting, maintaining and monitoring it over time. Mature organizations are also responsible with data and respect the security of the data they handle and create.

Organizations handle enormous amounts of data every day. If you remember our zettabyte framing in Chapter 3, it can be said that much of this data is created and stored by organizations – commercial and otherwise. Some of this data can be specific to an individual (including personal details such as age, address, contact details) or more general data.

Individual or personal data has been the focus of significant attention in the last five years since the globally influential European General Data Protection Regulation (GDPR) came into force on 25 May 2018. GDPR focuses on personal data – a subset of the wider world of data that organizations collect, use and transfer. Don't get personal data confused with 'data' more generally. The intense focus on compliance with GDPR often has compelled boards and executive teams to focus on this data subset specifically.

While compliance with all types of data protection regulations (depending on what jurisdiction you are in) is essential, it is not the only data you as a leader need to be concerned with.

General data covers all the other data an organization uses to run its business, which takes many forms. It can include, for example, how long users visit a web application, how they interact with it (what they click on, etc) and how likely they are to return. This data can be essential to a digital organization. To other organizations, data on product sales in various cities across Spain may be crucial to their profitability. In others, data on the price of cotton used to make the company's bestselling T-shirts is fundamental to the success of the business. In a service-based business, data on time spent by employees on projects would be critical in understanding business efficiencies and calculating project plans. What data is essential to a business depends on the knowledge it gleans from the data, and how that knowledge is used.

Insights can be derived from data. How these insights are used varies widely from organization to organization. As data maturity increases, taking actions based on the organization's data accelerates.

Celebrating an Example

Take the example of an immature data organization whose business is in selling greeting cards: HoHoNotes Inc. HoHoNotes may collect data quarterly on both regional sales and costs of paper. If there is a spike in paper prices (based on comparison to previous quarters or years) in the run-up to the Christmas season, but HoHoNotes does not act on that data (i.e. no moves are made to switch suppliers, renegotiate contracts or put in place options on future prices of inputs, etc), there is a real chance the company would not have a very happy holiday season. Quarterly data may not be what HoHoNotes needs *or* it may not use the data gathered to make changes. Without action the company could generate poor margins at a critical time of year.

Alternatively, if a competitor greeting card company, JollyGreetings Ltd, actively tracks pricing data in real time and uses the data insights to predict the spike in paper costs, it has different options to HoHoNotes. If JollyGreetings acted on the data it collected by mitigating the costs of its inputs or raising the costs of its holiday cards, it could be in a much better position through acting on the knowledge and insights brought to it via data. In this example, it could be the difference between a stocking filled with coal or diamonds.

Classifying your organization by how 'data mature' it is can help ensure you make the most of the data you have. There are tonnes of different data maturity models out there, because there are a lot of different types of data and organizations.

Having an understanding of the principles governing data maturity models can help you to classify and sort through your own data. It can be an intense process to determine your organization's data maturity level. Many organizations undertake detailed consulting projects with external experts to advise them specifically on their data maturity. Your organization may have undertaken some form of review already. If not, that isn't a requirement for the purposes of this exercise. As a business leader, you should have a fair idea of how integral data is to your organization's decision-making processes.

For this process, you can leverage any research your organization has already done or go with your experience as a leader in the organization. You can always dig deeper and get more specific on your organization's data maturity, together with your colleagues, in the future.

Mapping your organization's data maturity

To map your organization on the Data Maturity Index, review Figure 4.3.

The index breaks organizations down into four data maturity categories. Briefly, here is how those categories are defined, and what a company must be doing to reach each of the four levels:

- **Data Conscious:** At the entry level, a business will compile any reports and forms manually. Being aware of data is about as basic as your relationship with data can be. You as a leader would likely feel that you do not get enough data to make decisions, or that the data is not granular or timely enough to be meaningful for assessment. You do not wait for data to take business decisions.

- **Data Capable:** The second level begins to demonstrate more automated processing of data and a clearer understanding of what that data can do. The concept of standardized data inputs for various parts of the organization's product or service delivery helps to embed reliability and accuracy in both data collection and review. As a leader, you feel that you receive some data, but you may still be asking 'So what?' The data may not be easy to use for planning or projections. Historical data dominates in this category.

- **Data Confident:** A company's awareness of their data reaches new heights here, by using the data to make decisions that can have a huge impact on

Figure 4.3   The Data Maturity Index

Data Conscious	Data Capable	Data Confident	Data Compelled
Manually compile non-standardized reports from different systems	Standardized data reporting on an organization-wide platform	Data is used to make critical business decisions	Data is embedded in all business processes and extracted in good time
Your view: It would be good to have more data	*Your view: We could improve data detail, density and timeliness*	*Your view: We use data to predict and plan some important areas of the organization*	*Your view: No data, no decisions*

Data maturity

the business. This is where data starts becoming powerful to the organization and to you as a leader. You receive data that can help you make critical decisions about the business including processes, product development, sales plans and predictions, costs and value chain judgements. You notice that the data is available to you and you use it to make decisions.

- **Data Compelled:** The biggest tech companies in the world and the smartest CEOs and boards will strive to reach this level. At this point, data is everything. Not a single decision is made in the business without data being involved. As a leader, you will expect data to be a part of reports you receive and that the data can be analysed, projected and interrogated to answer your questions. You use data to answer the question 'Why?' and to stress test trends and predictions.

Naturally, businesses are going to want to find themselves at level four: Data Compelled. This might not always be possible due to the nature of the business, or the expense of putting in place these systems, but going as far up the scale as you can is never going to be a bad idea.

Where is your organization? This is your first chance to use your actual or mental pen in this book. Using Figure 4.4, circle where you believe you are on the scale.

Figure 4.4 Where does your organization sit on the Data Maturity Index?

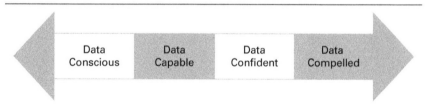

Data Conscious | Data Capable | Data Confident | Data Compelled

2: The ESG Data Disclosure Index

Seeing as we are looking to recommend how your organization can best engage with ESG data, it is logical to ask how much data specifically about sustainability metrics and outcomes you as a leader see today.

To answer this question, you need to assess where you sit on the ESG Data Availability Index. This index represents the information available to track, measure and manage sustainability impacts by the business. This includes data on your organization's impact on and adoption of:

- air pollution
- water scarcity
- diversity of workforce
- fossil fuel consumption
- methane emissions
- single use plastics usage
- waste management
- governance of human rights
- business travel policies
- transparent procurement
- land usage
- etc.

ESG data categories have become vast. Thousands of data points and qualitative data disclosures could be attributable to either E, S or G categories. This can feel daunting. Don't panic.

There are some data points that are fundamentally sought out across the ESG spectrum (at the time of writing). In Table 4.1 the most fundamentally sought data points (in my experience) are listed alongside categories to track how available they are to your organization. Consider this table and what level best describes your organization's data availability today.

Table 4.1 ESG data disclosure high-level assessment

ESG data	No data	Some ESG data available internally	Required ESG data available externally	ESG data openly disclosed
GHG emissions data				
Energy usage (broken down by type of energy source)				
Waste volumes and treatment				

(continued)

Table 4.1   (Continued)

ESG data	No data	Some ESG data available internally	Required ESG data available externally	ESG data openly disclosed
Water consumption				
Employee demographic breakdown including gender, race and ethnicity				
Employee turnover				
Governance policies in place (regulation, HR, privacy, etc)				
Modern slavery policies and governance				

Of course, the above data points are still not standardized globally in terms of what exactly is reported (as our GHG example in Chapter 3 illustrates), but for this exercise in mapping your own organization on the ESG Data Disclosure Index, you can take column one of Table 4.1 as a guideline. If your organization collects/shares/reports on this data or very similar outputs, tick the box most closely reflecting the availability of that data with your mental or physical pen.

Let's define those assessment columns in the table above in a little more detail to help you decide:

- **No data:** This indicates that your organization does not collect or calculate this data for the organization. It may be true that some of the data is collected in some divisions but not others. This would put you in the next category (some ESG data available internally). If you assess that your organization has 'no data' available, this indicates that the organization does not collect or calculate the data anywhere on these subjects.

- **Some ESG data available internally:** This category reflects that your organization collects some of the data points, but does not disclose them externally. For these purposes the word 'internally' includes all levels of management, including the board of directors.

- **Required ESG data available externally:** In this case, your organization may be asked by external stakeholders to disclose the indicated information to them either confidentially or in a more open format. However, the data that is disclosed is specifically driven by external demand and not internal interests. This may include regulatory requirements, supply chain requests for information, association or industry-specific group requests, etc.

- **ESG data openly disclosed:** Tick this box if your company discloses the data listed to the public. This can be done via sustainability data platforms (such as CDP, GRI or others to be outlined later in this chapter), or though the organization's sustainability report or similar. The information needs to specifically address the subject matter indicated. Just having a sustainability report – no matter how many pages of beautifully flowing text there is – does not count unless it contains the data in column 1 of Table 4.1!

Now that we have distinguished between the columns, go back and tick the boxes where you believe your organization sits today. An example is shown in Table 4.2 using a fictitious company called Dogfood Forever Inc. (DFI).

Table 4.2   DFI's ESG data disclosure high-level assessment

ESG data	No data	Some ESG data available internally	Required ESG data available externally	ESG data openly disclosed
GHG emissions data				X
Energy usage (broken down by type of energy source)				X
Waste volumes and treatment		X		
Water consumption	X			
Employee demographic breakdown including gender, race and ethnicity			X	
Employee turnover		X		
Governance policies in place (regulation, HR, privacy, etc)			X	
Modern slavery policies and governance				X

DFI is a dog food producer and distributer in Europe and the Middle East. They have produced a sustainability report distributed alongside their annual report last year, which included information on their GHG emissions and energy usage. They also collect data on the waste volumes and what happens to that waste (i.e. recycling, landfill, incineration, etc) at all their sites across Europe, but only one site in the Middle East.

They have extrapolated data based on assumptions they have shared internally to account for the waste volumes and how the waste is dealt with for the sites for which they don't have raw data. This waste data is only shared with the executive management team at present – nothing is released in their sustainability report or in press releases. DFI doesn't measure their water consumption.

DFI's HR team tracks the data on employee demographics, including breaking down the data by percentage along gender, race and ethnicity lines. It uses this data to calculate its gender pay gap and to assess if it is reaching its diversity goals at all levels of DFI's employee hierarchy. The DFI team shares this with some associations it is a part of, including the prestigious Pet Food Diversity Institute based in Bern, Switzerland. The DFI team also collects employee turnover data, which it shares with the management and board of directors annually.

In order to maintain its licence with its EU regulator, the Pet Consumables Commission, DFI discloses its governance policies around production welfare processes for both human employees and canine taste testers as well as its robust governance of data privacy, employee rights, etc.

This information should help you to understand how DFI's leaders have filled in their ESG data disclosure high-level assessment.

A health warning

It is impossible for you to tick the boxes in the 'ESG data openly disclosed' column if you have assessed your organization at the basic level of data maturity (i.e. Data Conscious) in the previous section. It just doesn't make sense. If your organization is not collecting and using data in its central business processes, the likelihood of it offering ESG data openly to the market is very low.

If you find yourself in this situation when conducting your ESG data high-level assessment, I suggest you take a moment to review both of the previous sections again.

Figure 4.5   Where does your organization sit on the ESG Data Disclosure Index?

Once you've filled in Table 4.1 based on your own organization's experience, how do you map that to where you sit on the ESG data disclosure continuum?

After completing Table 4.1, all you need to map yourself on the continuum presented in Figure 4.5 is to determine which column has the most ticks in it. This maps to the ESG data disclosure continuum categories as follows:

- No data = ESG Data Novice
- Some ESG data available internally = ESG Data Newbie
- Required ESG data available externally = ESG Data Numerate
- ESG data openly disclosed = ESG Data Nirvana

Do this mapping now to commit to the level you believe your organization is at today. This will add 'data' as you map your overall Sustainability Data Category later in this chapter.

3: The Regulatory Pressures Index

This is a big one to assess accurately, and will directly influence your company's ESG data disclosure requirements.

To say that ESG data disclosure regulations are rapidly evolving is a monumental understatement. In 2023, the global discussion on regulation of companies' requirements to disclose is a hot topic. The discussion is being backed up by actions. In particular, the development of standards for disclosures is moving at pace. We deep dive on the state of play for disclosure regulation in Chapters 7 and 8.

It would be a fool's errand to outline in this book the current regulatory requirements for your organization. It most certainly will have changed between the point of publication and when you are reading this. Instead, I encourage you to review Chapter 8 and to get the up-to-date information for your business based on its location, size of business, sector and governance requirements (i.e. public vs private company vs not for profit, etc).

With that being said, you may already know the sustainability regulations that apply to you. Let's review some framing before we map your organization to the indicators.

When considering regulatory pressures, we need to first define what we mean by the terms 'voluntary' and 'mandatory':

- **Voluntary disclosure** indicates that the regulator or supervisor has identified a framework for ESG data disclosure and made public their encouragement for those in their jurisdiction to use that framework to disclose data. Increasingly this framework is based on the Task Force on Climate-related Financial Disclosures (TCFD) principles, which include high-level categories and increasingly more detailed descriptions of what should be disclosed. Notably the TCFD has taken a principles-based approach which is not completely specific about which datasets match up to each of its disclosure categories. (This is where the standards-setters are stepping in to bring added granularity.) For the purposes of your analysis, 'voluntary' means that your organization is not required to report ANY sustainability data. Reporting on ESG is entirely the decision of the organization. BUT voluntary disclosure guidance exists in your geography, and you are aware of it.

- **Mandatory disclosure** is another kettle of fish. When your regulator mandates disclosure of data, you need to comply or risk not being able to operate. The data that is mandated for disclosure varies. As stated before, this is a moving target. What we do know is that it is changing. In the most advanced regulatory regimes, mandatory disclosures are increasing year on year.

Not all geographies have either voluntary or mandatory disclosure guidance in place. Some areas of the world are completely silent on the topic of ESG disclosures. But this group of silent jurisdictions is already in the minority. Moreover, some regulations are putting in place requirements to disclose worldwide data – not just the data relevant to their jurisdiction. We discuss this 'extraterritorial reach' in more depth in Chapter 7, but for the purposes of this section, it is something to be aware of.

Another element to consider is the scope of regulation within a jurisdiction. Frequently, regulation is rolled out first to include the largest organizations or those that are most publicly held. This eases the way for a wider range of organizations to come under regulation in the future. Larger companies will have more resources overall to manage the compliance burden and regulators can assess how regulations are delivering on their intended outcomes.

How does this affect your assessment? If you are a publicly listed organization, or a large player in your jurisdiction, you may be top of the list for regulators to require sustainability data disclosure. You will likely be in the first group of organizations within the scope of mandatory disclosure requirements. If you are a smaller or private organization, this does not mean you are free from any disclosure obligation. Certainly, it means you need to monitor developments to be sure you are aware when and if you fall into scope for regulation in the future.

As in most things, there is a sliding scale between one extreme and the other. 'No disclosure regulation' vs 'mandatory sustainability disclosure requirements' has some points in between. If your organization has no disclosure requirements today, it is possible that it will be subject to voluntary or mandatory disclosures in the future. With the pace of change in this space, do not be surprised if that future comes very quickly! Sometimes regulations start with voluntary disclosure suggestions. Sometimes they jump straight into mandatory requirements. It depends on where you operate and which regulators supervise your business.

Most typically, there will be some publicly available indications that regulation is on its way to being mandatory. These phases of governmental and regulatory discussions are often easy to pick up through the media. You can often track regulation through its phases of discussion, consultation, finalization, adoption and enforcement. These phases can take decades, years, or months. They may overlap or be very regimented as to their process. Again, it depends on who is regulating what where. You as a business leader are best placed to have the detail behind the current status of your organization's sustainability data disclosure requirements – or you will know who to ask.

A model mapping the regulatory reality for your organization today is presented in Figure 4.6. Choose where you are on this Regulatory Pressures Index to help further build up your understanding of where you land on the ESG Data Maturity Journey overall.

Figure 4.6   Where does your organization sit on the Regulatory Pressures Index?

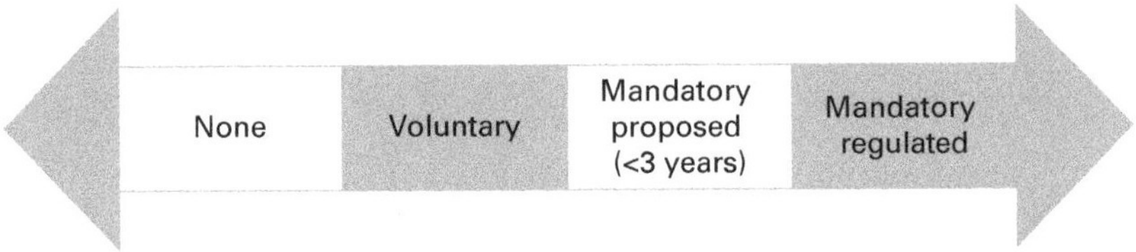

4: The Stakeholder Engagement Index

All organizations have external stakeholders. How your organization is perceived and engaged with by these stakeholders can make or break your success. Through the lens of sustainability data, these stakeholders can play a critical role. They can demand information or outcomes about your organization's impact on the climate and society. They will need data to do this – and so we are back to the question of what, how and why you disclose your ESG data.

This time we are considering the question of 'why' you should disclose, based on the pressures from your current stakeholders. You need to get a handle on their demands and the consequences of not meeting those demands. Some consequences may be game-changing for your success. Others may not matter significantly.

In this section we will review some stakeholder groups and describe how their engagement can impact your organization's ESG data journey, with the objective of helping you decide how impactful these stakeholders are for your organization today. This will shape your overall Sustainability Data Category.

We will review six key stakeholder groups. Your organization may have others that are important to running your business. Consider these alongside the six shown in Figure 4.7:

- customers
- suppliers/partners
- employees
- investors
- shareholders
- government

What should you consider when thinking about how these six important stakeholders engage with your organization on the topic of sustainability data?

Customers

What your customers want plays an important role in the success of your business. The definition of a customer can vary. For this purpose, the

Figure 4.7   Stakeholders for your organization

customer is the business or individual you sell to or that your distributors sell to. Your distribution network is simply a means to access the customer, and what we are looking to uncover here are the interests and needs of your actual customer.

The question here is, what does your customer want from you as an organization in order to continue to buy from you? If the answer includes sustainability minimum standards or information on your company's environmental, social or governance practices, your customer is an engaged stakeholder in sustainability.

This results in pressure on you as an organization to supply the information the customer needs on an accurate and timely basis. Without this information, an engaged customer may not buy from you. You are putting revenue at risk by not offering the necessary sustainability-related information to them.

Suppliers/partners

As with customers, suppliers may want or need sustainability-related information in order to do business with you. Suppliers are the companies providing the inputs you need to conduct your business. In the broadest sense, this includes partners in your ecosystem you rely on to create and deliver your product or service. Your organization's suppliers are unique to your business. However, every company has suppliers – they may be supplying significant physical inputs such as carbon fibre to the high-end bicycle industry, or flights to the management consulting industry.

Suppliers increasingly are aware of their own supply chains and who they are doing business with. They may request to know how their products are being used, and how they are reused or disposed of at end of life (to fulfil their circular economy commitments, for example).

Requests for sustainability information work both ways in the value chain of an organization, and being cognizant of suppliers' needs for information helps you be fully aware of the implications on reporting.

Employees

Your organization delivers through the efforts of your employees. As referenced earlier, the employee is a critical stakeholder in your organization's sustainability journey. A highly engaged employee may demand information from the businesses they work for to get comfortable in being a part of the organization. This information can include ESG data or sustainability or transition plans. The information can be shared confidentially with the internal audience of employees, or it can make up the externally available information about your company.

The internal audience of existing employees may choose to stay with the company based on disclosure of sustainability data and practices. The external audience of potential future employees may demand disclosure before they commit to working with you.

Investors

Investor stakeholders may have specific ESG disclosure requirements from your business. Depending on the investors' own regulatory requirements and disclosure needs, their engagement with you on topics of sustainability may vary from light touch to deeply demanding. The requests for information may come from existing investors or potential new investors. Trends indicate a one-way trajectory towards greater demand from investors for data – you may already be experiencing this.

Shareholders

As distinct from investors, shareholders already hold some of the stock of your company. They have the right at most annual general meetings to comment on management and corporate priorities and objectives (as well as voicing these questions and challenges throughout the year).

Increasingly, shareholder activism has pivoted to the topic of sustainability and companies' shareholders want proof that companies are acting responsibly. This is not only true in public or large companies – smaller companies are also being challenged by shareholders who prioritize sustainable growth.

Government

We will talk a lot about regulators in this book, and they are important. Governments are also important stakeholders. It is governments that show up at the COP meetings each year and make emissions-based and net zero target commitments on behalf of their countries. These commitments will increasingly shape the economies our companies and organizations work in. The views and priorities of governments can influence your business directly through tax credits or increases, or indirectly through influencing buyer sentiment.

Now that we have defined these stakeholders and their interests, think about your own organization. Which stakeholders are engaged in requesting ESG data in one form or another? By this we mean directly requesting datasets or indirectly asking for your organization to act sustainably, to a point where you feel pressure to respond. You may not actually take action – but you feel the pressure to consider doing so from these stakeholder groups. Take a look at Table 4.3, and mark the columns associated with each stakeholder group as yes or no.

Table 4.3 Stakeholder engagement – yes or no?

Stakeholder	Requesting ESG data = YES	Not requesting ESG data = NO
Customers		
Suppliers/partners		
Employees		
Investors		
Shareholders		
Government		

Figure 4.8   Where does your organization sit on the Stakeholder Engagement Index?

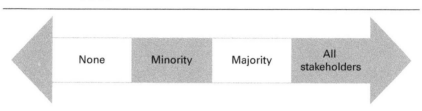

This is a simplified test of your stakeholder engagement, but as a leader you should be aware of the needs of these groups on this topic. Your views on stakeholder engagement and pressures will help you make business decisions now and into the future. For the moment, your answers in Table 4.3 will help you map where you are as an organization on the Stakeholder Engagement Index (Figure 4.8).

If there are zero stakeholders marked as 'Yes' in Table 4.3, your organization maps to 'None' on the scale below. If you counted two or fewer stakeholders as 'Yes', you are in the Minority category below. If three to five stakeholders were assigned a 'Yes' in Table 4.3, your organization is in the Majority category. Finally, if all the stakeholders in Table 4.3 were engaged in requesting ESG data of some sort from you, your organization is mapped to the 'All stakeholders' category.

Take a moment to circle the category your organization is in on the Stakeholder Engagement Index outlined in Figure 4.8.

5: The Climate vs Sustainability Index

I have used the word 'sustainability' a lot already in this book – and there will be a lot more references coming up. I am specifically using the term to encompass all the elements of environmental, social and governance issues that make up ESG and the full range of ESG data.

However, not all organizations or active players in the sustainability ecosystem include all elements of E, S and G in how they engage with sustainability-related data. Some have their definition of sustainability focus on climate change. Some define their sustainability interests even more narrowly as a focus on carbon specifically, rather than water or other elements included in a climate change envelope.

Other organizations prioritize the social elements of sustainability first. These groups may prioritize equality or diversity of workforce, human rights, active participation in community projects, etc. These discrepancies in ESG focus are a natural product of the evolution of sustainability and ESG reporting.

Often, organizations first focus on climate change – the environment and protecting the planet from rising temperatures brought on by GHG emissions. In data parlance, this is a focus on the E in ESG. This 'climate-first' strategy is also reflected in many organizations embedded in the ESG ecosystem. For example, CDP, a non-profit that runs a global environmental disclosure platform we will describe further in Chapter 6, publishes a questionnaire annually. When CDP began more than 20 years ago, it was extremely focused on collecting data on carbon emissions specifically. CDP has expanded significantly beyond collecting carbon data and into other key environmental themes, such as water security, forests and, more recently, biodiversity and plastics. CDP largely remains focused on E data vs S data.

The same is true for the International Sustainability Standards Board (ISSB), which is intent on climate data standards formation. The ISSB has actively decided to focus on climate-related data in the first instance during its initial data definitions (the first of these was released in June 2023), before expanding to other datasets including S and other specific data categories including biodiversity/nature solutions data.

No matter where your organization sits today on the Climate vs Sustainability Index, it may change focus over time. The choice of what to prioritize in the spectrum of sustainability is often influenced by increasing confidence and comfort in the act of reporting your data. It may also be forced upon you by regulatory requirements. Again, this is evidence of a journey still underway. Your organization is no different. It's a journey. So let's take it a step at a time.

Before we get to the underlying data supporting either a climate focus or a wider sustainability focus, you can map where your organization is today in its business strategy and philosophy. Ask yourself these questions:

- Does your company strategy include recognizing your organization's impact on climate – the E?

- Does your company strategy include recognizing your organization's impact on society – the S?

- Does your company strategy include recognizing your organization's adherence to governance best practice – the G?

Based on your answers above, map yourself onto Figure 4.9.

Figure 4.9   Where does your organization sit on the Climate vs Sustainability Index?

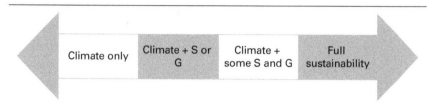

| Climate only | Climate + S or G | Climate + some S and G | Full sustainability |

Mapping to the ESG Data Maturity Journey – finally!

As has probably become abundantly clear, navigating what ESG data reporting suits your business is a seemingly simple question with enormous complexity. It can be helpful to align yourself with a category of companies engaging with ESG data to help to break down what is most important at your stage of maturity. This can help you to gauge what you're doing well today and what are your potential next steps.

This methodology of categorizing your organization is specifically focused on ESG data maturity, and takes into account the type of business you are – product-led or services-led. The implications of these two different types of organization on their ESG data needs and opportunities differ enough to call them out separately while they sit at the same point on the ESG Data Maturity Journey.

The journey is intended to be used as a map for leaders to understand where their organization sits today. The categories of organization will also help leaders to consider immediate next steps for their businesses, identify critical ESG data points needed for the use cases we reviewed in Chapter 2, recognize risks and opportunities associated with their level of ESG data maturity, and make better informed decisions.

When you know where your organization sits on the ESG Data Maturity Journey, you are better equipped to make decisions on sustainability KPIs you need as a leader. This helps you to moderate your own personal sustainability aspirations to align with your organization's reality. If you are less ambitious than your organization, it is a useful tool to help analyse where the value lies in ESG disclosures. If you are more ambitious than your organization, it allows you to plan how to successfully influence organizational change.

Below is a description of each of the five Sustainability Data Categories. As you read through them, think about where your organization is placed on the journey and which of the descriptions best describes your business. Refer to the work you've just done in mapping your organization to the five indicators:

1 Data Maturity Index

2 ESG Data Disclosure Index

3 Regulatory Pressures Index

4 Stakeholder Engagement Index

5 Climate vs Sustainability Index

Alongside the descriptions of the categories presented in Figure 4.2, there is also a characteristics section. This section allows you to revisit each indicator to guide you to the category that best reflects today's reality. Don't be tempted to map yourself to where you would *like* to be. We'll deal with your ambitions and future plans in the next chapter. For now, be honest about today.

The five Sustainability Data Categories

Figure 4.10   An organization's ESG Data Maturity Journey

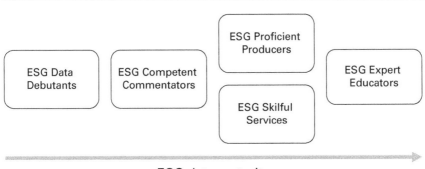

ESG data maturity

ESG Data Debutant

Characteristics:

- Anywhere on the Data Maturity Index.
- Low on the ESG Data Disclosure Index.
- Ranked 'None' on the Regulatory Pressures Index.
- Ranked 'None' on the Stakeholder Engagement Index.
- Anywhere on the Climate vs Sustainability Index.

You are the new kid on the block in terms of embracing ESG data. It's all up from here! You are currently not known in the marketplace as an organization that is proactive on sustainability topics. If others in your industry are in different Sustainability Data Categories, you may even be considered a laggard in this area. It may be that your industry or geography is not focused on hearing about your sustainability metrics and so the topic doesn't affect you as an organization at all.

Your current position as an ESG Data Debutant likely reflects the priority the board, C-suite and leadership of your organization give to the topic of sustainability. It is low on the management agenda or doesn't play a role at all. ESG data production is similarly low volume – for both your internal and external stakeholders. As a result, you do not include sustainability considerations in your business decisions. You may or may not be data-centric in other areas of your business, but ESG data specifically does not appear in management discussions

As a Data Debutant, you can't have regulatory requirements to disclose ESG data – if you did you would be woefully out of compliance (and out of business?). Currently, your shareholders are not demanding sustainability data from you. You have no sustainability or climate targets such as net zero or carbon neutrality goals set or commitments made. Your organization does not yet have a climate transition plan in place.

You have at least some interest in understanding the use and value of ESG data – that is evident from you reading this book! However, you would also recognize your organization has currently very low engagement in the sustainability agenda. As an ESG Data Debutant, you have ample opportunity to expand your engagement with ESG data should you choose to.

ESG Competent Commentator

Characteristics:

- Anywhere on the Data Maturity Index.
- Medium on the ESG Data Disclosure Index.
- Medium to high on the Regulatory Pressures Index.
- Low to medium on the Stakeholder Engagement Index.
- Likely closer to the 'climate' end of the Climate vs Sustainability Index.

Your organization is not known externally as a sustainability champion, but neither are you completely off the radar. Typically, you look at sustainability through a risk-mitigation lens as opposed to proactively embracing opportunities to seek out data for positive outcomes such as improving efficiency, winning business, improving image, retaining talent, etc.

You already collect and share some ESG data and you comply with sustainability disclosure regulations where they apply to you (financially driven or industry-centric). You disclose a minimum of ESG data to the public and may have more data you see and use internally. You may be data savvy in other areas of your business, and you at least are aware of how to use data to improve decision-making in some areas of your business.

You may or may not have a net zero target, carbon neutrality goal or other pledge or commitment in place. You may already be carbon neutral but are likely to use carbon credits and offsets to reach this goal. You do not have a transition plan in place. You are unlikely to benchmark your sustainability credentials against others in your industry or sector. You take more of a 'only the necessary' approach to ESG data collection and production.

You will likely have at least Scope 1 GHG emissions numbers for your business, and may already be confident in the Scope 2 GHG emissions disclosures for your organization. You are unlikely to have Scope 3 GHG emissions data available, and certainly not published externally. You are aware of sustainability pressures from the market, but are not putting sustainability at the top of your corporate agenda. Your ESG data coverage is competent but nothing more.

The next two categories are similar in their ESG data maturity levels, but represent two different organization types: one predominantly a product company, the other predominantly a services company.

ESG Proficient Producer

Characteristics:

- Medium to high on the Data Maturity Index.
- Medium to high on the ESG Data Disclosure Index.
- Anywhere on the Regulatory Pressures Index.
- Medium on the Stakeholder Engagement Index.
- Anywhere on the Climate vs Sustainability Index.

You are a product-dominant organization that may be known in the market as sustainably credible. Your board of directors, C-suite and leadership teams are aware of sustainability as a macro-trend affecting the organization and take ESG data considerations into account when making business decisions.

Some level of ESG-related claims are part of the organization's public communications and brand association. There may be reference to how the organization or product is sustainable on packaging, marketing or sales literature.

You produce ESG data either voluntarily or in line with regulatory requirements. The data certainly includes GHG emissions data and energy usage details. You have disclosed Scope 1 and Scope 2 emissions in multiple years, and may have disclosed Scope 3 emissions. Your dominant emissions are from Scope 1. You are likely to have set targets (for example, net zero or carbon neutrality with target deadlines before 2030), and may have already achieved these targets. (We will define these targets in the next chapter if you are unsure of what they are all about.) You may have a transition plan or are in the process of designing or publishing one.

Overall, sustainability plays an important role in your business and you have data on climate (the E), together with some significant elements of data from the S and/or G categories. Your role as a business leader includes discussions on the business's sustainability and how it compares to competitors and others in the sector, industry, product category or geography. You or your colleagues may be involved in some sustainability councils/associations/working groups or policy development forums.

You are a solid ESG data contributor and your organization recognizes the benefits of collecting, disclosing and analysing this data for both the business and the planet. You do more than the bare minimum when it comes to collecting and disclosing ESG data internally and externally.

ESG Skilful Services

Characteristics:

- Medium to high on the Data Maturity Index.
- Medium to high on the ESG Data Disclosure Index.
- Anywhere on the Regulatory Pressures Index.
- Anywhere on the Stakeholder Engagement Index.
- Medium to high (high being full sustainability) on the Climate vs Sustainability Index.

You are a services-dominant organization that includes sustainability in its external communications. Similar to the ESG Proficient Producer category, your board of directors, C-suite and leadership teams are aware of sustainability as a macro-trend affecting the organization and take ESG data considerations into account when making business decisions. Some level of ESG-related claims are part of the organization's public communications and brand association.

You produce ESG data either voluntarily or in line with regulatory requirements. The data certainly includes GHG emissions data and energy usage details. You have disclosed Scope 1 and Scope 2 emissions in multiple years, and may have likely disclosed Scope 3 emissions. Your dominant emissions are from Scope 2. You are likely to have a net zero or carbon neutrality target deadline before 2030, and may have already achieved these targets. You may have a transition plan or are in the process of designing or publishing one.

Overall, sustainability plays an important role in your business and you have data on climate (the E) and are particularly strong in data on the S category. Your service offering relies heavily on people as an input. You will also likely have strong data on the G categories. Your role as a business leader includes discussions on the business's sustainability and how it compares to competitors and others in the sector, industry, or geography. You or your colleagues may be involved in some sustainability councils/associations/working groups or policy development forums.

You are a solid ESG data contributor and your organization recognizes the benefits of collecting, disclosing and analysing this data for both the business and the planet. You do more than the bare minimum when it comes to collecting and disclosing ESG data internally and externally.

ESG Expert Educator

Characteristics:

- High on the Data Maturity Index.
- High on the ESG Data Disclosure Index.
- Anywhere on the Regulatory Pressures Index.
- Anywhere on the Stakeholder Engagement Index.
- High (full sustainability) on the Climate vs Sustainability Index.

You produce, analyse and disclose a wide range of ESG data internally and externally. You go beyond where regulation or stakeholder pressures require data – you are looking for data that can be helpful to positively impact society and our natural world. Your leaders – from managers up through the board of directors – consider sustainability a priority. You may link some or part of your executive and employee compensation to sustainability targets or ESG data improvements.

You produce a sustainability report that is published and you report to an external ESG data collection platform. You use (or plan to use) TCFD guidance to disclose material climate-related information about your organization. You are already carbon neutral or carbon negative and have set or achieved a net zero target no later than 2040. You have a published transition plan in place.

Data plays a critical role in your business strategy and governance – you value data and invest in producing, managing and analysing data for continuous improvements – in the area of sustainability and elsewhere. You track your sustainability and ESG data against disclosures by your peers and strive to be best in class.

You calculate and disclose Scope 1, 2 and 3 GHG emissions and most other widely used ESG data metrics. You are not satisfied with stopping there. You are investigating other areas for data disclosure, potentially including biodiversity and nature impact data, inclusion of geospatial and asset location data, and impact measurement data. You play a role in developing policy and industry best practices for sustainability and disclosure by participating in knowledge sharing in a variety of ways: through think tanks, regulatory consultations, sitting on working groups, associations, policy formation bodies, etc.

You are known in your industry for prioritizing sustainability as one of your business drivers and your brand messaging includes sustainability credentials which have been verified as appropriate and accurate.

Deciding which category you are and what is next

After reading through the descriptions above and doing your mapping on the five indicators earlier in this chapter, you should now have decided on the correct category for your organization on the ESG Data Maturity Journey.

A reminder: this is your starting point. The categorization you have just done reflects where you are today. As we know from previous chapters, much can change rather quickly in the area of sustainability. It may be that you are in the absolutely right category for your organization for the foreseeable future. It may be that your category does not reflect where you could or should be. For example, if you mapped your organization to the ESG Data Debutant category, and you are aware of regulation that affects your organization in force now or imminently, you may need to consider how to move up to a different category in order to meet these obligations.

As an ESG Competent Commentator organization, you may feel you are spot on and you are comfortable that your disclosures are being led by regulation. You may not feel the need to make changes until external factors force that change. On the other hand, if you are an ESG Proficient Producer, you may believe there is significant business upside to transitioning to an ESG Expert Educator. It may win you new business and improve your profile to stakeholders that matter to you.

How you decide what to do next will be based on the use cases for ESG data that are most important to your organization. Your organizational ambition will also play a role. Remember our steps to mapping your sustainability data journey outlined in Figure 4.1?

You have now completed your action for the M: mapping your ESG data maturity. You may need to do this periodically as you make changes within your organization. But for now, you can tick that step off your to-do list.

In the next chapter we will review the use cases for the sustainability data your organization may want or need to collect and disclose. Onwards and upwards.

Prioritizing sustainability data use cases

5

REFLECTIVE QUESTIONS

- Which ESG data use cases are most important to me?
- What is a sustainable finance taxonomy, and how does it affect me?
- What are carbon credits and how do they work?

In your sustainability data journey, it is time to ground the 'why?' in your core business objectives. The 'why?' is the *reason* for thinking about, collecting, analysing, sharing or disclosing ESG data. It needs to be valuable for your business to engage with this type of data – otherwise why do it?

Our next steps are to prioritize the use cases we reviewed in Chapter 2 and determine how they match with your organization's operations and growth plans. We will review your use case priorities now and your ambitions in Chapter 6. No matter if you are an ESG Data Debutant, an ESG Competent Commentator, an ESG Proficient Producer, an ESG Skilful Services or an ESG Expert Educator, there is room to move, improve and change along the journey.

Let's check if your Sustainability Data Category is fit for purpose for the ESG data use cases most important to your organization. We're going to look into the U in our journey through the 'MUD' (see Figure 4.1 for a reminder). It will clear off the dirt obscuring your view of your organization's current ESG data needs.

Through this review, you will get a steer on the minimum data requirements your organization needs to collect and review today so that you don't close off business-critical options for the future. Now is the time to be clear about your priorities so that you can use ESG data to future-proof your business. A reminder of the ABCs of data use cases: Access to Capital; Business Growth and Efficiency; and Compliance.

Access to capital – is it your priority?

In order to assess the impacts of the access to capital use case to your organization, ask yourself the following questions:

- Do you plan to raise capital or restructure your finances?
  - If yes: Do you plan to access capital through an equity-based IPO or a secondary placement?
    - If yes: Do the stock exchanges you are considering accessing consider ESG disclosures to be mandatory?
- Do you plan to access capital through a debt-based placement?
  - If yes: Do you plan to issue a bond? Are you considering a Green Bond?
    - If yes: Do you know what data is needed to qualify as a Green Bond?
- Do you plan to apply for a loan from a bank?
  - If yes: What are the bank's standard ESG/sustainability related questions?
- Do you plan to access private equity funds?
  - If yes: Have you identified a funding group, and do you know their required ESG disclosure requirements?

Essentially, if you have said yes to any of the questions above, you will encounter some level of ESG disclosure requirements. Some funding sources have very clear disclosure requirements, and others have developed their own unique data disclosure requests before agreeing funding. If you are seeking funding, your organization must understand the financial sector's disclosure requirements or you risk being shut out of capital-raising activities.

I would recommend you ensure you have absorbed the journey of regulation and disclosure policies pertaining to financial institutions in the deep dive in Chapters 7 and 8. This will give you a good handle on your organization's level of data disclosure requirements.

In the meantime, let's consider the case of a simple loan.

Show me the money – show me the ESG data

Banks are at the forefront of financial intermediation, and their lending decisions can significantly impact the economy, society, and the environment. Traditional lending criteria often focus on financial performance alone, neglecting other critical aspects that can affect long-term viability and sustainability. By incorporating ESG data into their loan approval process, banks can assess a borrower's overall risk profile, including potential non-financial risks that may not be immediately apparent.

Environmental factors

Banks are increasingly considering a borrower's environmental practices and their impact on the ecosystem. To evaluate a company's environmental performance, the bank may request data on:

- **Carbon footprint:** Measuring the company's greenhouse gas (GHG) emissions enables banks to assess its contribution to climate change and identify potential regulatory risks, such as carbon pricing.
- **Energy efficiency:** Understanding a company's efforts in reducing energy consumption demonstrates its commitment to sustainability and may indicate cost-saving potential.
- **Water usage:** Companies operating in water-scarce regions may face significant risks that can affect their long-term operations and financial stability.

Social factors

The social impact of a borrower's activities is another crucial consideration for banks. ESG data can help banks gauge a company's commitment to social responsibility and employee welfare. Relevant data may include:

- **Employee diversity and inclusion:** Companies with diverse workforces tend to be more innovative and resilient in the face of challenges.
- **Labour practices:** Banks may assess a company's adherence to fair labour standards and worker rights to mitigate reputational and legal risks.
- **Community engagement:** Understanding a company's involvement in the communities where it operates can reflect its commitment to sustainable business practices.

Governance factors

Governance forms the backbone of a well-managed and sustainable company. To evaluate governance practices, banks may request data on:

- **Board diversity:** A diverse board with varied expertise can contribute to better decision-making and risk management.

- **Executive compensation:** Transparency in executive pay ensures alignment with long-term shareholder value and minimizes conflicts of interest.

- **Anti-corruption measures:** Companies with robust anti-corruption policies are less likely to face legal and reputational risks, safeguarding the bank's interests.

ESG integration in loan approvals has gained significant momentum in recent years. A 2020 Organisation for Economic Co-operation and Development (OECD) publication revealed that over 60 per cent of major global banks have incorporated ESG considerations into their lending criteria (OECD, 2020). This represents a collective commitment within the financial industry to sustainable financing practices.

The most important point to make here is that if access to capital is a priority use case for you based on the questions above, you need to establish a system for collection, data reporting and disclosure on critical datasets.

What are these critical datasets? They still vary depending on your funding source. However, let's be clear: if you are going to choose only one data point to collect and be ready to disclose, it is GHG emissions. This data point will establish your ability to monitor your carbon emissions, which is a key to unlock many funding sources today and many more in the future.

Business growth and efficiencies – are they your priorities?

In order to assess the importance of the business growth and efficiencies use case to your organization, ask yourself the following questions:

- Is your supply chain interested in your ESG data?
  - o If yes: Is your opportunity to win business affected by your sustainability data? Are you ruled out as a supplier if you do not have credible

ESG data available? Is your end customer adding sustainability considerations to their buying decisions?

- Are your employees asking about the organization's sustainability priorities?

  o If yes: Are you losing talent seeking a more proactively sustainable company to work for? Are there challenges in attracting new talent based on your sustainability profile?

This is a rapidly moving space. The questions above may impact you subtly today, but quickly become a dominant force for your business. When you're contemplating the business growth and efficiencies use case, you consider both the situation today and the trends you are seeing. This will help you get ahead of any future requests from stakeholders by having data available to share with your audience. This is why collecting data today is beneficial, for you to be able to quickly disclose credible data when you decide it is important to do so.

You may be wondering – either as a Data Debutant or an Expert Educator – why we have not broken down ESG data maturity definitions by industry type. Surely certain areas of the economy are more squarely in the spotlight for disclosing their sustainability data than others? Shouldn't we be thinking about this sectorally?

This is a slippery slope. No sector is untouched by climate change, and therefore no sector is excused from monitoring their impacts on the world we live in. With that clearly stated, understanding which sectors are the biggest emitters of GHGs can help you as a business leader assess the potential intensity of stakeholder interest.

Which sectors are the world's heaviest emitters?

In 2021, total global GHG emissions were estimated to be around 37.9 gigatonnes of carbon dioxide equivalent ($GtCO_2e$) (International Energy Agency, 2022). Which sectors are responsible for the largest share of these global GHG emissions?

1. Energy sector

The energy sector is the largest contributor to global GHG emissions. In 2021, it accounted for approximately 73 per cent of the total emissions.

This sector includes fossil fuel-based activities such as the burning of coal, oil and natural gas for electricity generation, heating, transportation and industrial processes. The combustion of fossil fuels releases significant amounts of carbon dioxide (CO_2) and other GHGs into the atmosphere, making it the primary driver of anthropogenic climate change.

2. Industrial activities

Industrial activities, including manufacturing, cement production and chemical processes, contributed around 19 per cent of global GHG emissions in 2021. The cement industry is particularly notable for its CO_2-intensive nature, as limestone is converted into clinker during cement production, resulting in substantial carbon emissions.

Additionally, certain chemical processes release potent GHGs like hydrofluorocarbons (HFCs) and perfluorocarbons (PFCs) that have a much higher global warming potential than CO_2.

3. Land use and forestry

Land use and forestry activities play a significant role in GHG emissions and sequestration. In 2021, they accounted for approximately 8 per cent of global emissions. Deforestation, land clearing for agriculture and peatland degradation release substantial amounts of CO_2 into the atmosphere. On the other hand, reforestation, afforestation and sustainable forest management can act as carbon sinks, sequestering CO_2 from the atmosphere and mitigating emissions.

4. Agriculture

The agriculture sector is responsible for about 10 per cent of global GHG emissions in 2021. Livestock farming, particularly ruminant animals like cattle and sheep, produces methane (CH4) during enteric fermentation. Additionally, rice paddies and manure management also contribute to methane emissions. Furthermore, the use of nitrogen-based fertilizers in agriculture releases nitrous oxide (N_2O), another potent GHG.

5. Transportation

Transportation, including road, air, rail and maritime travel, is a significant emitter of GHGs. In 2021, the transportation sector contributed approximately 16 per cent of global emissions. The combustion of fossil fuels in vehicles, airplanes and ships releases CO_2, while aviation and maritime transport also emit other GHGs like nitrous oxide and HFCs.

6. Residential and commercial

The residential and commercial sectors contributed around 8 per cent of global GHG emissions in 2021. This category includes emissions from buildings for heating, cooling, lighting and appliances, as well as commercial activities. Fossil fuel-based energy consumption for electricity and heating plays a major role in these emissions.

Many other sectors contribute to GHG emissions, but the above highlights some of the dominant sectors and quantifies their contributions.

Understanding the sectors responsible for the largest share of GHG emissions can help you determine if your organization is considered a significant emitter and therefore global interest in your emissions and sustainability practices may be high.

In prioritizing the ABCs of sustainability data use cases, the intensity of shareholder interest – even if you don't experience it acutely today – may bump the business growth and efficiencies use case up your priority list. It also may drive your organization to be more public about your ESG data and transition plans based on the demand from interested parties.

Part of this data, especially as a company operating in a high emissions sector, is the amount and type of carbon credits your organization buys. A primary driver for organizations to buy carbon credits is to comply with carbon caps imposed on them. A link between the business growth and efficiencies ESG data use case and the compliance and regulation use case is this concept of the carbon emissions cap. These caps may be in place for your organization or may be in the future. Emissions caps directly affect your business's bottom line and put pressure on you to build in efficiencies.

An emissions cap is a limit set by a government on the GHG emissions allowed by either the whole of the economy or a specific industry. Economy- or industry-wide caps then break down into the maximum allowable GHG emissions allocated per company. This limit decreases year on year to drive down overall carbon emissions. The emission 'cap' is allocated to the company (or industry or economy) by governing bodies.

If a company exceeds its carbon cap, it must pay for credits to offset this infraction. In many jurisdictions this is done through a trading system that provides a market for trading carbon credits – companies under their allocated carbon cap sell credits to those that exceed their carbon cap. This is a 'cap-and-trade' system, also called an emissions trading system or scheme (ETS). The credits generated from these systems can be traded on a carbon market.

How does this affect your organization's business growth and efficiencies use case? Carbon credits are not free. They cost real money and will affect your business's bottom line. If you are in the position of needing to buy carbon credits (and in some jurisdictions pay fines for exceeding your GHG emissions to boot), you will need to pay for them. This means you may not have the capital to invest in other areas of your business. Your growth or investment in innovation for future efficiencies may be impaired.

Since it restricts your business's bottom line, let's understand how all this works a bit better.

The what and how of carbon credits

A carbon credit market, or ETS, is a system that seeks to reduce GHG emissions by creating a market for such reductions. They are based on two basic mechanisms, carbon credits and emissions allowances, which correspond to the carrot and the stick, respectively.

A carbon credit is generated when an organization achieves a reduction in its carbon emissions. This is based on GHG emissions and uses CO_2 equivalents (designated by the symbol CO_2e) as a unit of measurement. Calculating carbon credits relies on an organization's baseline disclosures.

Let's look at an example in the high-emitting steel sector. Let's say Greensteel Inc establishes to its regulator's satisfaction that its baseline CO_2e emissions level is 525 tonnes per year. Greensteel's year one emissions cap was set to 500 tonnes of CO_2e. Every tonne of savings Greensteel achieves below this cap equals a carbon credit, which can be sold. Buyers of these carbon credits are organizations, like Brownsteel Ltd, which have sadly exceeded their own established emissions cap.

Incentivizing organizations that achieve reductions by allowing them to benefit financially is the carrot in the system. Everyone likes carrots in this scenario. This is the true bedrock of the carbon credits and offsets system: organizations that decrease carbon usage are rewarded financially, and organizations that are over-using carbon are penalized financially.

Greensteel gets the delicious carrot in our simple scenario above. Brownsteel has to swallow the stick. In theory, this redistribution of capital supports organizations and whole industries to take more and more carbon out of the system and be financially compensated for this effort.

In our example above, Brownsteel bought the carbon offsets from Greensteel. Both of these fictious firms were in the steel business. However, buying and selling carbon offsets does not and should not be limited to transactions between firms within a sector. An intra-sector trading system could become limiting or impossible to use. This would depend on how efficient firms in that sector were overall. Sticking to the steel sector example, if the entire steel industry exceeded their permitted CO_2e allowance, it would be impossible for anyone in the market to acquire offsets. There wouldn't be any in existence.

This is where a wider market for carbon credits comes into play. Through the establishment of a market for units of emissions, the law of supply and demand makes reductions in GHG emissions financially valuable. It incentivizes organizations to reduce their own emissions in order to have carbon credits to sell on the market and generate value. The carbon credit, once on the market, can be sold to anyone in any industry. This is the essential logic of a carbon market which is based on an ETS.

ETSs and how they work

Carbon markets are based on having carbon credits generated by an ETS. A crucial aspect of the effectiveness of any ETS system is the limit – the cap – that is placed on the amount of GHG emissions the actors in a given economy are permitted to produce. As noted above, baselines are established for specific organizations, and these are usually lowered year on year to drive overall lower carbon emissions. This is what creates the opportunity for carbon credits to exist. Without carbon credits, a carbon market would have nothing to trade.

If organizations want to avoid increased costs driven by their need to buy more and more carbon credits, they need to find ways to lower their emissions at least to align with their emissions caps. If a firm does nothing, every year it will be more difficult not to exceed decreasing emissions limits and increasing carbon credit costs. This financial incentive for year-on-year reduction in carbon usage is in line with the concept of transition we discussed in Chapter 3.

This is the direction of travel for most carbon planning – an organization targeting lower emissions year on year not only by buying more carbon credits, but by fundamentally changing their emissions profile. Therefore, for you as a business leader, getting your head around carbon markets, carbon offsets, and carbon credits is increasingly important so that you can make business decisions that change that emissions profile. Doing so will save you money.

Costing the future: carbon prices

So how do we work out what carbon emissions cost? The price of carbon credits is established via two primary mechanisms: carbon taxes and cap-and-trade systems. We reviewed the cap-and-trade (or ETS) system above, including its relationship to carbon markets. A carbon tax directly sets a price on carbon by defining a tax rate on emissions, whereas a cap-and-trade system lets the market decide the price of carbon. Cap-and-trade systems do this by placing a limit on the amount of GHG emissions and allowing carbon markets to establish a market price for emissions based on buying and selling carbon credits.

The World Bank has been tracking carbon markets for around two decades, and currently about 23 per cent of global GHG emissions are covered by 73 carbon pricing instruments. Revenues from carbon taxes and ETSs have grown steadily, with 2022 representing a high to date of $95 billion, and 2023 projected to surpass this level (World Bank, 2023).

There is significant variation in carbon pricing globally, as illustrated by the World Carbon Pricing Database (Resources for the Future, 2023). This database tracks carbon prices around the world since 1990. The database provides an emissions-weighted carbon price, which is the average carbon price across all sectors of a jurisdiction's economy, weighted by each sector's share of the economy's total emissions. The price of carbon is determined by factors such as the rigour of emissions reduction targets, the availability of low-carbon technologies, and local market conditions.

This can lead to significant variations around the world. For example, as of 1 April 2022, Uruguay had a carbon tax rate of $137.00/tCO$_2$e, while Poland's was less than $1.00/tCO$_2$e.

How does a company use carbon credits and the carbon markets?

Getting back to your role as an organizational leader, what does this mean for you? How do carbon prices, credits and ETSs impact your organization?

An organization operating in an ETS jurisdiction will have a stipulated emissions allowance. You may fall into this camp. If you do, measuring and managing your GHG emissions is essential. If you exceed your emissions targets you must act. You can buy carbon credits from an ETS, or you can earn them.

Carbon credits can be earned in a variety of ways. Most directly, organically reducing your organization's emissions by adapting your processes can bring down your emissions to below your cap. This yields the opportunity to package the carbon you saved as a carbon credit and sell it as outlined above. You don't *have* to sell it. But you can.

Some ETSs also permit the offsetting of emissions. In carbon offsetting, an organization can claim carbon credits by setting up initiatives including renewable energy projects or forest conservation initiatives, or by creating carbon capture and storage technologies, even if these activities are ancillary to its primary operations. If the organization can demonstrate that the initiative in question achieves a given reduction in CO_2e, it can offset this against its own emissions (providing the ETS in which it operates permits this).

Ways carbon credits can be generated are illustrated in Table 5.1.

Table 5.1   Activities that generate carbon credits

Afforestation and reforestation	Planting new trees or re-growing previously forested areas
Renewable energy projects	Projects such as wind farms, solar power plants or hydroelectric dams
Energy efficiency improvements	Projects that increase the efficiency of industrial processes, reduce energy consumption in buildings or improve the fuel efficiency of vehicles
Methane capture	Projects that capture methane from landfills, coal mines or agricultural waste
Carbon capture and storage	Capturing carbon dioxide at its source (e.g. a power plant) and storing it underground to prevent the carbon dioxide from being released into the atmosphere
Agriculture, forestry, and other land use projects	Projects that aim to reduce emissions or increase carbon sequestration in the agriculture and forestry sectors, such as improved forest management, agroforestry, oceanic farming or changing agricultural practices to increase soil carbon storage

NOTE It would be impossible for me to write this book without mentioning kelp. Seaweed has great potential for sequestering carbon and for providing agriculture alternatives to land-based activities. As my daughter has said since she was 6: kelp is the future (she may have picked that up from me). It may not be the total solution, but kelp can help.

Royal Dutch Shell (Shell) provides an example of how these are employed in practice. As an EU-based company, Shell is subject to the EU ETS. In this system at present, allowances are applied to specific plants and factories, rather than the company as a whole. But large organizations are implementing a wide range of equivalent initiatives too.

Shell has committed to becoming net zero by 2050, which includes the emissions from the production of its energy products (Scope 1 and 2), as well as the emissions from its supply chain (Scope 3). Shell has implemented a combination of methods to meet its net zero emissions goal, including increasing the efficiency of its operations; supplying low-carbon energy products; capturing and storing carbon; and using nature-based solutions. Shell also uses the purchase of carbon credits in its strategy.

In Shell's case, in the effort to reach net zero the use of carbon offsetting is pretty much inevitable. The organization's primary business is selling fossil fuel, so, short of replacing its product with a totally different business output, it's going to be generating carbon emissions. To balance its emissions, and as one step to comply with its ETS caps, Shell plans to plant forests to offset 120 million tonnes of CO_2 by 2050.

It has been pointed out that an area of land three times the size of the company's native Netherlands would be required to achieve this reforestation plan, with potentially negative consequences for the countries in which land is to be acquired by Shell to achieve its plans (Action Aid, 2021). This calls into question the strength of Shell's net zero plan. Is this a realistic balance of activities to bring the company into ETS compliance? Should buying carbon credits be used to achieve its net zero goal?

Carbon credits and offsets used by many companies are being challenged based on their risk of manipulation and misrepresentation. We look at this aspect of carbon markets in greater detail in the final section of this chapter. As it stands, Shell is also targeting direct reduction of its Scope 1 and Scope 2 emissions by 50 per cent by 2030 alongside other internal actions and external offsets to achieve its goals. It isn't all down to collecting credits from planting trees. Nor should this ever be in any organization's sustainability strategy.

Engaging in the carbon markets is not only an option for organizations operating in jurisdictions directly covered by an ETS. Many organizations that do not have a cap imposed on their emissions are reducing carbon emissions and offsetting activities, for a range of reasons linked to the organization's priority use cases for ESG data. The near certainty of the value of carbon credits increasing in the future also makes them an attractive prospect for speculators.

Some organizations are starting to think about how they can begin preparing themselves to cash in on developments in carbon credits. This includes organizations not regulated under an ETS that voluntarily want to participate in the carbon markets. This is leading to increasing interest in voluntary participation in ETSs, which the Taskforce on Scaling Voluntary Carbon Markets (TSVCM) is responding to.

The Taskforce on Scaling Voluntary Carbon Markets

TSVCM is a private-sector initiative focused on exploring the feasibility of the creation of voluntary carbon markets, and their potential role in helping organizations achieve net zero (TSVCM, 2021).

Many organizations have net zero as an aim, but it is often not yet feasible to get rid of emissions entirely. Carbon credits are thus likely to continue to play an important role, allowing organizations to offset emissions they can't phase out through changes to processes, technologies, and other more fundamental means. Creating a voluntary carbon market has the potential to channel these ambitions into beneficial activity, and to create value in the process.

The TSVCM projects that demand for carbon credits could rise 15 times or more by 2030, valuing the potential market for carbon credits at upwards of $50 billion (Blaufelder et al, 2021). Such a market would make it attractive for organizations to invest in the initiatives and technologies required to bring emissions down, and harness market forces to extend the reach of ETSs.

There are a range of challenges for ETS markets and credits. The TSVCM groups these under three categories: market concerns, integrity and quality concerns, and regulatory linkages. Market concerns include the difficulty for new buyers in navigating the market, significant information asymmetry between buyers and sellers, insufficient risk management tools (contractual, insurance, etc), and limited access to financing and resources for suppliers. Integrity and quality concerns include measurement methods and lack of transparency, which undermines confidence in the instrument.

The risk of double counting that results from the fragmented regulatory and registration frameworks also challenges the integrity of the carbon credits being traded (are they really making a difference?). Also noted is the concern that use of offsets can promote greenwashing and forestall engagement in more ambitious approaches by providing a temporary fix. The main challenge posed by regulatory linkages is the weak interconnection between any voluntary market and the compliance markets that are being established.

The TSVCM has accordingly proposed six key action areas to address these challenges:

1 **Core carbon principles (CCPs) and attribute taxonomy**. Quality thresholds need to be established to ensure that credits represent environmental and market integrity. These should be administered by an independent third party, which would also create a taxonomy of additional attributes (for example, project type) to classify credits.

2 **Core carbon reference contracts**. Liquid reference contracts (spot or futures) with a daily price signal need to be used to help participants manage the risk of prices changing and ensure the availability of funds to support the whole supply chain. Information from such reference contracts could also be used in over-the-counter transactions.

3 **Infrastructure: trade, post-trade, financing and data**. Such contracts would be facilitated by the establishment of a resilient and scalable infrastructure. For example, the establishment of clearing houses and meta-registries would enable post-trade activities (on-exchange and over the counter) and protect against counterparty default. Data infrastructure would enhance the availability of important data and boost the integrity and transparency of the market.

4 **Consensus on offset legitimacy**. A generally accepted set of conventions needs to be created on the legitimate and helpful use of offsets, and standards for organizational claims regarding these.

5 **Market integrity assurance**. Voluntary carbon markets need to be made more reliable with respect to oversight, who is permitted to participate, and the operation of market mechanisms.

6 **Demand signals**. Demand signals need to be made clearer if such markets are to develop reliably and scale up supply. This can be done via industry-wide commitments, new point-of-sale offerings, simplified buyer experience, and clear guidance for investors on the use of offsetting.

The TSVCM proposes that such principles could provide the foundation for a reliable voluntary carbon credit market. While emphasizing that decarbonization should remain the primary priority, the task force indicates that carbon credits can nevertheless play a valuable role in helping organizations, and the economy as a whole, get to net zero.

Pros and cons of ETSs and carbon credit systems

Carbon credits and ETSs are not universally considered unambiguously reliable and beneficial tools. The Science Based Targets Initiative (SBTi), for example, argues that they should be considered a temporary measure, to be superseded as we move along the path to a sustainable economy.

While they present certain benefits, there are drawbacks that don't seem like the kind of thing that can be ironed out with minor tweaks. It's worth getting an idea of what the pros and cons of ETSs are, as a way of obtaining a deeper understanding of how your organization can make use of them and contribute to the goals they're intended to foster.

The *benefits* of ETSs are largely connected to the way they enable market forces to be harnessed to promote sustainable ends:

- **Cost-effectiveness:** By allowing market forces to drive emissions reductions, carbon trading systems can potentially achieve reduction targets in a more cost-effective way than direct regulation. Companies that can reduce emissions cheaply have an incentive to do so and can sell their extra allowances to companies for whom reduction would be more expensive.

- **Flexibility:** Companies have the flexibility to choose how they will reduce emissions. They can innovate and find the most efficient ways suited to their specific circumstances.

- **Revenue generation:** Governments can raise revenue by auctioning off emission allowances. This revenue can be invested in renewable energy, energy efficiency, and other climate-friendly projects.

- **Stimulate innovation:** By creating a financial incentive for reducing emissions, cap-and-trade systems can stimulate technological innovation and the development of cleaner technologies.

But the *drawbacks* of ETSs are connected to the limitations of market forces for achieving something as complex and globally interconnected as sustainability:

- **Enforcement challenges:** Carbon trading systems require reliable monitoring, reporting and verification of emissions, which is a challenge with our current systems. There's also the risk of non-compliance and fraud. A study by the World Economic Forum identifies this as a major threat, given the complexity and labour-intensive nature of the auditing systems currently in place (World Economic Forum, 2023).

- **Uncertain environmental effectiveness:** The environmental effectiveness of cap-and-trade systems can be uncertain. If the cap is set too high, it may not lead to significant emissions reductions. Furthermore, emissions can be displaced rather than reduced through the phenomenon of 'leakage', whereby the measures simply cause the harmful activity to move elsewhere, rather than genuinely reducing it.

- **Price volatility:** The price of emission allowances can fluctuate, leading to uncertainty for businesses. This can also impact the effectiveness of the system, by making uncertain the returns for organizations taking action to reap the rewards of reduced emissions in the long term.

- **Potential for inequity:** Companies that can't afford to buy allowances or reduce emissions might face significant costs, which could be passed on to consumers. There's also a concern that pollution could be concentrated in certain areas if companies in those areas choose to buy allowances rather than reducing emissions. This ultimately places in question the long-term effectiveness of such mechanisms and helps clarify why they are often perceived to be a stepping stone to more fundamental solutions.

Given these drawbacks, numerous authorities consider carbon markets to present a potential threat to long-term sustainability.

As you think about prioritizing the business growth and efficiencies use case for your organization, your obligations under an ETS directly affect your business's resource availability. This can impact your growth and may drive you as a business leader to make decisions to drive efficiencies. These efficiencies will ultimately reflect in your ESG data disclosures. On the positive side, if your business generates carbon credits and offsets, you may consider increasing activity to generate more credits you can sell on carbon markets.

Either way, ETSs, carbon taxes and carbon markets are part of a regulatory-led framework that influences business growth and efficiencies. They should be part of your considerations when prioritizing this use case alongside the factors outlined above and in Chapter 2.

Compliance and regulation – are they your priorities?

Turning our minds to the compliance and regulation use case – above and beyond compliance with a cap-and-trade system and the financial compliance requirements outlined above! – there is still more to consider.

Even if you rated yourself as 'none' or 'voluntary' on the Regulatory Pressures Index, compliance and regulation may be a high priority for your organization. It may be that you wish to voluntarily disclose data to be seen as best in class, or it may be that you foresee mandatory disclosure regulations coming down the track and need to get prepared.

To prioritize the compliance and regulation use case, ask yourself the following questions:

- Do you have regulatory requirements to disclose ESG data?

  o If yes: Is the requirement principles-based or framework-based?

- Do these principles or frameworks have established guidance on which data points are needed to meet the regulatory requirements? Are there ESG data disclosure standards that have been or are in the process of being established that will apply to you?

  o If yes: Is the guidance specific about the source/calculations/framing of the disclosure output?

- Is the guidance specific about the timing of the data point for compliant disclosure?

  o If yes: Do you know if there is a stipulated maximum elapsed time from collection of data to disclosure to fulfil obligations?

As is evident from the questions above, having a regulatory obligation to disclose is quickly followed by the need to be clear about what data is needed to comply. This requires a link between the regulatory principles or frameworks and information that comes in the form of datasets.

What do we mean by principles and frameworks?

Principles, frameworks and data differ in two ways. Firstly, they differ in purpose. Principles are the high-level statement outlining what is trying to be achieved through any actions.

A framework is a tool for organizing information. Frameworks can be based on principles that govern the rationale for why the information is needed or important. Data is the information that feeds into the framework. Data is needed to give a framework power and to make it useful. A framework that supports overarching principles needs data to be able to determine if organizations that say they align with the principles and framework really are aligned or not. Data becomes the tool for adjudicating an organization's adherence to the framework, and ultimately the principles.

You can think of the relationship between these concepts as depicted in Figure 5.1.

In the diagram below we see that standards, guidance and calculations all feed up into 'data'. All three of these elements help to define the data that is needed to adhere to the framework. Standards, guidance and calculations also allow the data used to align organizations to frameworks to be comparable. This helps to contrast levels of alignment between organizations and set benchmarks for best practice.

Not all principles and frameworks designed for sustainability transparency have been adopted into regulation. They are certainly not all mandatory for organizations to comply with. Increasingly, some of the principles and frameworks are being moved from concept through voluntary reporting into the world of mandatory compliance. Chapters 7 and 8 will help you navigate the signposting on this journey.

Figure 5.1   Principles vs frameworks vs data

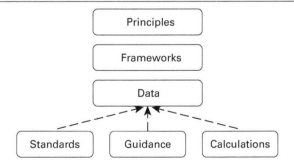

Table 5.2   Sustainability themes and associated principles, frameworks and standards

Themes	Taxonomies for sustainable finance	Sustainability data disclosure	Nature and biodiversity
Principles	Creation of a green classification system that translates climate and environmental objectives into criteria for specific economic activities for investment purposes	Reporting disclosures on sustainable topics should be reliable, verifiable and objective	Risks and impacts on biodiversity through operations, portfolios and supply and value chains should be monitored, assessed and transparently disclosed
Example frameworks	EU Taxonomy	TCFD	TNFD
Example standards	Links to EFRAG standards	ISSB, GRI, SEC	TBC

Embedding the concept of principles and frameworks in our sustainability discussion, Table 5.2 gives you some examples of some sustainability themes at work.

We will outline how sustainability taxonomies and the Task Force on Climate-related Financial Disclosures (TCFD) are influencing the ESG data disclosure ecosystem below. To be plain, at the time of writing, the detailed standards, guidance and calculations for all of the above and many more themes are far from complete. However, the journey is robustly pushing forward. As you assess the priority of the regulation and compliance use case, you should consider if your organization is currently aware of the principles and frameworks that are or are likely to become mandatory for you.

TCFD is an important framework that has been embedded in many jurisdictions as a model for ESG data disclosures. There are many standards that loosely or tightly link to TCFD.

TCFD seems important. What exactly is it?

The TCFD task force was established in 2015 to develop recommendations for companies to disclose information about their climate-related risks and opportunities. Note that TCFD covers the E in ESG only.

The TCFD framework provides a voluntary, consistent and comparable way for companies to disclose information on their climate-related risks and opportunities. To be TCFD compliant, companies need to disclose information on four key areas: governance, strategy, risk management, and metrics and targets. A bit more detail on each will help you to understand the scope of TCFD and the data that your organization will need to collect and disclose to align with its framework.

Governance

The first area that companies need to disclose information on is governance. To be TCFD compliant, companies need to disclose information on the following:

- the board's oversight of climate-related risks and opportunities
- management's role in assessing and managing climate-related risks and opportunities
- the processes for engaging with stakeholders on climate-related risks and opportunities
- the role of the board and management in overseeing and monitoring the company's climate-related risks and opportunities

To calculate this data, TCFD guidance suggests that companies review their governance structure to incorporate climate-related risks and opportunities into their decision-making processes. Companies should also review their board and management structures to ensure that they have the necessary expertise to oversee and manage climate-related risks and opportunities.

Strategy

The second area that companies need to disclose information on is their strategy. To be TCFD compliant, companies need to disclose information on the following:

- the processes for identifying and assessing climate-related risks and opportunities
- the impact of climate-related risks and opportunities on the company's business strategy
- the processes for managing climate-related risks and opportunities

To calculate this data, companies should integrate climate-related risks and opportunities into their strategic planning processes. A company's risk management processes should also be reviewed to ensure that they are incorporating climate-related risks.

Risk management

The third area that companies need to disclose information on is risk management. To be TCFD compliant, companies need to disclose information on the following:

- the processes for identifying and assessing climate-related risks and opportunities
- the processes for managing climate-related risks and opportunities
- the integration of climate-related risks and opportunities into the company's existing risk management processes

To calculate this data, companies should review their existing processes to determine how climate-related risks and opportunities are embedded into their risk assessments. This area overlaps somewhat with the requirements of governance and strategy.

Metrics and targets

The fourth area that companies need to disclose information on is metrics and targets. To be TCFD compliant, companies need to disclose information on the following:

- the metrics used to assess climate-related risks and opportunities
- the targets set to manage climate-related risks and opportunities
- the processes for tracking progress towards meeting those targets

To calculate this data, companies should review their existing metrics and targets to determine how they are measuring and reporting on climate-related risks and opportunities. This area of TCFD most directly requires data to be collected, measured and managed.

In all four key areas, there have been many organizations offering TCFD guidance for compliance. TCFD is a framework and not specifically a detailed data standard. Therefore, there remains some ambiguity on some of the datasets required to be fully comparable under TCFD. This gap is being filled by data disclosure standards-setters like the International Sustainability Standards Board (ISSB), the Global Reporting Initiative (GRI), the Securities and Exchange Commission (SEC) in the US, etc.

What *is* absolutely clear is the need for detailed definitions of datasets to allow you as an organization to confidently comply with any principles and frameworks you choose to adopt. One tool being used around the world today to get this clarity is the development of sustainability taxonomies. Let's look at what these taxonomies are and why they are important.

It's taxomania out there

In language, to ensure we all understand each other, we have created dictionaries to accurately reflect the meaning of the words we use. Without a common understanding of the definitions of words we write and speak, there would be an abundance of misunderstandings. This seems obvious.

In speaking about sustainability topics it has grown essential to create a common language to ensure we minimize misunderstandings and are all singing from the same song sheet.

This becomes essential when we consider what is at stake when misunderstandings are the basis for making investments or considering the value of companies and organizations. Without a common language there is risk of misrepresenting (intentionally or unintentionally) the 'green-ness' of a company, which can result in a charge of greenwashing.

On the other hand, without a clear definition of what is included and excluded in the definition of sustainability, data demonstrating an organization's leadership in certain areas (i.e. carbon emissions or renewable energy usage) may not be given full weight or value. 'Green-ness' is now only one element of sustainability and it sits alongside categories such as social impact – we need concrete definitions to support the marketplace in using all of these terms with confidence.

Enter the concept of the taxonomy. Simply put, a taxonomy is a guide to determine whether an investment is sustainable or not. A taxonomy's aspiration is to be the dictionary for sustainable finance in the region/jurisdiction where it is adopted. It would make a business leader's life a lot easier if that jurisdiction was global. However, there is not one global jurisdiction and not one global taxonomy. In fact, at the time of writing, there are currently 27 taxonomies in development around the world.

While this may instinctively make you as a leader throw your hands in the air in frustration, there are reasons for sustainable taxonomies to develop in this way. Some of these are logical, and some are political.

Why are there so many taxonomies?

A taxonomy is a dictionary, but it is also a mechanism for categorization of what is 'in' and what is 'out' of the overall definition of sustainability. This top line definition varies from region to region and country to country. This is because views on what activities are sustainable or not differ around the globe. In particular, the inclusion of certain energy sources such as nuclear and gas are hotly contested questions in currently developed taxonomies.

Another reason why taxonomies differ is that they are developed to represent the interests of the country they aim to be adopted by. This influences the overarching path taxonomy development takes. The first path develops a carbon-based taxonomy which is focused on carbon usage and emissions minimization. The second path develops a transition-based taxonomy which is focused on changes being made by industries towards sustainability.

We already know both carbon measurement and transition planning are prime ESG data territory. Basing a taxonomy on either path has strong science-based logic.

Science aside, it would be impossible not to note that differences in taxonomies also reflect the political realities of different countries. Some countries are heavily dependent on fossil fuels to drive their economies. In these scenarios, limiting the inclusion of any companies that are involved with the hydrocarbon value chain in that country's adopted taxonomy may limit the options of that country's industry to participate in any positive sustainability investment initiatives. These countries may take the view that the goal is to reward and support companies that are showing progress on transition. These countries tend to lean towards a transition-centric taxonomy.

Countries with a stronger services sector overall are less dependent on fossil fuels and may opt for a carbon-based taxonomy, with less concern over what is being excluded in their country's corporate landscape.

Politics and regulatory philosophy also play into *who* is developing taxonomies within a jurisdiction. In some countries, the taxonomy is being developed by the government or regulators. In others, it is a private sector-led initiative. This distinction is relevant when considering the taxonomy's path to adoption. Top-down work by governments may give the private sector opportunities to consult, but, in the end, the resulting taxonomy will be pushed down into implementation through legislation and supervision. Bottom-up work by the private sector may reflect market sentiment, but may not match government commitments and plans for a sustainable future. It may therefore make taxonomy adoption a bumpy ride.

So what and where are these taxonomies? See Figure 5.2 for an international overview.

Figure 5.2 Taxomania: an international overview

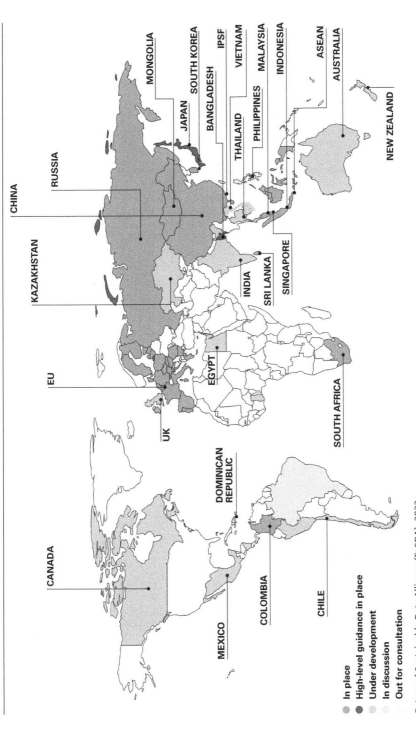

In place
High-level guidance in place
Under development
In discussion
Out for consultation

CANADA
MEXICO
DOMINICAN REPUBLIC
COLOMBIA
CHILE

UK
EU
EGYPT
SOUTH AFRICA

KAZAKHSTAN
CHINA
RUSSIA
MONGOLIA
JAPAN
SOUTH KOREA
BANGLADESH
IPSF
THAILAND
VIETNAM
PHILIPPINES
MALAYSIA
INDONESIA
INDIA
SRI LANKA
SINGAPORE
ASEAN
AUSTRALIA
NEW ZEALAND

Future of Sustainable Data Alliance (FoSDA), 2022
Special thanks to Climate Bonds and Bloomberg

Making sense of taxonomies, and how to map data to be practical

While taxonomies have proliferated, remember that they all have the same purpose: to define what is considered green or sustainable in order to give clarity to investors. All taxonomies have some overlap. Your job is to be aware of what taxonomies are being adopted or developed in your region. Your business activities may fall clearly into or outside the taxonomy. This has implications for how your business is categorized by your audience.

Together with your direct regulatory obligations, understanding the taxonomy structure and your obligations under any ETS schemes should help you prioritize the compliance and regulation use case for your business.

Now that we have unpacked more detail on the ABCs of sustainability data use cases, it is time for you to prioritize them for your organization. You can have more than one use case as your top priority, but if you are early in your sustainable data journey, it may be wise to push yourself to prioritize by giving each of the ABCs a ranking from one to three.

Use your mental or physical pen to mark these down for your reference in Table 5.3. If you are regulated, you must rank compliance and regulation as a top priority (i.e. a 1 in the table). This is the only hard and fast rule to this prioritization exercise. The rest is based on your perspective as a business leader.

Let's marry up what we've learned in the last two chapters to give you a snapshot of your organization's positioning today. You have identified the Sustainability Data Category your organization is most similar to within the five categories of the ESG Data Maturity Journey, from Data Debutant to Expert Educator.

You also have prioritized the ESG data use cases for your organization. This allows you to use Table 5.4 to get a feel for what ESG data would be appropriate for your team to measure and manage today.

Table 5.3 Use case prioritization table

Use case	1 = Top priority	2 = Medium priority	3 = Low priority
Access to capital			
Business growth and efficiencies			
Compliance and regulation			

Table 5.4 Useful ESG data for your organization today

Sustainability Data Category	ABCs of ESG data use cases		
	A	B	C
Data Debutant	GHG emissions Scope 1 and 2	GHG emissions Scope 1, 2 and 3	GHG emissions Scope 1 and 2 (3 where required)
Competent Commentator	GHG emissions TCFD-aligned data discourses	GHG emissions Scope 1, 2 and 3 Energy consumption Human rights governance	GHG emissions TCFD-aligned data disclosures All regulatory obligations
Proficient Producer	All Competent Coverage PLUS G data	All Competent Coverage PLUS Product level E data Waste management data	All Competent Coverage PLUS Product level E data
Skilful Services	All Competent Coverage PLUS G data S data (diversity metrics)	All Competent Coverage PLUS S data (diversity metrics)	All Competent Coverage PLUS S data (diversity metrics)
Expert Educator	All above PLUS Climate-related targets Carbon credit data	All above PLUS Climate-related targets Carbon credit data	All above PLUS Climate-related targets Carbon credit data

As you move through the categories you will be building up the ESG data you collect and manage. Alongside the content of data, you will also be increasing the amount of data you disclose publicly. This is an important decision for you as a leader – what data you collect for internal use and what data you release to the public. Some of this decision will be taken out of your hands: when you are required to report sustainability data based on a regulation or requirement by your clients or other external stakeholders, this will bring your data into the public domain.

Table 5.4 gives you a high-level flavour of the depth of data your organization should be measuring and managing at your current level of ESG data maturity. It may be that you don't believe your organization is at these levels yet, or that your organization far exceeds the volume of data associated with your category above. Use this table and these categories as a guide only. Each organization is unique and will collect data that is most useful to their core business as a priority. It may be that you have been convinced that some of the data you have previously considered 'nice to have' is actually a core priority for your organization going forward, based on the importance of your ABC use cases.

Wherever you are today, tomorrow may bring new priorities and new data requirements. In the next chapter we will link up where you are today and where your ambitions can take you tomorrow.

It's time to find out what to do next.

References

Action Aid (2021) Shell's net zero climate plans need land up to three times the size of the Netherlands for carbon offsets, https://actionaid.org/news/2021/shells-net-zero-climate-plans-need-land-three-times-size-netherlands-carbon-offsets (archived at https://perma.cc/6Z9T-JZU3)

Blaufelder, C, Levy, C, Mannion, P and Pinner, D (2021) A blueprint for scaling voluntary carbon markets to meet the climate challenge, McKinsey Sustainability, www.mckinsey.com/capabilities/sustainability/our-insights/a-blueprint-for-scaling-voluntary-carbon-markets-to-meet-the-climate-challenge (archived at https://perma.cc/842Z-YLL3)

FoSDA (2022) Taxomania! International overview update 2022, https://futureofsustainabledata.com/taxomania-international-overview-update-2022/ (archived at https://perma.cc/GQ6M-B6T3)

International Energy Agency (2022) Global Energy Review: CO_2 Emissions in 2021, www.iea.org/reports/global-energy-review-co2-emissions-in-2021-2 (archived at https://perma.cc/SL8K-3AV8)

OECD (2020) *OECD Business and Finance Outlook 2020: Sustainable and Resilient Finance*, https://doi.org/10.1787/eb61fd29-en (archived at https://perma.cc/WA5K-2XLE)

Resources for the Future (2023) The World Carbon Pricing Database, www.rff.org/publications/data-tools/world-carbon-pricing-database/ (archived at https://perma.cc/9ZKK-CRJV)

TSVCM (2021) *Summary Pack*, Institute of International Finance, www.iif.com/Portals/1/Files/TSVCM_Summary.pdf (archived at https://perma.cc/2FZT-MXV4)

World Bank (2023) Press release: Record high revenues from global carbon pricing near $100 billion, www.worldbank.org/en/news/press-release/2023/05/23/record-high-revenues-from-global-carbon-pricing-near-100-billion (archived at https://perma.cc/QE5P-MK7V)

World Economic Forum (2023) *Briefing Paper: Recommendations for the digital voluntary and regulated carbon markets*, www3.weforum.org/docs/Recommendations_for_the_Digital_Voluntary_and_Regulated_Carbon_Markets.pdf (archived at https://perma.cc/VSN3-HUQW)

Determine your sustainability data ambitions   6

REFLECTIVE QUESTIONS

- What ambitions drive my organization's ESG data requirements?
- What data is essential for all organizations to disclose?
- How do the UN Sustainable Development Goals relate to ESG and how important are net zero, carbon neutrality and transition planning?
- Which tools are useful for meeting sustainability targets?

Today's media focus on climate change makes it impossible to avoid the topic in our daily lives. As leaders, the subject of sustainability is seeping into all aspects of business life too. We see it every day – via the news, government announcements, events, panel discussions, webinars, education sessions, surveys and advertising.

In this chapter we will unpack how that external buzz translates into your internal engagement. There is no right or wrong level of corporate involvement with sustainability. It is increasingly difficult to ignore the topic completely. As a professional, it is appropriate to make a conscious choice about the engagement of your organization with sustainability as a topic and as a dataset. You may choose greater engagement. You may choose to limit its priority in the business. This choice is the result of defining your sustainability ambitions. So long as you choose, and do not ignore the topic, you can effectively govern the organization to success.

We have made it partway through the MUD we referenced in Figure 4.1. In this chapter we will complete our journey by determining your ambitions.

We will take your current Sustainability Data Category into account as we scope your organizational ambitions. Data Debutants through to Expert Educators all have opportunities to do more – or less – or to be content with the category they are in today.

We will explore sustainability targets such as net zero commitments, carbon neutrality and alignment to the Paris Agreement – and the data tools you can use to meet those targets.

Critically, you'll come away from this section of the book with an understanding of the ways you as an organization can choose to disclose your data.

What is your sustainability ambition?

Whether you are an ESG Expert Educator, Competent Commentator, Proficient Producer, Skilful Services or Data Debutant, your organization will have sustainability ambitions. They may not be top of the business priority list today or tomorrow, but there will be some level of ambition associated with the topic of sustainability. Your ambition may be modest and driven primarily by outside forces. Your ambition may be bold and aspire to be at the leading edge of sustainability-driven action.

Whatever it may be, your ambition is underpinned by ESG data. Without data you will not be able to know that you have attained your goals – no matter what they are or how humble they may be. Without data you will not be able to prove to internal and external stakeholders that your actions are taking steps towards long-term goals.

Up until now, we have asked you to consider your current data maturity and ESG data disclosure levels. This is an essential step to create a data baseline. A baseline will allow you to compare your future ESG data points to this baseline. From there you can celebrate a pathway to successfully achieving climate and social goals – or course-correct should the data tell you that your organization is off track.

What happens beyond the baseline? Your organization's ESG ambition will determine what's next. It should help you decide if you are comfortable in your current ESG data maturity category, or if you strive for a category further along the Data Maturity Journey.

For this purpose, we are defining ESG ambition as the level at which you wish to embed sustainability data in your organizational DNA to drive your business. Again, there is no wrong answer here. It is essential – even more so than when you assessed your business's data and ESG data capabilities – to answer the question of ambition with brutal honesty. Ambition will drive the choices you make as a business leader in moving your organization from where you are today to where you want to be tomorrow. This will inform – or at least influence – resource allocation, talent acquisition, supply chain management, pricing and communications.

My recommendation is to take a moment to get it right and to consider not only your view, but the view of the management team, board of directors and stakeholders. That may seem overly serious, but being accurate with your ambitions will set you on the path to success. It will help you navigate the future for your organization in a sustainable world.

Best in class vs bare minimum

A good question for you to consider when setting out your sustainability ambitions is if you want to be best in class or if you are content to do the bare minimum to meet requirements. Fundamentally, this asks whether your organization aims to make sustainability one of its strategic objectives or not. If not, the bare minimum may be an appropriate ambition.

A very simplistic view of what constitutes the bare minimum is the organization's compliance with current regulations. This is pretty much a bottom-line requirement. If you are required to disclose ESG data to a industry regulator, financial regulator, ETS governance body or government agency, not doing so risks incurring financial fines or business restrictions. Not complying may lead to your inability to trade or do business at all. An ambition to comply with regulatory requirements would put you at the lowest level of the ambition scale. You would sit as an ESG Data Debutant or Competent Commentator.

There are benefits to minimizing your ambitions. You lower your risks associated with disclosing data that is poorer than industry average. Poor data could reflect badly on your organization if taken without any narrative on your plans to address the deficit (if indeed you have plans to do so). If your baseline suggests you will not come top of a comparable pack, you may choose to minimize your ESG data disclosure ambitions rather than invest in a transformation plan to address it.

At the other end of the spectrum sits the ambition to be best in class for sustainability data disclosures. In a rapidly moving environment, it can be challenging to define what is leading edge. You will need to dedicate resources to horizon scan the commercial and policy environments to remain up to speed on current trends and where ideas are being developed and debated.

You will then need to participate in the earliest versions of data disclosures to lead the rest of your industry or geographic pack.

As with holding ambitions at the bare minimum end of the scale, high ambitions for sustainability data can bring risks as well. Being the first or one of the first organizations to disclose data on a topic within the ESG scope may reveal that the data is not best in class over time. Being at the vanguard of disclosures may open your organization up to challenges on data quality or relevance. It may also make you a target for competitors or activists to challenge your disclosures and claims – especially when data definitions have not been codified.

What ambition costs

Deciding your level of ambition can't be decided without addressing the costs of ESG data disclosures. Collecting, compiling and publishing data can be costly. Particularly when your organization operates across borders and includes many lines of business. A 2022 study surveyed US-based corporate issuers and institutional investors on what they spend on measuring and managing climate-related disclosure activities. The cost for a company to disclose was calculated to be $533,000 per year (SustainAbility Institute by ERM, 2022). These costs were incurred in the following four categories:

1 GHG analysis and/or disclosures

2 climate scenario analysis and/or disclosures

3 internal climate risk management controls

4 assurances/audits related to climate

The cost was relatively consistent with the Securities and Exchange Commission's (SEC's) predicted cost analysis for its proposed disclosure regulations published in 2022 (and not implemented at the time of writing). The SEC predicted costs to a business of $530,000 per year (Office of the Federal Register, 2022). This number isn't insignificant. Bear in mind that this reflects the costs for listed companies who already carry a cost burden of financial data transparency that non-public companies do not have.

Participating in ESG ratings, analyses and data isn't free. Corporates incur ratings-related costs including direct payments to raters for evaluations and benchmarks, employee time, consulting support and digital tools. Another survey in March 2023 specifically on ratings-related costs to companies found that publicly traded companies reported an average annual spend of $220,000–$480,000 to engage with these tools. Private companies surveyed, all of which had institutional investor shareholders, reported an average annual spend of \$210,000–\$425,000 (Sustainability Institute by ERM, 2023). Again – not cheap.

So it would be wise as you set your ambitions to run a cost analysis at the level of disclosure you are aiming for. It is a realistic component of ensuring you can be successful in your aims.

An important part of your ambitions: setting targets

Your organization may not have made commitments to sustainability goals. Many already have. This trend was accelerated in 2021 during COP26 in Glasgow when many of the world's largest companies voluntarily made commitments to climate change through 'net zero pledges' and similar agreements between themselves and the public.

Announced at the conference, 60 of the UK's FTSE 100 companies signed up to the United Nations Race to Zero campaign. This campaign is a global alliance committed to achieving net zero carbon emissions by 2050. This is a good example of organizations using a global event to make commitments to climate goals which they will take forward as an integral part of their business decision-making from the point of commitment.

With these FTSE 100 companies, the largest 100 businesses by market capitalization on the London Stock Exchange, it is very likely that they had some data to base their commitments on. They were at least in the Competent Commentator category in the ESG Data Maturity Journey. They must have tracked ESG data in advance of their commitment so that their boards of directors could assess their chances of success in their drive to net zero by 2050.

It is certainly sensible for any leader to consider the current state of the organization before committing to change – especially when that change is on a strict schedule. You should be doing the same. Be aware of your ESG data capabilities today. If you are not collecting data already, the likelihood of you as an organization being ready to commit to targets is low. If you have committed to targets and you are not collecting, tracking and managing ESG data, you are opening yourself up to significant risks.

Before we get ahead of ourselves, let's review some of the more popular targets and commitments to help you determine which ones your organization is already moving forward on and which you want to consider adopting.

Sustainability pledges, goals, commitments and targets

What targets and goals are we talking about here? There are many global types and varieties of pledges and commitments associated with sustainability. Some of these will be a perfect fit for your organization's sustainability data maturity level and ambitions. There are a few that merit calling out specifically based on their popularity and global reach.

Out of many options you can consider adopting as an organization's target, we will review:

- net zero
- carbon neutrality
- transition plan
- science-based targets
- Task Force on Climate-related Financial Disclosures (TCFD) alignment
- UN Sustainable Development Goals (SDGs)

Net zero and carbon neutrality pledges

We have used the term 'net zero' many times already. You have undoubtedly heard it hundreds if not thousands of times before picking up this book. It is high time we define what we mean by the term.

Net zero refers to a state in which the greenhouse gases (GHGs) going into the atmosphere are balanced by carbon removal out of the atmosphere. When organizations claim to be 'net zero', they are saying that the GHGs they emit have been reduced by actions they have taken, and any residual carbon or carbon equivalent that is emitted is offset. These offsets play a 'last resort' role, and are not relied on exclusively to reach net zero.

The balance of emissions and action to reduce atmospheric carbon results in a calculation reflecting that organization's GHG contributions to the planet. When that calculation equals zero, the goal of net zero is realized.

Net zero means that a company reduces its absolute emissions across its whole supply chain, in order to support the target to limit global temperature increases to 1.5°C, as agreed at the 2015 Paris climate summit.

So you may think that net zero sounds a lot like being carbon neutral. You aren't wrong. It is certainly a similar concept, but the difference is in how the balance of emissions and reductions is achieved. The terms also differ in that net zero takes into account all GHG gases. Carbon neutrality includes only carbon in its definition.

> *Carbon neutrality* refers to a balance achieved between carbon emissions and carbon offsets to result in reporting zero excess carbon released into the atmosphere. This is achieved through offsetting carbon in various ways, but does not necessarily require reductions in carbon emitted compared to historical periods.

When setting either a net zero or a carbon neutrality target, a target date is essential. In the case of net zero, target dates for achievement vary radically – some have been achieved today, and others have a target date late into the 21st century. Overall, net zero dates after 2050 are considered too late to be meaningful in aligning with the Paris Agreement goals.

When you plan to use these targets, you may wish to research your industry peers to ascertain their publicly stated commitments and target dates. Your pledges need to be realistic, but they should also be competitive.

When companies claim carbon neutrality, they are counterbalancing carbon emissions with carbon offsets without necessarily having actively reduced emissions by an amount consistent with reaching net zero at the global or sector level. Net zero is considered the gold standard of claims since it is actively supporting reductions in overall GHGs. It is not something an organization can simply throw money at buying carbon credits to achieve. You can achieve carbon neutrality through only buying carbon credits.

This is a big difference between the definition and ethos of net zero and carbon neutrality. Carbon neutrality may be a stepping stone along the way to being net zero, and it is faster to achieve. This is because the ability to buy carbon credits is a faster route to balancing emissions than making changes to the way you conduct your operations.

The opportunity to become carbon negative exists as well. Being carbon negative means that you are taking out more carbon from the atmosphere than you are putting in. This can be done by acquiring more offsets than you need to become neutral, or by conducting activities outside your core business activities that reduce carbon in the atmosphere. These can include carbon capture and storage. If these activities are tracked and measured, they can reduce your carbon output and drive your organization towards being carbon negative.

Transition plans and science-based targets

We have already explored the concept of transition plans in Chapter 3 and touched on science-based targets. As you consider targets and goals to set as part of your organization's ambitions, these opportunities are worth understanding further.

A climate transition plan is a time-bound action plan that outlines in detail how an organization will change how it uses its existing assets, operations, and business model to align with the Paris Agreement goals of keeping global warming to below 1.5°C. Interest in and demand for setting transition plans is growing. In reality, this demand is a logical extension of the popularity of setting net zero targets. The market and external stakeholders are now asking how organizations and countries plan to achieve net zero. This infers an element of scepticism about the ability of some pledges to be achieved.

To make a long-term goal like net zero more plausible, a step-by-step plan helps both the organization or country know what it needs to do by when, and the external stakeholders to believe it can happen.

Transition planning at the country level: the UK's Transition Plan Taskforce

The UK's Transition Plan Taskforce (TPT) is a strategic initiative established in 2022 by the British government to pave the way for a successful transition to a net zero economy by 2050. The country's net zero strategy was put under a microscope in 2021 by an independent review looking at how the UK was planning to achieve its stated goal. The UK emerged from the review wanting.

The main objective of the task force is to develop a comprehensive roadmap that outlines the necessary steps, policies and actions required to achieve the country's ambitious climate goals.

The task force has set several key goals to guide its efforts towards sustainability and environmental stewardship. These include:

- carbon emission reduction
- renewable energy integration
- green infrastructure development
- just transition

While specific deadlines for individual goals may vary, the overall target of achieving a net zero economy by 2050 remains constant. The TPT is an example of a transition plan in action at the country level. In October 2023, the TPT published a framework outlining what good looks like for any entity's transition plans.

We mentioned the Transition Pathway Initiative and Race to Zero as two initiatives designed as a platform for organizations to develop and report progress on transition plans. Others include Climate Action 100+, the Net Zero Asset Managers initiative and 1.5°C Supply Chain Leaders.

A particular mention is needed for the Science Based Targets Initiative (SBTi). The SBTi is dedicated to supporting organizations to set a science-based target and develop a transition plan. This can be kicked off online through the SBTi web portal. It has grown significantly since its inception in 2015.

Getting started sounds easy. However, successfully achieving a transition plan in line with science-based targets requires making changes to your business as usual. These changes can include alterations to your energy mix to increase the use of renewables or wholesale changes to your business model to reuse resources and minimize carbon emissions.

A cornerstone of transition planning is the core belief in achieving net zero at the organizational, industry and country levels. Transition and science-based targets include pathways to net zero embedded in their plans. The focus is on reducing GHG emissions at every level and only using carbon offsets and buying carbon credits as a last resort.

Net zero, carbon neutrality and science-based targets all require an understanding of how to use the carbon credits and carbon markets we discussed in Chapter 5. Let's find out a bit more about these tools and how they fit into net zero and carbon neutrality plans.

Net zero, carbon neutrality, science-based targets and the appropriate role of carbon markets

Setting your organizational targets for sustainability is an important step in your journey in reporting climate data. Getting to your targets can take many paths and require many substantive actions from you as a business. Using carbon credits to offset your emissions and reach a voluntary or mandatory limit is a tool at your disposal. This tool can turn from helpful to harmful if you aren't conscious of the role carbon credits play in your overall emissions calculations.

Let's take a net zero target as an example. If 90 per cent of your GHG emissions are attributable to burning fossil fuels, and you only use carbon credits to offset these emissions to zero, you may have nominally achieved net zero, but you may face some challenges. Stakeholders may call you out for 'buying your way out' of the commitments you made to net zero.

If instead, alongside using carbon credits as offset tools, you actively change your energy sources to include 10 per cent renewable energy this year, and plan to increase that percentage year on year while reducing your reliance on carbon credits, you are in much stronger sustainability territory.

The SBTi affords carbon offsets no role in efforts to reach net zero. This is clear in its Corporate Net Zero Standard, a framework to help organizations set targets for achieving net zero (SBTi, nd). The SBTi Corporate Net Zero Standard requires organizations to halve their emissions by 2030, and to aim for a >90 per cent reduction in direct and indirect value chain emissions by 2050. The remaining <10 per cent that cannot be eliminated by such direct means should be captured by permanent carbon removal and storage.

The principle at the heart of the SBTi Corporate Net Zero Standard is the 'mitigation hierarchy'. According to this hierarchy, companies should commit to reducing value chain emissions and implement strategies to achieve these commitments as their main priority before acting outside their value chains (such as utilizing carbon offsetting strategies), which includes buying carbon credits. Emission reductions must be the overarching priority for companies, and the central focus of any credible net zero strategy.

In light of this, carbon credits are best seen as a transition tool, to be implemented while more fundamental adjustments are put in place.

Carbon credits play a role in a path to lower carbon emissions by acting as a tool to move investment into activities that are positive for the environment. The hope is that this investment will pump-prime and/or accelerate activities and industries that lower carbon emissions, trap carbon from processes and actively remove carbon from the atmosphere. There is a strong case for parts of the economy that are emitting carbon to create incentives through these tools to spur innovation by other entities in carbon capture and reduction.

But what happens when that investment doesn't result in lower carbon in the atmosphere?

Credits up in smoke? An example of real-world challenges to carbon offsetting

Alphabet, the parent company of Google, provides a good example of the dangers of using carbon credits. Alphabet is one of the largest buyers of carbon credits in the world, having purchased 3.5 million tonnes of CO_2e in carbon credits between 2017 and 2019 (Silverstein, 2022). This is an important component of the strategy that has enabled the company to claim to have been carbon neutral since 2007. This claim has been the subject of significant market scepticism.

Alphabet buys many of its carbon credits from Nature Conservancy, an organization which generates them through projects such as reforestation, sustainable land management, and the protection of threatened ecosystems. It has been claimed that the accounting for such credits is unreliable. In many cases, the basis for carbon reductions that underpin the credits' creation would have occurred anyway, or has already been factored into other carbon credits. This results in the purchaser of the credit writing off emissions without the write-off genuinely corresponding to a reduction in carbon.

A cause for further concern is the fact that many of these credits can go up in smoke in the blink of an eye – quite literally. Trees remain one of the best carbon-capture 'technologies' available to us, by some substantial distance (Mulligan et al, 2023). Except maybe for kelp (see previous notes in this book admitting my seaweed obsession). For this reason, reforestation, afforestation and conservancy projects comprise a significant percentage of the initiatives organizations are engaging in to offset their own emissions.

As we've seen in recent years, climate change is making forest fires larger and more frequent. So it's to be expected that some portion of these forest-based projects will themselves succumb to the flames. The carbon credit calculation is based on the carbon being sequestered over the full lifespan of the forest, and credit for the full lifespan is being credited at the beginning of the project. If these trees subsequently burn in forests fires, they are not sequestering the carbon that has already been credited to the organization that bought the credit. It could all be a tinderbox.

Some buffer is built into the calculation of the carbon credits from such afforestation initiatives to account for these hazards. In California, for example, the regulator requires that some portion of the credits to be achieved by a given project be set aside into a collective 'buffer pool', rather than sold. But analysis shows that a buffer pool that was expected to be sufficient for the whole of the 21st century was consumed by just five wildfires.

There is nowhere near enough buffer to make up for the rate at which forests are burning. With organizations seeking to maximize the carbon sequestration from the land they have access to, they're squeezing in as many trees as possible – worryingly increasing the likelihood of fires.

It is in recognition of the potential mismatch of the value of carbon credits to offset long-term mitigations of climate-related harms that the SBTi argues for treating the instrument as a temporary one, to be superseded in due course. Some such recognition appears to be shaping policy wherever carbon credits have been put into practice. For example, reducing reliance on carbon credits year on year drives organizations to find ways to genuinely reduce their emissions, rather than displacing them, and incentivizes innovation to drive this purpose.

TCFD alignment

Another goal or target organizations can choose is to be TCFD aligned. The Task Force on Climate-related Financial Disclosures was established in 2015 by the Financial Stability Board to provide a framework for organizations to disclose their climate-related risks and opportunities.

Becoming TCFD aligned allows businesses to effectively assess and address climate-related risks, enhance resilience, and demonstrate commitment to sustainability. TCFD has been encouraged as the framework that underpins mandatory disclosures in many public markets the world over.

In 2023, the TCFD was disbanded to cede the way for the ISSB (the body creating environmental data disclosure standards that we have mentioned earlier in this book). This consolidation should add to the detail behind what data is needed for good alignment and transparency.

Alignment with the UN SDGs

You may already be familiar with the 17 United Nations SDGs. They are a framework for promoting positive action on a number of topics important to the UN and, arguably, sustainable and equitable life on earth.

The SDGs are not the same as ESG. You would be surprised how many people confuse the two. They are both three-letter acronyms (TLAs!), but are not interchangeable. Let's get clear on what these terms are so they can be used appropriately.

The *UN SDGs*, also known as the Global Goals, are intended as a universal call to action to end poverty, protect the planet, and ensure that by 2030 all people enjoy peace and prosperity (UN Development Programme, 2023). Adopted by the UN in 2015, they are a set of 17 development goals to frame a better world. Their predecessor was the Millennium Development Goals (the MDGs – another TLA!).

The SDGs were developed through a highly inclusive process that involved UN bodies and members alongside 1,500 businesses globally. They primarily target actions by governments but, notably, the SDGs take a step up in ambition from the MDGs by calling on all businesses to apply their creativity and innovation to solve sustainable development challenges (UN, 2015).

The SDGs were agreed by all UN countries, and call for worldwide action among governments, business and civil society around a common set of goals and targets (Figure 6.1).

The SDGs are, by their nature, quite high-level concepts. Some of the SDGs resist the opportunity to quantify progress easily. This offers a challenge for those of us obsessed with quantitative data. For example, both SDG 2: Zero Hunger and SDG 3: Good Health and Wellbeing have inherent qualitative characteristics, which are often difficult to capture and connect with a company's performance. This makes it hard to track an organization's positive progress on these targets.

The 17 SDGs are integrated together, and the hope is that action in one will also create positive change in others. Many companies make some or all of these 17 SDGs a part of their own goals, vision or mission statements. The UN itself recommends as a first step for organizations to prioritize which SDGs they are looking to tackle – 17 is a lot for any business to manage!

Figure 6.1 The UN Sustainable Development Goals

SUSTAINABLE DEVELOPMENT G⚙ALS

1 NO POVERTY

2 ZERO HUNGER

3 GOOD HEALTH AND WELL-BEING

4 QUALITY EDUCATION

5 GENDER EQUALITY

6 CLEAN WATER AND SANITATION

7 AFFORDABLE AND CLEAN ENERGY

8 DECENT WORK AND ECONOMIC GROWTH

9 INDUSTRY, INNOVATION AND INFRASTRUCTURE

10 REDUCED INEQUALITIES

11 SUSTAINABLE CITIES AND COMMUNITIES

12 RESPONSIBLE CONSUMPTION AND PRODUCTION

13 CLIMATE ACTION

14 LIFE BELOW WATER

15 LIFE ON LAND

16 PEACE, JUSTICE AND STRONG INSTITUTIONS

17 PARTNERSHIPS FOR THE GOALS

UN, nd

Figure 6.2   Mapping ESG to the SDGs

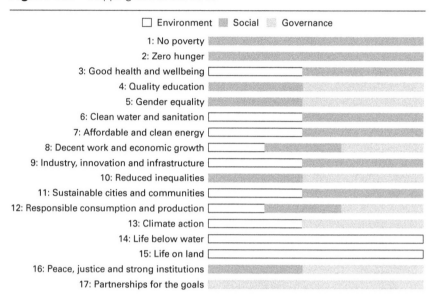

How are the SDGs and ESG interrelated?

The SDGs are a sweeping UN-led framework for improving the world. ESG is a data-centric definitional term guiding data disclosures. ESG data can be used to track SDG targets. SDG targets need ESG data to measure progress.

To get an idea of how the 17 SDGs can be attributed to the various elements of ESG, Figure 6.2 is a good guide.

As you consider including SDG targets in your sustainability ambitions, take note of the types of data that underpin the tracking of each SDG as illustrated in the diagram above. If, as in SDGs 1 and 2, this requires primarily S data, you may need to check on your confidence that your organization can track this sort of data accurately. SDGs 14 and 15 are focused on E data. Is that a strength of your organization? If so, it may make a good fit.

How can you as a business set goals and targets in line with the UN SDGs?

Before you can answer this question, you should ask why your organization should align with the UN SDGs. The overarching concept of the UN and the

UN SDGs is that business cannot succeed in societies that fail. The SDGs aim to:

- lift billions of people out of poverty, thereby growing consumer markets around the world
- strengthen education, thereby fostering a more skilled workforce
- make progress on gender equality and women's empowerment, thereby creating a 'virtual emerging market' equivalent in size and purchasing power to that of China and India
- ensure the global economy operates safely within the capacity of the planet to supply essential resources such as water, fertile soil, metals and minerals, thereby sustaining the natural resources that companies depend on for production
- foster accountable and well-governed institutions as well as open and rule-based trading and financial systems, thereby reducing the costs and risks of doing business

These intentions guided the development of the SDGs, and companies are encouraged to also believe in these intentions as a basis for their engagement with the SDGs. Before you as a leader set SDG-aligned goals for your business, you should ask yourself some probing questions:

- Do the SDG intentions match with your organization's ethos?
- Do they align with your culture?
- Do they play a role in your mission, vision and values?

If they do, you can move forward to plan your targets to align with the SDGs that you choose to include in your strategy. If not, and you aspire to bring your values in line with these principles, you should proceed with the understanding that some efforts need to be made to adapt your organizational culture first.

If you want to proceed with taking on SDG-related targets, there exists a baseline responsibility set out by the UN for businesses to respect universal rights. The established list of principles that apply universally to all companies include:

- International Labour Organization (ILO) Tripartite Declaration of Principles Concerning Multinational Enterprises and Social Policy
- UN Global Compact Principles
- UN Guiding Principles on Business and Human Rights

In your SDG alignment journey, this is where you must start. These principles are not optional or aspirational, and must be a solid criteria by which businesses decide to do more and aim higher through SDG targets.

From this starting point, how do you channel the efforts of your organization to support the SDGs? Take it one step at a time. Below is a logical path to pursue should you wish to move forward with the SDGs as one of your organizational targets:

- Recognize that not all 17 SDGs will be equally relevant for your company.
- Consider that you operate within a value chain and identify where your efforts can make an impact to minimize negative impacts and scale up positive impacts across the value chain.
- Choose which SDGs are most logical for your business.
- Set a timeline and level of ambition.
- Set business goals against the SDGs.
- Leverage work and processes that already exist to decide KPIs and collect data.
- Be sure your team knows their responsibilities in both implementing and tracking these goals.
- Share widely.

What other targets could I be considering? What about nature and biodiversity?

An area that is growing in interest is monitoring and managing organizations' impact on nature and biodiversity. In the face of escalating environmental challenges and the urgent need to address climate change and biodiversity loss, there has been growing recognition of the crucial role played by nature-based solutions in promoting sustainable development. As corporations and financial institutions increasingly recognize the material risks and opportunities posed by nature-related issues, the Taskforce on Nature-related Financial Disclosures (TNFD) has emerged as a transformative initiative aimed at driving disclosures related to nature-based risks and opportunities.

The TNFD was launched with the purpose of developing a framework that encourages businesses and financial institutions to assess, manage and report on their nature-related risks and dependencies. The objective is to enhance transparency and decision-making by integrating nature-related considerations into financial disclosures, similar to the way in which climate-related risks are being addressed through the TCFD. By doing so, the TNFD aims to foster sustainable investment, promote the preservation of biodiversity, and drive transformative change in the global economy.

The mission of the TNFD is to catalyse a shift towards a nature-positive economy by promoting the mainstreaming of nature-related information in financial reporting. The TNFD is a collaborative effort involving a wide range of stakeholders, including governments, financial institutions, corporations, scientists and civil society organizations. This multi-stakeholder approach ensures that the framework is robust, comprehensive and credible.

The scope of the TNFD's work encompasses all sectors of the economy that impact nature and depend on nature's services. This includes, but is not limited to, industries such as agriculture, forestry, fisheries, mining, infrastructure, tourism and finance. The TNFD framework seeks to capture not only the direct impacts of these industries on nature, but also the indirect risks and dependencies that may arise from nature-related issues.

Data in the TNFD's mission

Data is a foundational element in the TNFD's mission to promote nature-based disclosures. To achieve its objectives, the TNFD relies on comprehensive, accurate and reliable data from various sources. This data-driven approach ensures that nature-related risks and opportunities are adequately identified, assessed and integrated into decision-making processes. How do they do that?

- **Assessment of nature-related risks and opportunities:** Data is instrumental in assessing the exposure of businesses and financial institutions to nature-related risks, such as biodiversity loss, habitat degradation, water scarcity and climate-related impacts. By analysing relevant data, entities can identify potential vulnerabilities and develop effective risk management strategies.

- **Dependency on nature's services:** Many economic activities are dependent on nature's services, such as pollination, water purification and carbon sequestration. Data is crucial in quantifying and understanding these dependencies, enabling entities to appreciate the value of nature and take appropriate measures to preserve it.

- **Scenario analysis and stress testing:** Similar to the TCFD, the TNFD encourages organizations to conduct scenario analysis and stress testing to assess their resilience to nature-related risks under different future scenarios. Data-driven models and projections help in simulating potential impacts and designing strategies that are adaptable to changing environmental conditions.

- **Performance measurement and reporting:** Transparent and consistent reporting of nature-related metrics is essential to track progress and compare the performance of different entities. Data-driven metrics enable investors and stakeholders to evaluate an organization's sustainability efforts and nature-positive contributions accurately.

- **Policy formulation and impact assessment:** Policymakers also benefit from robust data and analysis provided by the TNFD. Data helps in formulating effective policies to encourage nature-positive practices, and can be used to assess the impact of existing regulations and initiatives.

The TNFD plays a critical role in driving the integration of nature-related information into financial disclosures. By leveraging data and adopting a collaborative approach, the TNFD aims to transform the global economy towards one that recognizes and values nature's contributions.

Your targets, your choice

What should be clear to you now is that there isn't just one sustainability-related target you can set for your organization. There are many. The choice is yours. It needs to make sense based on your current Sustainability Data Category and your ambition. It may be a long-term goal or it may be something you are able to achieve in a short number of months or years. In any case, targets, goals and organizational commitments are a powerful tool to align your entire team. Setting targets sends an internal message to your organization that sustainability plays a role in your priorities.

Targets can also signpost to external stakeholders your commitments to the sustainability agenda. Set them thoughtfully and carefully and be conscious about how you share them externally. As soon as your organization makes public its targets, there will be a very reasonable assumption that data on your progress to achieving those goals will be public too. Disclosing your ESG data publicly is part of the sustainability journey.

So how does your organization do that? How do you publicly disclose the ESG data you have collected and calculated?

How to disclose your ESG data

Once your organization's unique priorities and objectives are set, you need to tell people about them through your data. You're in luck. There are already many tools available to help you do this. Some may say that there are already too many tools – thereby creating a layer of confusion and complexity to the act of ESG disclosure.

In the following section we first define some of the most significant routes to disclosure and suggest how to decide which of these routes best match your current and future organizational sustainability objectives.

As an organization you have a number of avenues available to you to disclose your sustainability information. There are two routes to consider:

- disclosing through your own publications
- disclosing through a reporting platform or tool

Each method has its advantages and disadvantages, which we'll explore in detail below.

Disclosing through your own publications

Your organization could disclose its ESG data directly through a sustainability report or financial report. The pros of this approach are:

- **Tailored approach:** By generating an organization-specific sustainability report or integrating ESG metrics into the financial report, companies can customize the data presentation to align with their unique goals, material issues and industry context.

- **Comprehensive and in-depth information:** Direct reporting allows companies to include a wide range of ESG information, diving deep into their initiatives, performance, targets and progress. This level of detail fosters transparency and fosters a deeper understanding of the organization's sustainability efforts.

- **Branding and storytelling:** Sustainability reports provide companies with a platform to showcase their commitment to ESG principles, detailing their contributions to society and the environment. This branding opportunity can enhance the organization's reputation and attract like-minded stakeholders.

- **Investor interest:** Investors are increasingly considering ESG factors when making investment decisions. By including ESG data in financial reports, companies can cater to investor demand for more holistic information, potentially attracting socially responsible investors.

The cons are:

- **Data overload:** Publishing a standalone sustainability report alongside the financial report may lead to data overload for some stakeholders, potentially hindering comprehension and meaningful engagement with the ESG data.

- **Lack of standardization:** Without a standardized framework, companies may choose to disclose only selective ESG data, leading to inconsistency and difficulty in comparing performance across different organizations.

- **Time- and resource-intensive:** Preparing comprehensive sustainability reports can be time-consuming and resource-intensive, especially for smaller organizations with limited capacities.

Disclosing through a reporting platform or tool

Alternatively, you could choose to disclose your ESG data through a disclosure platform. The pros of this approach are:

- **Standardization and comparability:** Utilizing recognized disclosure platforms ensures consistency and comparability of ESG data across different organizations. This allows stakeholders and investors to evaluate and benchmark performances objectively.

- **Streamlined reporting:** Companies can benefit from streamlined reporting processes as these platforms often provide structured templates and guidelines, reducing the burden of data collection and organization.

- **Enhanced visibility:** Disclosure platforms are widely accessed by investors, analysts and stakeholders seeking ESG information. Being featured on these platforms can increase an organization's visibility and attract potential investors aligned with ESG values.

- **Independent verification:** Some disclosure platforms offer options for third-party verification of reported data, adding credibility and trust to the disclosed information.

The cons are:

- **Limited customization:** Companies might find it challenging to convey their unique sustainability story as disclosure platforms generally follow standardized formats, potentially limiting the level of detail and narrative.

- **Cost and complexity:** Using disclosure services on comprehensive platforms may incur a fee; however, given the increase in expectations of organizations, this is a service that more should expect to pay for. Meeting specific reporting requirements at a level sufficient to supply robust, reliable data can be complex. There are tools available to help those new to disclosing.

- **Reporting fatigue:** Larger organizations may have to comply with multiple disclosure frameworks, leading to reporting fatigue and duplication of efforts. Work continues by allowing existing platforms to streamline and simplify.

Both routes of disclosing ESG data to the public have their merits and limitations. A direct sustainability report or financial report allows for a tailored and comprehensive approach, providing an opportunity for storytelling and branding. However, it may lack standardization and could be resource-intensive. On the other hand, using disclosure platforms like CDP or GRI offers standardized reporting, comparability and enhanced visibility. It streamlines the reporting process and allows for independent verification. However, it may limit customization and entail additional costs.

Organizations need to carefully consider their priorities, resources and stakeholders' preferences when choosing the most suitable method or a combination of both. Regardless of the approach, transparent ESG disclosure fosters accountability and trust, and drives positive change towards a more sustainable future.

If you choose to disclose through a reporting platform, here are some of your options.

CDP

CDP, formerly known as the Carbon Disclosure Project, is a global not-for-profit focused on motivating and supporting companies, cities, states and regions, and capital markets to measure and disclose their environmental impacts. Leveraging both investor and supply chain influence, CDP runs a global disclosure system, known as the CDP Online Response System (ORS), that organizations use to report sustainability information requested by their stakeholders. CDP also uses the data supplied through ORS to benchmark organizations on their sustainability performance across multiple areas, including environmental impacts and supply chain management.

Your organization can disclose your sustainability data through CDP by completing their questionnaire. CDP does not set reporting standards like the International Sustainability Standards Board (ISSB) or GRI, but provides a reporting platform to disclose data. It aligns its questionnaire with the TCFD's framework (and will align with ISSB and TNFD) and evolves its platform to encompass standards as they develop – in 2024, CDP will be fully ISSB aligned.

- Founded: 2000.
- Number of companies reporting: Over 23,000.
- Typical audience: Investors and customers who are requesting disclosure.
- Purpose: To motivate governments, companies and investors to disclose their environmental impacts and take action to reduce them.
- Focus: External environmental impacts for requesting stakeholders.
- What is reported: The E and G pillars. Environmental disclosures related to climate change, water security, forests, biodiversity, plastics use and supply chain management.
- Who reports: Global companies, financial institutions, cities, states and regions, either through voluntary submission or via investor or customer requests.
- Industry-specific versions: High-impact industries have additional reporting requirements.
- Output used for: Response to investor or customer inquiry, CDP public scoring (optional), availability via financial and other data providers.

The Sustainability Accounting Standards Board (SASB)

SASB standards are designed to help companies disclose financially material sustainability information to their investors. They outline the subset of ESG issues most relevant to financial performance in 77 industries.

The standards are organized by sustainability dimensions (broad ESG themes), general issue categories (industry-agnostic topics), disclosure topics (industry-specific versions of general issue categories), and accounting metrics (performance measurements for each topic). In 2021, SASB was folded into the newly formed ISSB.

- Founded: 2011.
- Number of companies reporting: 1,300.
- Typical audience: Financial stakeholders and investors.

- Purpose: Accounting/reporting standards to guide the disclosure of financially material sustainability information by companies to their investors.

- Focus: Internal impact of ESG risks on financial performance.

- What is reported: All three ESG pillars. These standards help businesses report on financially material issues across environmental, social capital, human capital, business model and innovation, and leadership and governance.

- Who reports: Any organization can use the SASB standards.

- Industry-specific versions: 77 industry-specific standards.

- Output used for: Company's public ESG report and other (sustainability indices, awards, etc).

GRI

GRI is an independent, international standard-setting institution and collaborating centre of the United Nations Environment Programme (UNEP). One of the most widely used systems for disclosing ESG performance, GRI standards provide a comparable, interconnected system that organizations can use for their impact reporting and/or decision-making.

The standards are organized into universal standards that apply to all organizations, sector-specific standards for 40 high-impact industries, and topic standards for specific topics such as waste, health and safety or tax.

- Founded: 1997.

- Number of companies reporting: 10,000+.

- Typical audience: Broad stakeholder base.

- Purpose: To help organizations be transparent and take responsibility for their impacts by creating common global standards for reporting that include an independent, multi-stakeholder process.

- Focus: External environmental, societal and economic impacts.

- What is reported: All three ESG pillars. General disclosures, sector-specific disclosures and topic-specific disclosures.

- Who reports: Most large companies globally use the GRI standards.

- Industry-specific versions: 40 industry-specific standards coming, starting with high-impact sectors.

- Output used for: Company's public ESG report and other (sustainability indices, awards, etc).

There are other local, regional or industry-specific platforms to disclose ESG data – these are just a few. There are fully commercial platforms, such as EcoVadis, that also offer ways to disclose. Taking some time to consider what is the best fit for your organization will allow you to confidently create the internal resources needed to report ESG transparently to the outside world.

Are you ambitious for your organization?

This chapter has focused on giving you the tools to assess your organization's sustainable data ambitions. This is the final stage of removing the dirt from your view of sustainable data's role in your organization using our handy MUD methodology outlined in Figure 4.1.

Determining your ambition builds on your current level of data capability and how you plan to use that data. However, unlike the assessments you've done before, it is completely forward looking. It is about where you want to be versus where you are today.

In assessing your ambition, we have reviewed the following areas for you as a leader to determine how the topics fit with your organization:

- being best in class versus doing the bare minimum
- costs of ESG data collection and disclosure
- targets you could set
- how to disclose – internally and externally

After reviewing these topics – how ambitious do you want to be? If you are striving to be ambitious, you would be gravitating towards being best in class, budgeting for resources to collect and manage ESG data, setting at least one target and planning to disclose your ESG data publicly. You may be less ambitious and dial down the plans on each or any of these scales. Corporate ambitions must come from inside the organization. In this process you are the expert on the topic of your organization's ambition.

Elvis Presley once said, 'Ambition is a dream with a V8 engine.' Maybe a better quote for this book is: 'Sustainability data ambition is a dream powered by perpetually renewable energy.' The ambitions for your organization cannot be realized without the entire organization being aligned with their implementation and doing their part in making the ambitions a reality.

What's next for your organization? Putting your ambitions to work

You have done a lot of work in the last few chapters. You have considered the current state of your organization's sustainable data savviness and mapped that to a Sustainability Data Category in Chapter 4. You have prioritized the use cases for sustainability data for your organization in Chapter 5. In this chapter, you have reviewed your sustainability data ambitions.

Based on where you are today, here are some suggested next steps for your organization to move along the ESG Data Maturity Journey.

If you are an ESG Data Debutant, what are your next steps?

It should be evident that ESG data is valuable to your core business. No matter which of the ABCs of sustainability data use cases you prioritize, they all require data. To be even more specific, they all require GHG emissions data as an absolute minimum. As a Data Debutant, you may not collect, manage, compare, review and disclose this data point yet. You should consider prioritizing this action as a first step. You would be wise to do this GHG emissions collection in line with the guidelines of the GHG Protocol, and start with Scopes 1 and 2. Scope 3 can be tricky and take time.

Accuracy and not falling into the traps of the three Es of data need to be guiding principles for your organization. This allows you to start as you plan to continue.

You can do more than just working on your Scope 1 and 2 GHG emissions, but be clear – this is your first and most important priority as a Data Debutant.

You can also plan to collect and review other increasingly important ESG datasets including data on water usage, waste management, employee safety and security governance, workforce diversity and inclusion, etc. An important building block on your journey to more and better ESG data is the creation of good governance for your organization.

Formally written and agreed policies governing your organization's environmental and social commitments can go a long way. They can offer you the opportunity to report that you have these policies in place and build transparency in your governance structure for external stakeholders. They can also set a clear standard that the organization must meet to achieve its governance goals. Be aware that having a policy is good. Having a process by which that policy is implemented and enforced is miles better. Putting in place a plan for governance must include rolling out the details of the policy to the whole of the organization.

In the same vein, a Data Debutant should be upskilling its leadership team on ESG and its role in the organization. This includes learning the ESG basics and inspiring leaders at all levels to find data that has dual purpose for your business – to drive the decisions you are making today, and to support sustainability-driven decisions. Auditing the data you already collect may surprise you. You may have some elements of ESG data disclosures already well underway.

As in all organizations, Data Debutants will already be planning ahead to identify the organization's capital needs in the next three to five years. A next step is to identify the data requirements financiers currently demand from potential investee organizations and be aware of the trends in this space. It may be that transition plans are required for accessing some capital in the future. Without a baseline of data collected today, you may find this requirement difficult to meet.

To help you frame your sustainability data levels against others, identify industry peers' ESG data disclosures. How do you measure up to their breadth of data disclosed? How do you measure up against the values of the data they make public? Understanding where you are at today can help you benchmark your business. You can keep this knowledge to yourself should you choose. It can be a powerful tool for you and your teams internally or can be an excellent story to tell your external stakeholders.

If you are an ESG Competent Commentator, what are your next steps?

You already collect some ESG data points, so you have something to build on. You should question whether you collect the sustainability data you have only for compliance purposes, or if you use it more widely across the organization. It may be that you have data sitting in your compliance department that can drive decisions that bring efficiency and growth to your core business. Don't waste the chance to use what you already have.

It is an excellent time for a Competent Commentator to assess where you sit compared to others in your industry. What rank are you overall in sustainability scores or ratings? How do you line up against peers on important raw datasets such as GHG emissions, gender diversity, waste management and energy usage? Could you be top quartile? If not, would it improve your business to become top quartile?

You may have some ESG data, but not all. Assess how you could fill in the blanks that align to all your priority use cases – not only compliance and regulation. It may be that you need more than you have already to access capital or win business. Leverage the systems you have in place to collect the sustainability data you have to build new datasets that directly add value to your core business. If the systems you have in place now are inefficient and unreliable, consider how you can improve the system.

By creating an efficient data collection, review and disclosure engine, you are building future data flexibility into your organization. During this period of rapidly changing rules for ESG data disclosures, this can be invaluable for your future.

If you are an ESG Proficient Producer or an ESG Skilful Services, what are your next steps?

Both Proficient Producer and Skilful Services organizations have and use ESG data. Their biggest difference is their output: is it a product or service? When we seek to marry our ambition with our level of ESG maturity today, it becomes less important what you produce and more important how you engage with data for your use cases.

As a Proficient Producer or Skilful Services company, you should be actively marrying ESG data with your use cases and ensuring the data you collect and analyse is decision useful. Is it granular enough? Is it timely enough? Does it cover a wide enough range of your geographical coverage, employee base, customer needs, shareholder requests? This is the phase of your sustainability data life cycle in which you build out your datasets. These may include water usage, recycling commitments, hiring policies, energy storage and production strategies, etc.

Especially as a Proficient Producer, you should be considering how the circular economy affects the data you need to collect and assess. It may be that you need to build out your knowledge on your product's end of life. Are there environmental impacts? Can they be mitigated? Increasingly, ignorance of this stage of your product's life cycle is not bliss. It may need action by you that could be very new for your business – and can both require and yield resources to your firm.

As a Proficient Producer or Skilful Services business, you are likely to be engaged with some sustainability targets. If not, it is reasonable at your stage of the sustainability data journey to set some. You should consider net zero and carbon neutrality targets in particular and get familiar with the use of carbon credits and offsets on your plan to achieve these goals.

Your relationship with sustainability data is already well established. This allows you to consider where you would like to rank versus your competitors and industry on the topic of ESG data. Do you want to be a leader and best in class? Do you want to choose some specific metrics to ensure you are the top of your class? By achieving these relative successes, you are able to share your leadership with your stakeholders. Internally, a leadership position in lowest GHG emissions or most gender diversity may inspire pride from your employees and attract top talent. Externally, being a leader in sustainability metrics allows you to justifiably shout about the achievements to your customers, shareholders and supply chain.

Keep one eye on the dangers of greenwashing we will review in Chapter 9, but, with this proviso, being a top performer on ESG metrics can benefit your business immensely.

If you are an ESG Expert Educator, what are your next steps?

As an organization in the top-level category of the ESG Data Maturity Journey, you may think your job is done. Think again. In this rapidly moving area, your excellent standing may easily slip if you don't focus on maintaining your data focus. More importantly, you have established a position to credibly offer your views, your experience and your resources to others in the market.

There are some data-driven actions you may not already have in place. For example, sustainability key performance indicators (KPIs) in the business may need updating. Board-level KPIs can help your organization's top decision-makers and stewards of governance embed sustainability data into their decisions. By ensuring the top table of leaders regularly interact with ESG data, your organization can ensure these data points are used for decisions on core business activities and objectives.

ESG metrics embedded into objectives should cascade through your organization. Including sustainability KPIs based on data in employee bonuses and compensation is becoming more common. It is a tool used to bring the need for sustainably driven action top of mind for everyone within an organization. We will add more thought to the question of sustainability data KPIs in Chapter 10.

If you are already collecting, analysing and disclosing ESG data publicly to promote comparability, coherence and comprehensiveness, you may consider adding more data types to this group. In particular, there is a growing interest in how organizations impact nature and biodiversity. This could be an area where you collect additional data and work with standards-setters in this burgeoning topic set.

As an Expert Educator you can also use that name literally. Your experience with ESG data allows you to teach others in your ecosystem about how to engage with sustainability data to bring out its value. That value is not only for advancing action to fight climate change. It is also valuable for your business and its central activities. Sharing this understanding with others in the value chain allows you to be seen as a leader by stakeholders that matter to your business: partners, customers, suppliers, investors, shareholders and employees.

Your knowledge can also help shape the future of data disclosures and climate action in your industry and beyond. There are many associations, initiatives, groups, task forces, working groups and other constructs actively working on sustainability topics. The recommendations coming out of some of these groups shape policy and regulations that may affect your business. Your level of knowledge and experience in ESG data can be a welcome voice in these groups. It can benefit your business directly if you help to bring added efficiency to requirements your business will be subjected to in the future. It can benefit your business indirectly through building good governance of sustainability to help fight climate change. That's beneficial for us all.

Your category, your ambition

Congratulations. You have completed your journey to assess your organization's sustainability data positioning today and plans for tomorrow.

The next steps are for you to truly embed some of the areas that will affect your decisions and the ESG data you will need as a business. Three areas that merit a deeper dive will be outlined in the following four chapters: regulatory trends in Europe and worldwide, greenwashing, and setting KPIs.

References

Mulligan, J, Ellison, G, Levin, K, Lebling, K, Rudee, A and Leslie-Bole, H (2023) 6 ways to remove carbon pollution from the atmosphere, World Resources Institute, www.wri.org/insights/6-ways-remove-carbon-pollution-sky (archived at https://perma.cc/Z6GB-A53P)

Office of the Federal Register (2022) The Enhancement and Standardization of Climate-Related Disclosures for Investors, A Proposed Rule by the Securities and Exchange Commission, www.govinfo.gov/content/pkg/FR-2022-04-11/pdf/2022-06342.pdf (archived at https://perma.cc/A3ZX-ZSNS)

SBTi (nd) The corporate net-zero standard, https://sciencebasedtargets.org/net-zero (archived at https://perma.cc/7KDL-CXQA)

Silverstein, K (2022) Not all carbon credits are created equal, Forbes, www.forbes. com/sites/kensilverstein/2022/06/22/not-all-carbon-credits-are-created-equal-heres-what-companies-must-know/?sh=1fad611c5328 (archived at https:// perma.cc/SPE8-TEEZ)

SustainAbility Institute by ERM (2022) Cost of Climate Disclosure: Fact sheet, www.sustainability.com/globalassets/sustainability.com/thinking/pdfs/2022/ climate-disclosure-survey_fact-sheet-april-2022.pdf (archived at https://perma. cc/4AMZ-39EJ)

SustainAbility Institute by ERM (2023) *ESG Ratings at a Crossroads*, www. sustainability.com/globalassets/sustainability.com/thinking/pdfs/2023/rate-the-raters-report-april-2023.pdf (archived at https://perma.cc/3VG7-VY6C)

UN (2015) Transforming Our World: The 2030 Agenda for Sustainable Development, https://sdgs.un.org/2030agenda (archived at https://perma.cc/ J2LW-FMGN)

UN (nd) Sustainable Development Goals, www.un.org/sustainabledevelopment/ (archived at https://perma.cc/DP6X-YSTX)

UN Development Programme (2023) The SDGs in action, www.undp.org/ sustainable-development-goals (archived at https://perma.cc/J269-D2DA)

Sustainability regulations – Europe's biggest export?

Now that we have mapped your organization to its Sustainability Data Category and considered what your next steps are for the future, we will turn our minds to a deeper dive on market pressures. These market pressures are set to affect your organizational strategy on collecting, using and disclosing ESG data.

The four deep dives on data coming up are:

1 Regulatory trends – the case of Europe

2 Global trends

3 Greenwashing

4 Data and key performance indicators (KPIs)

In this chapter we will look at the global regulatory and disclosure pressures facing organizations, and use Europe as a case study. Europe is breaking

Table 7.1   Acronym buster 1

Acronym	Full name	What is it?
CBAM	Carbon Border Adjustment Mechanism	A policy proposal by the European Union to tax carbon emissions embedded in imports from countries that lack equivalent carbon pricing.
CDP	CDP (previously Carbon Disclosure Project)	A not-for-profit charity that runs the global sustainable data disclosure system for investors, companies, cities, states and regions.
CEAP	EU Circular Economy Action Plan	A plan to promote sustainable resource use and waste reduction within the European Union.
CSDDD	Corporate Sustainability Due Diligence Directive	EU Directive to foster sustainable and responsible corporate behaviour and anchor human rights and environmental considerations into companies' operations and corporate governance. The CSDDD requires disclosure of direct impacts as well as those from their value chains inside and outside Europe.
CSR	Corporate Social Responsibility	A company's commitment to ethical, social and environmental responsibilities in its business practices.
CSRD	Corporate Sustainability Reporting Directive	A proposed directive by the European Commission to revise and strengthen the Non-Financial Reporting Directive, which requires certain large companies to report on their sustainability impacts.
EFRAG	European Financial Reporting Advisory Group	An organization that provides advice on accounting standards to the European Union.
EMAS	Eco-Management and Audit Scheme	A voluntary environmental management system that enables organizations to assess, manage and improve their environmental performance.
ESRS	European Sustainability Reporting Standards	A set of standards for the disclosure of sustainability information by companies operating in the European Union.

(continued)

Table 7.1 (Continued)

Acronym	Full name	What is it?
ETS	Emissions trading system	A market-based mechanism that allows companies to buy and sell permits to emit greenhouse gases, with the aim of reducing emissions at the lowest possible cost.
GRI	Global Reporting Initiative	A non-profit organization that provides a framework for sustainability reporting, including guidelines for companies to report on their ESG impacts.
IFRS	International Financial Reporting Standards	A set of accounting standards developed and published by the International Accounting Standards Board, which are used in many countries around the world.
ISSB	International Sustainability Standards Board	A board of the International Financial Reporting Standards Foundation that aims to develop a set of sustainability reporting standards that are globally accepted.
NFRD	Non-Financial Reporting Directive	A European Union directive that requires certain large companies to report on their social and environmental impacts, as well as their diversity policies.
PAI	Principal Adverse Impact	An impact that has, or may have, a negative effect on sustainability factors, such as the environment, society or human rights.
SASB	Sustainability Accounting Standards Board	A non-profit organization that develops and publishes industry-specific sustainability accounting standards to help companies report on their sustainability performance.
SFDR	Sustainable Finance Disclosure Regulation	A European Union regulation that requires financial market participants to disclose how they integrate sustainability risks into their investment decisions.

(continued)

Table 7.1   (Continued)

Acronym	Full name	What is it?
TBL	Triple bottom line	A framework that measures a company's performance based on its social, environmental and economic impacts, also known as the three Ps: people, planet and profit.
TCFD	Task Force on Climate-related Financial Disclosures	An international initiative that aims to develop a framework for companies to disclose climate-related financial risks and opportunities.

new ground on sustainability data policy and wider sustainability legislation that requires ESG data. It is a sound place to start before we look at other global trends.

You'll encounter many acronyms in this chapter and the next. Some we have already used earlier in this book, and others are new. To help you follow the alphabet soup, Table 7.1 provides a quick and easy reference if you lose track. There is another one at the start of the next chapter too. Use both where you need to remind yourself of the shorthand. No doubt soon you will be fully conversant in sustainability acronyms!

Regulations in ESG data disclosures are not dull

Resist the urge to skip this chapter. In truth, regulations *can* be dull. But they are critically important. Rarely do organizations celebrate being regulated. Regulation imposes a burden of cost, compliance and scrutiny on an organization. This burden impacts the allocation of your organization's resources and may divert funds to servicing compliance over building your business. Many industries are already heavily regulated – just think of the rules governing the launch of new drugs in the healthcare industry or the rules on minimum reserve requirements in the banking sector.

Overall, regulations attempt to protect the economy, markets and consumers by offering requirements to keep people and organizations safe. They also allow for a measure of levelling of the playing field so that all of the participants in the market compete on the basis of equal minimum standards. This can come in especially handy in new areas of the economy where market players do not have a common understanding of what 'good' looks like.

In the case of sustainability, as we have seen in previous chapters, this common understanding of what is best practice and optimal transparency is not yet fully formed – certainly it has not yet harmonized globally. This can cause challenges for organizations, and if we consider regulations to be a way to bring clarity to this relatively new area of the business marketplace, perhaps we can see some benefits to having regulations in place.

It may still be a stretch to expect participants to celebrate the ESG data regulations that are arriving thick and fast, but arriving they are. So, perhaps our energy would be better spent finding ways to navigate them effectively rather than railing against their existence. As a business leader you don't need to celebrate them. You do need to accept them.

In almost all jurisdictions globally, there are now a variety of mandatory requirements regarding ESG reporting. As outlined in Chapter 2, organizations need to be sure that they are in compliance with these requirements when their organization falls into regulatory scope. The material penalties for not doing so can be severe. Alongside financial penalties, the material impact on factors such as reputation cannot be ignored. We go deeper into this impact in Chapter 9 on greenwashing.

Organizations cannot afford to be cavalier with ESG reporting. It's vital to know what's required, and to ensure that your operations and policies are in alignment with these requirements. As an added challenge, reporting requirements are changing rapidly. This makes it difficult for your organization to set a long-term plan for compliance. There are year-on-year changes to requirements, and you will need to review and renew your plans regularly. Your team will need to keep their wits about them.

The EU has been a front-runner in these developments and continues to set the pace in numerous areas. Reviewing how ESG reporting requirements have developed in the EU therefore provides a good overview of where global regulations have come from, and where they're likely to be headed. We will consider the history of ESG data regulation and standards in the EU and their current state of play (at the time of publishing!). We can use the EU as an example of wide and deep sustainability regulation. In the next chapter we'll look at equivalent developments in various other jurisdictions.

At the outset it is important to clarify the difference between regulations and standards, as they aren't the same thing.

- **Regulations** are detailed instructions issued by regulatory bodies or public authorities on how laws are to be carried out or enforced. Regulations are usually the detailed rules underpinning legislation which has been passed by a government or governing body. They carry the force of law – their application is mandatory.

- A **standard** is an agreed upon way of doing things. Standards make things work by providing specifications (guidelines or requirements) for products, services and systems. If used consistently, they ensure quality, safety and efficiency. They may take the form of a reference document that provides details about the criteria involved.

At the time of writing, ESG data disclosure regulations are seeing rapid change, development and adoption. Keep in mind that new developments may take the form of regulations (which must be complied with) or standards.

The EU at the vanguard of sustainable regulation

The development of corporate sustainability disclosure regulation in the European Union offers a glimpse into the reasoning that has shaped global frameworks. In my experience walking the halls of the European Commission and engaging with officials across a range of departments, the sustainability agenda has captured a significant amount of mindshare from the most senior policymakers since about 2016.

There was talk in Brussels about creating a framework to support a sustainable consumption society long before this, and the earliest shoots of what is now the European Green Deal, as we will see, existed before 2016. But I pick out this date specifically as the point when I sensed a pivot of priority towards sustainability from the very top of the European political house.

Times change, and certainly the pressures emanating from the war in Ukraine that began in February 2022 have strained European policymakers as an energy crisis, humanitarian and refugee crisis, and economic burdens on households through high inflation in the early 2020s needed attention. As inflation in the Eurozone sat at 10 per cent in January 2023 – with many countries in Eastern Europe and the Baltics displaying greater than 15 per cent year-on-year inflation over the same period – there were heavy demands on policymakers in Brussels to help ease the burden on the economy of inflated prices.

However, my conversations in Brussels and in the capitals of the 27 European member states (with some exceptions) continued to prioritize sustainable growth throughout this period. Prolonged pressures on the near-term economies across Europe will continue to challenge the longer-term priority of climate change policy. However, Brussels' dedication to finding solutions to the global problem of sustainability throughout EU President Ursula von der Leyen's first term in office remained strong. We see that dedication manifested in the forward leap in sustainability related regulations and frameworks developed.

We will dig deeper into the detail here so we can not only understand Europe's position and projections for regulations in this area, but also see where other geographies may use Europe as a guide to their own regulatory plans. Sustainability data disclosure regulation itself underpins and supports other sustainability-focused policies. We will look at the wider policy context to understand how and why data fits in.

It is often said that Europe's biggest export is regulation. In the area of sustainability this may end up being very true indeed.

Europe's sustainable regulatory journey

So, how did Europe start creating its sustainability policymaking machine? A crucial piece of legislation in the development of the sustainable finance landscape was the Non-Financial Reporting Directive (NFRD), introduced by the EU in 2014. The NFRD was the first instrument to mandate the reporting of 'non-financial' information, alongside and complementing organizations' financial reporting.

The idea of non-financial reporting has been around for a long time. The OECD's 1976 'Guidelines for Multinational Enterprises' was probably the earliest framework. These non-financial reports – also called 'sustainability reports' – encouraged companies to disclose information about their operations relating to environmental, social, economic and governance issues understood in the broadest sense. The goal of these disclosures was to make businesses more transparent and accountable, helping investors make better-informed decisions and fostering a more sustainable economy.

In many ways you can think of regulating disclosures as the regulatory system picking up the concept of the triple bottom line, which we discussed

in Chapter 2. The NFRD, as the name suggests, is not financial reporting...
but acts a bit like it. Back in 2014, its genesis from the financial corridors of
the European Commission rather than the environmental offices was also
remarkable and indicative of the purpose of the disclosures. They were designed from the beginning to be used by the financial community.

We will follow the development of the EU's NFRD through its journey as
an early example of ESG disclosure entering the regulatory mainstream.

However, before we continue our journey on the EU's regulatory development pathway, we should take a moment to remember what came before.
An important precursor to these frameworks was the idea of corporate social responsibility (CSR). CSR can be defined (at the acknowledged risk of
insulting the reader's intelligence) as the concept that businesses should not
only focus on their financial performance, but also consider their broader
impact on society, the environment, and the wellbeing of all their stakeholders, rather than just the owners.

CSR encourages companies to integrate social, environmental and ethical
concerns into their business practices and decision-making processes. The
idea of CSR emerged in the mid-20th century as a response to growing concerns about the social and environmental consequences of industrialization
and the role of businesses in society. It challenged the traditional assumption
that the sole purpose of a company is to maximize shareholder value.

The economist Milton Friedman – notably not a sustainability guru –
famously argued that the only social responsibility of businesses is to increase profits while abiding by the law. This hasn't necessarily changed, as
you recall we discussed the idea of profit vs social outcomes in Chapter 2.
The primary legal obligation of managers remains that of promoting the
interests of the owners of the business they work for.

But CSR has made possible a more encompassing perspective on the organization's relationship with its context, and the implications of this for its
operations. CSR caught on because it offers several concrete benefits to corporations, which can contribute to their long-term success and
competitiveness.

CSR 'box ticking'

CSR is often perceived a bit of a box-ticking exercise, of no real benefit to
organizations and something to do so they look good. Something that 'ticks
the box' on the corporate to-do list rather than having any impact on the
core business.

This perception has emerged due to a range of reasons, but the challenge of measurement is no doubt high among them. As has been demonstrated previously, the availability of metrics for ESG factors has lagged behind the desire to measure them. Early metrics therefore often seemed highly arbitrary. Organizations, in turn, struggled to see the value or purpose of the collection and reporting of such data, and considered associated requirements an unnecessary burden. They responded by doing what they needed to do to satisfy the letter of the law, without any real appreciation for the spirit informing it.

But as is shown below, the market is embracing the substantial benefit of this kind of data. Firms showing strong sustainability credentials through their ESG disclosures are outperforming their counterparts, and finance is following CSR in this respect.

Corporate sustainability disclosure regulation emerged from a place in which the importance of CSR was increasingly being acknowledged, and a range of stakeholders wanted more information to be accessible. Regulators and legislators needed to know how organizations were operating. Investors began to see this data as providing valuable insights. Executives spotted the benefit of capitalizing on the signals they could send to prospective customers, partners and employees.

The earliest non-financial reporting frameworks were established on a voluntary basis and tended to be promoted on the merits of the practical benefits of the measures they advocated. 'Doing well by doing good' is a slogan that captures this rationale. But a general trend in corporate sustainability disclosure regulation has been for suggestions to transform into *requirements*.

This brings us back to the EU's NFRD regulation which began in 2014. The NFRD clearly demonstrated the change from 'nice to have' (encapsulated in CSR-style disclosures) to 'must have' (actual regulations legally requiring compliance). The NFRD became mandatory for large companies in 2018 and is continuing to evolve to incorporate more firms in its regulatory scope.

In keeping with its place at the front of the ESG data disclosure pack, the EU is also pushing boundaries on how sustainability fits into overall legislation – not limiting it to an area of financial disclosure alone. The trend in sustainable regulation demonstrated in the EU has been towards an increasingly wide scope and ambition in the frameworks associated with sustainable goals.

The NFRD, for example, has fed into the European Green Deal, a comprehensive plan to make the European Union the world's first climate-neutral continent by 2050. This ambitious initiative has developed and enhanced the aims and approaches of the NFRD by introducing a set of policies and strategies to decarbonize the economy, promote clean energy, and protect the environment. The EU Green Deal demonstrates the growing trend of integrating regulation and comprehensive policy frameworks to address the complex challenges of climate change and associated issues. ESG issues compound throughout society; regulatory responses are recognizing the need for their provisions to do so too.

Thinking it through – the case of the Gilet Jaune

The Gilet Jaune protests, also known in English as the 'Yellow Vest' movement, were a series of demonstrations that began in France in November 2018. The movement was named after the high-visibility yellow vests (*'gilets jaunes'* in French) that protestors wore as a symbol of their grievances.

The protests began as a reaction to the French government's proposed fuel tax rise. The ostensible purpose of the increase in fuel tax was to promote the greening of the economy and the reduction of carbon emissions in France. Opponents of the measure, however, saw it as disproportionately affecting rural and working-class citizens, who are more dependent on their private vehicles for transportation. The increase in fuel prices directly affected their livelihoods. It was not an amorphous tax. It was personal. The movement quickly grew to encompass a broader range of issues outside just fuel tax, including economic inequality and social injustice.

The Yellow Vest protests provide a good demonstration of the interconnection of environmental, social, economic and household impacts. On the face of it, a higher fuel tax would seem a sound and straightforward measure to address the role of private vehicles in carbon emissions. But, as the protestors recognized, it would disproportionately affect those who are already less well-served by public transport, and economically marginalized. The environmental benefits would therefore be contradicted by social and economic harms. Regulators appear to have recognized the complexity this poses, with the most recent frameworks having adopted additional perspectives.

As in the case of the Gilets Jaunes, the European Green Deal has also explicitly taken account of the social, economic and equality issues that live (closely!) alongside environmental ones.

As we explore in the following box, under the European Green Deal, the EU has developed a classification system called the EU Taxonomy. As the EU developed its framework for sustainable regulation, it needed a reliable and agreed nomenclature on which to base its rules. Without a common definition, the ambitious EU plans for sustainability regulation would be difficult to implement and police.

The EU Taxonomy is a key component of the EU's sustainable finance strategy. The primary goal of European sustainability regulation is to channel private and public investments into sustainable projects and businesses, thereby supporting the transition to a low-carbon, climate-resilient and resource-efficient economy. The EU Taxonomy is a critical tool to ensure all parties are speaking the same language when defining sustainability (see Chapter 5 for more details on taxonomies).

A special note on the EU Taxonomy

In June 2020 the EU Taxonomy was made public after an intense period of development supported by the EU-commissioned Technical High Level Expert Group (the TEG). This development created waves through the European and global financial markets based on the taxonomy's extensive set of definitions and controversial inclusions of nuclear energy and gas.

The EU Taxonomy was written with the belief that it would become the global gold standard and that it would be ratified quickly by the European Parliament and regulators and adopted into law by the European member states. At the time of writing this still has not happened. Why?

There are a number of sticky points that remain unsolved. Firstly, the EU is a special creature requiring 27 member states to agree to ratifying a legislation such as the taxonomy. Not all of these countries have the same view of sustainability. Put these differences in position between EU countries against the backdrop of the global need to build back after the Covid-19 setbacks and economic pressures from the war in Ukraine that began in 2022. In these circumstances, negotiations to get the taxonomy ratified become very testing.

The EU Taxonomy sets out six environmental objectives:

1 **Climate change mitigation:** Activities that contribute to reducing greenhouse gas (GHG) emissions or enhancing GHG removals.

2 **Climate change adaptation:** Activities that reduce the negative impacts of climate change and increase resilience to its effects.

3 **Sustainable use and protection of water and marine resources:** Activities that contribute to preserving and restoring water and marine ecosystems.

4 **Transition to a circular economy:** Activities that support waste prevention, recycling and the efficient use of resources.

5 **Pollution prevention and control:** Activities that contribute to preventing or reducing pollution and its impacts on the environment and human health.

6 **Protection and restoration of biodiversity and ecosystems:** Activities that contribute to protecting, conserving and enhancing biodiversity and ecosystems.

As one of the most ambitious sustainable taxonomies in development, the EU Taxonomy's journey is one to watch.

Europe in constant forward motion: all hail the new NFRD

From its start as one of the world's first sustainable finance legislations through to becoming a mandatory part of the EU's financial system, you would be forgiven for thinking the NFRD acronym was here to stay. As we hinted at earlier, Europe is at the cutting edge of sustainable finance regulation. It should therefore be no surprise that the EU decided that even the NFRD was not good enough. Instead, the Corporate Sustainability Reporting Directive (CSRD) was born, to replace the already leading-edge disclosure regulation with something even more robust.

The CSRD is a piece of European Commission regulation that aims to revise and expand the pre-existing NFRD. The CSRD came into force on 5 January 2023, marking a significant update to the earlier instrument. With this directive, a broader range of large companies, including listed SMEs, is now required to report on sustainability – encompassing approximately 50,000 companies in total.

Starting from the financial year 2024, the first set of companies will need to adhere to these new rules, with the first reports being published in 2025. The CSRD aims to promote a culture of transparency regarding the impact companies have on people and the environment.

Under the CSRD, companies must adhere to the European Sustainability Reporting Standards (ESRS). These draft standards are being developed by the European Financial Reporting Advisory Group (EFRAG), an independent body comprising various stakeholders. The ESRS will be aligned with EU policies and contribute to international standardization initiatives. The European Commission is expected to adopt the first set of standards by mid-2023, following the draft standards published by the EFRAG in November 2022.

The CSRD will also require companies to undergo an audit of their reported sustainability information. In the medium to long term, the directive is expected to reduce reporting costs for companies by standardizing the required information, and digitizing and streamlining the reporting processes.

As a reminder, CSRD is the regulation and EFRAG is creating the ESRS standards. Going back to our earlier definitions, these are tightly linked but need to be kept clearly understood when considering your role in your organization's governance. Complying with CSRD will require your organization to stay up to date on the EFRAG standards which aim to help create clarity for firms as to how to align their reporting with suitable standards of disclosure.

Also important is to call out the trend the CSRD is demonstrating when we consider the evolution of ESG data in regulation. The initial implementation of the NFRD regulation focused on large, publicly listed companies in the EU. The advent of the CSRD takes the scope of the regulatory requirement to disclose significantly wider. The stated plans are to increase the universe of organizations that fall into the scope of the CSRD (or whatever they may choose to call it next!).

An important point for you as a leader to take from this is that even if you are not compelled by regulation to disclose your ESG data points today, you may be required to do so tomorrow.

> ## A quick reminder
>
> We're first reviewing Europe as it is a leader in sustainability regulation at the time of writing. It would be wrong not to mention here that there are some global standards for disclosure being created in parallel with the work of EFRAG in creating the ESRS.
>
> Most notably, the International Sustainability Standards Board (ISSB) – referenced more fully in the next chapter – is a critical standard-setting initiative aiming for a globally relevant set of ESG disclosure standards. ISSB published its first set of standards in June 2023.

I'm not headquartered in the EU... should I care about European legislation?

European legislation on climate and sustainability can be relevant to all organizations no matter where they are headquartered if they are taken as a sign of things to come. Europe's early sustainability regulations may be used as blueprints – or at least inspiration – for other jurisdictions. This should make Europe of at least some interest to you.

More importantly, European regulations on sustainability are affecting companies that do business in the EU but are headquartered elsewhere. We will look at two of these regulations specifically: CSRD, which we have reviewed above, and the Corporate Sustainability Due Diligence Directive (CSDDD), which we will outline below.

The CSRD primarily targets companies incorporated within the EU. However, it can impact non-EU companies that have some operations within the EU. This is true particularly in cases where these non-EU companies have subsidiaries that are subject to the reporting requirements. Under the CSRD, non-EU companies themselves will not be directly subject to the reporting requirements – that would be an obvious extraterritorial stretch!

However, as the regulation stands at the time of writing, if a non-EU organization has a subsidiary that is either a large organization or an organization listed on a regulated market in the EU, that subsidiary will be required to comply with the CSRD reporting standards. In this situation the non-EU parent company would need to ensure that their EU-based subsidiaries have the necessary processes and systems in place to collect, manage and report the required ESG information in accordance with the CSRD.

Additionally, these parent companies may need to support their subsidiaries in adapting their governance structures, risk management processes and internal controls to meet the new sustainability reporting requirements.

In practice, the CSRD's indirect impact on non-EU companies looks likely to result in these companies adopting more consistent and comprehensive ESG reporting practices across their entire organization, even if they are not directly subject to the CSRD. It makes sense to build in this efficiency and comparability across all the countries where the company does business.

This harmonization can help non-EU companies align with the direction of travel for global ESG trends – i.e. towards some mandatory disclosure requirements. By creating a whole-of-company approach to what is currently the most stringent requirements, the organization can better meet the expectations of investors and other stakeholders and prepare for potential regulatory changes in their home countries.

Of course, given the broader trend towards mandatory and consistent forms of ESG disclosure, organizations are likely to need to implement some such measures sooner rather than later. Attention to how this kind of harmonization could be implemented may well give organizations a head-start on future developments.

Another European directive is the CSDDD, which was agreed by the European Parliament in June 2023. It needs to go through the process of negotiations and is projected to be formally adopted no earlier than 2024. After it is adopted, European member states will have two years to implement the CSDDD into national legislation. Talking about CSDDD is sustainable regulatory horizon scanning at its best. It is worth looking at the CSDDD since it has caused significant uproar in the global community due to its extensive reach.

The primary objective of the CSDDD is to enhance corporate accountability and transparency in sustainability matters. It aims to encourage businesses to conduct comprehensive due diligence throughout their supply chains to identify and address potential adverse impacts on the environment, human rights and social aspects. By enforcing responsible business practices, the EU intends to achieve a more sustainable and ethical business environment, fostering long-term value creation, and mitigating reputational and operational risks associated with irresponsible conduct.

The CSDDD applies to companies that meet the criteria outlined in Table 7.2.

Table 7.2 Criteria for the CSDDD

Company description	Global net revenues	Employees
EU-based companies	>€40M	>250 employees
EU-based parent companies	>€150M	>500 employees
Non-EU companies	>€150M (provided that at least €40M is generated from within the EU)	n/a
Non-EU parent companies	>€150M (from which at least €40M is generated from within the EU)	>500 employees

This is a broad catchment of organizations that will need to comply with the CSDDD.

One of the most notable features of the CSDDD is its extraterritorial reach. As we can see from Table 7.2, the directive applies not only to companies headquartered within the EU but also to non-EU companies conducting business activities within the EU market. This extension of jurisdiction is seen as crucial by the EU. It ensures that multinational corporations operating in the EU adhere to the same sustainability standards as EU-based companies. This move by the EU has significant implications for international businesses, as compliance with the CSDDD could become a prerequisite for accessing the EU market.

As illustrated by the examples of the CSRD and the CSDDD, the answer to whether you as a non-EU headquartered business should care about European legislation is: yes.

More disclosures upstream: the asset management case

Hopefully, we're now all on the same page with Europe's dedication to sustainability disclosure from companies, as evidenced by the evolution of the NFRD through CSRD and CSDDD and into the future. This dedication to disclosures does not stop at the organizational level. In the EU it has also been extended to the investor level, meaning that financial services companies that manage investments as funds on behalf of others must also disclose their sustainability data.

These financial services companies are called many things: fund managers, asset managers, portfolio managers, etc. For simplicity, we will refer to companies that take client money and pool it with others' money in order to allocate it to all types of investments (i.e. equity, fixed income (bonds), currencies, etc) as 'asset managers'.

The fact that asset managers must disclose the sustainability data of their portfolios creates a value chain for ESG data. ESG data has become critical to the fund management community to allow them to publicly declare their funds to be sustainable or green. This requirement on asset managers affects you as a business leader because the data an asset manager discloses on its portfolio needs to be gleaned from the portfolio companies themselves.

Therefore, if an asset manager has certain sustainability criteria guiding their investment decisions, and your business does not disclose the ESG data the investor needs to assess your business against its sustainability criteria, you will likely not get the investment you need from that asset manager. This can potentially have a direct impact on the health and future of your business.

Asset managers' regulatory obligations under the European Green Deal are governed by the Sustainable Finance Disclosure Regulation (SFDR), which came into force in 2021. The SFDR aims to increase transparency and standardization in the disclosure of sustainability information by financial market participants and financial advisers. That sustainability information will come from the investors' portfolio companies – and, as stated above, that could be you.

The primary objective of the SFDR is to promote sustainable investments by requiring financial market participants and financial advisers to provide clear, consistent and comparable information on the ESG properties of their products and services. This enables investors to make better-informed decisions based on the sustainability risks and opportunities associated with their investments.

Key elements of the SFDR applicable to asset managers include:

- **Disclosure requirements:** Organizations must disclose how they integrate sustainability risks into their investment decision-making and advisory processes. They are also required to disclose the potential negative impacts of their investment decisions on sustainability factors, such as environmental and social issues.

- **Transparency on remuneration policies:** The SFDR requires organizations to include information on how their remuneration policies are consistent with the integration of sustainability risks.

- **Product-level disclosures:** For financial products that promote environmental or social characteristics or have sustainable investment objectives, the SFDR mandates additional disclosures. These include information on how these characteristics or objectives are met and the methodologies used to assess, measure and monitor the sustainability impact of the products.

- **Principal Adverse Impact (PAI) reporting:** Large organizations (with more than 500 employees) are required to report on the principal adverse impacts of their investment decisions on sustainability factors. This involves disclosing information on indicators related to climate change, environmental degradation, social issues and corporate governance.

You may think that if your company is not seeking capital from an asset manager operating in the EU specifically looking at sustainable investments, the SFDR is irrelevant to you. However, as we saw in earlier chapters, if you intend to seek capital in the EU from investors that are regulated in the EU, the sustainability regulations these funds need to comply with become your problem too.

Moreover, we have seen in other areas of the implementation of the European Green Deal that there is a trend for scopes to be widened and voluntary suggestions to solidify over time into mandatory rules. It may be the same path for asset manager sustainability data reporting. Increasing requirements to a wider group of asset managers, or increasing the granularity of the ESG data needed from portfolio companies, could affect your business and its access to capital.

It may also be that the SFDR spawns similar regulation in other jurisdictions worldwide. The UK's Financial Conduct Authority is consulting on this topic at the time of writing.

Is the ESG investing market big enough for me to care about?

A Global Sustainable Investment Alliance (GSIA) analysis of the growth of ESG investing found that, between 2016 and 2018, the rate of sustainable assets under management grew by an average of 38 per cent in five major markets (US, EU, Canada, Japan, and Australia and New Zealand) (GSIA, 2018).

What's more, a PwC forecast from 2022 predicts a growth rate of more than 100 per cent in ESG-oriented investing in the US between 2021 and 2026 (from $4.5 trillion to $10.5 trillion) (PwC, 2022). In Europe, sustainable investing volumes are up 172 per cent in 2021 alone, and could increase another 53 per cent to $19.6 trillion by 2026. In the Asia-Pacific region, sustainable funds are expected to more than triple, reaching $3.3 trillion by 2026.

As this report notes, the rate of growth in ESG investing is significantly outstripping that of the market as a whole. ESG investment therefore represents a substantial and growing share of the finance that is available to organizations.

Organizations that want to take advantage of this growth would do well to consider the categorizations provided by the SFDR with regard to sustainable investment. The SFDR categorizes investment funds into three groups based on their sustainability objectives: Article 6, Article 8 and Article 9 funds.

Article 6 funds represent the most basic level of compliance with the regulation. These funds do not explicitly promote ESG characteristics or have specific sustainability objectives. However, they are still subject to certain disclosure requirements, such as transparency regarding their approach to the integration of sustainability risks into their investment decision-making process. They are also required to disclose any potential negative impacts their investment decisions may have on sustainability factors.

The other two types, in contrast, do have specific ESG orientations. Article 8 funds focus on promoting ESG characteristics, while Article 9 funds have a specific sustainable investment objective. Both fund types are subject to additional disclosure requirements under the SFDR to provide investors with greater transparency about their sustainability focus and impact.

Article 8 funds promote environmental or social characteristics but do not have sustainable investment as their primary objective. They integrate ESG factors into their investment process and often follow specific ESG criteria, industry best practices, or other sustainability benchmarks. However, they don't necessarily target a specific sustainable outcome. Article 9 funds have a specific sustainable investment objective. They aim to make a positive environmental or social impact, and their primary goal is to contribute to one or more of the UN SDGs or the objectives of the EU Taxonomy regulation, such as climate change mitigation or adaptation. Article 9 funds typically have a higher level of ambition in terms of sustainability compared to Article 8 funds.

Given the growth in the ESG investing sector, it's no surprise that demand for Article 8 and Article 9 funds is increasing. However, the number of such funds in the industry may in fact be decreasing. This may seem odd and counterintuitive to basic supply and demand principles. It is a direct outcome of the dark side of regulation – the risks of non-compliance!

One of the motives behind this trend of Article 8 and Article 9 fund numbers decreasing is the challenge in obtaining accurate, consistent and reliable ESG data from the companies in which these funds invest. To comply with SFDR disclosure requirements, fund managers need detailed and standardized ESG data from their portfolio companies. But, as noted previously, there are several factors that can pose a challenge, including inconsistency and a lack of standardization, and problems with the quality and coverage of the data.

Given these obstacles, businesses with robust ESG data and credentials stand to benefit significantly from the growing demand for sustainable investments. Companies that can demonstrate strong ESG performance through transparent, consistent and standardized reporting are more likely to attract investment from Article 8 and Article 9 funds. The demand from investors is strong – helping your potential investor create a portfolio that meets the criteria of sustainable investment funds will serve you well.

These developments demonstrate clearly how the frequently vague, voluntary and discretionary nature of early corporate sustainability disclosure regulation has steadily developed into a more encompassing and hard-nosed set of tools. The direction of travel is unambiguous. ESG data disclosure is going to be more and more important in order to secure investment. Organizations that can substantiate their credentials in this area will have a massive advantage.

European regulations: beyond ESG data disclosures

In keeping with this book's focus on sustainability data and the role of ESG data in company decisions at the board and executive leadership team level, the regulations focused on data reporting are critical to understand. However, the EU, in its self-appointed role as global sustainability regulation leader, has put in place other areas of regulation that any corporate leader should be aware of. They may reveal the ESG data requirements of the future.

Considering where they affect your business can help you to harness the data you decide to produce and disclose for multiple uses. Creating efficiency through a 'write once read many' approach to ESG data will give you an advantage.

If you are an Expert Educator, Skilful Services or Proficient Product organization you can use your experience to advocate on how new datasets driven by sustainable regulations can affect businesses in scope of compliance. Costs and complexities associated with disclosing this data are not necessarily known to regulators or other parts of the regulatory ecosystem. Your knowledge and voice can help shape a smooth path forward incorporating data requirements that are specific and easy to source.

In addition to such measures pertaining to reporting, the EU Green Deal is also incorporating a range of non-reporting instruments, which will impact on organizations' activities – for companies resident both inside and outside the EU. We saw this aspect of regulations in the CSDDD. One aspect of the increasing complexity of the EU's framework is a recognition of the need for global solutions. Many of the non-reporting regulations are geared towards tackling sustainability challenges without borders.

Stopping sustainability arbitrage

In a globalized economy, regulations can sometimes disadvantage companies resident in that jurisdiction compared to their counterparts resident elsewhere. To mitigate this risk, taxes or adjustments can be put in place as a form of regulation to level the playing field.

In the case of sustainability, there is an additional advantage to implementing these adjustments. Most legislation is only able to affect organizations inside the jurisdiction of the legislation. But by requiring the same standards for any goods/services that enter the zone – not only for those manufactured or provided within the zone – the regulator achieves a form of extraterritorial reach for its rules. This can be a very good thing for the global goals of limiting climate change.

Extraterritorial reach will have its opponents, and the principle of national self-determination should not be discounted. However, to achieve global goals, a global framework presents numerous advantages.

A carbon border 'tax' creates barriers to sustainability arbitrage. For example, a producer of electronic equipment based in Italy must adhere to the EU's laws and regulations. A competitive firm based in Turkey has no such requirements to adhere to the EU's laws. Therefore, the Turkish firm could choose to employ a manufacturing process that exploits high levels of carbon emissions and does not protect labour or employment rights.

This could present a competitive advantage for the Turkish firm over the Italian firm, through lower costs of production and costs associated with compliance. If the Turkish firm sells its products in Italy (or anywhere else in the EU), it may be able to sell its products at a lower price point due to its poorer sustainability standards.

This creates an incentive for the Italian firm to relocate to Turkey (or elsewhere that has lower standards of sustainability compliance than Italy). This relocation can harm the Italian and EU economy. It also creates a moral hazard by incentivizing a migration of industry to jurisdictions with low standards of environmental protections. None of this is helpful to our shared climate challenges. Of course, higher sustainability standards can be a selling point for businesses meeting the higher requirements within (in this example) the EU.

Implementing a border adjustment tax that levels the sustainability playing field helps to maintain healthy competition and seeks to promote a healthy planet and society as well. One such measure that has been agreed in Europe is the Carbon Border Adjustment Mechanism (CBAM).

The CBAM in Europe and elsewhere

The CBAM is a policy that has been developed by the European Commission, which enters into force in its transitional phase on 1 October 2023. It will initially apply to imports of certain goods and selected precursors whose production is carbon-intensive and at most significant risk of carbon leakage: cement, iron and steel, aluminium, fertilizers, electricity and hydrogen. If you do business with the EU in any of these fields and move your products into the EU, you will need to understand the implications of CBAM to your business – in terms of both taxes levied and compliance requirements.

When fully phased in, the CBAM is expected to capture more than 50 per cent of the emissions in sectors covered by the EU's emissions trading system (ETS). We outlined ETSs in Chapter 5. The broad motivation of the CBAM is to address the risk of carbon leakage and ensure a level playing field for companies operating within the EU's ETS.

To this end, the CBAM imposes a carbon cost on imports of certain goods from countries with less stringent climate policies. This cost is based on the emissions associated with the production of these goods, thereby levelling the playing field between EU and non-EU producers. By introducing this mechanism, the EU is taking a more proactive approach to address the issue of carbon leakage. This is a measure that again demonstrates the increasing scope and complexity of climate regulation.

An additional aim of the CBAM is to incentivize non-EU countries to adopt more ambitious climate policies. By imposing a carbon cost on imported goods, the mechanism will encourage foreign producers to reduce their GHG emissions in order to remain competitive in the EU market.

The CBAM also expands the scope of the pre-existing EU ETS by extending its reach to imported goods. Companies operating in the EU and beyond therefore need to be prepared to adapt to this evolving regulatory landscape. Instruments such as the CBAM will affect many operations directly, and will require organizations to disclose data to establish their compliance with the relevant regulations.

At the time of writing, there is also vigorous activity in favour of something like the CBAM in Canada, the UK and the USA, with lawmakers in all three countries having floated proposals. In the USA, while there is as yet no federal-level equivalent of the CBAM, some states have implemented their own approach.

California dreamin'

California's ETS imposes carbon border adjustments for electricity imported from jurisdictions without a carbon trading framework. For electricity generated outside California, in a state that does not have an ETS linked to California's, the first deliverer of the imported electricity is held liable for the GHG emissions. California's ETS was created in 2006, and operates in tandem with the state's cap-and-trade system for carbon.

Here's how it works in California. Organizations responsible for 25,000 metric tonnes of CO_2e per year are subject to the cap-and-trade system. There are in excess of 450 such companies in the state. In practice, this accounts for about 85 per cent of California's emissions. The Californian cap-and-trade system has been highly successful: the first objective was to reduce GHG emissions to 1990 levels by 2020, and it achieved this in 2016.

California has also attempted to mitigate the risk for carbon arbitrage. Its ETS imposes a fee on electricity imported from jurisdictions not regulated by another ETS. A proactive state of affairs.

Similar ends can also be achieved through a reverse approach to carbon border taxes. This can take the form of incentives offered to organizations that lower carbon emissions. One example of this is the Inflation Reduction Act (IRA) in the USA, which promotes environmentally positive production in the country. The IRA provides direct tax incentives to organizations, investors and consumers to transition to clean energy, along with grants and subsidies for associated purposes.

Passed in 2022, and made effective in 2023, the IRA has already significantly boosted the attractiveness of the USA as a place for green business and green investment. One result of this is that other countries are having to consider how they meet these incentives to keep their home firms at home, or to attract new green innovation.

Organizations need to start thinking about CBAM-type measures and how they will affect their business. New ESG data will be required if their products are in scope. As with all aspects of regulation and legislation considered in this chapter, the trend is unmistakable. Organizations' operations are going to need to be tracked with increasingly granular, and detailed data to meet these requirements will be necessary.

Those that fall behind will face a range of costs. In addition to the legal penalties for non-compliance, organizations that can't demonstrate their ESG credentials won't be able to compete in the interconnected systems that will emerge through instruments such as the CBAM. Reliable ESG data is vital to keep pace with the rest of the market.

The EU circular economy action plan

You may already be familiar with the concept of the circular economy. According to the Ellen MacArthur Foundation, a charity dedicated to promoting the circular economy:

> A circular economy is a systemic approach to economic development designed to benefit businesses, society, and the environment. In contrast to the 'take–make–waste' linear model, a circular economy is regenerative by design and aims to gradually decouple growth from the consumption of finite resources. (Ellen MacArthur Foundation, nd)

Running (consumption) in circles

The *circular economy* is a concept that aims to shift from the traditional linear economic model to a more sustainable and resource-efficient one. The former is often referred to as the 'take–make–waste' approach, relying heavily on resource extraction (take) and production (make), and generating a lot of waste in the process.

The circular economy, by contrast, focuses on designing out waste and pollution, keeping products and materials in use for as long as possible, and regenerating natural systems. The circular economy promotes a closed-loop system where resources are reused, remanufactured or recycled, reducing the depletion of natural resources and minimizing environmental impacts.

The idea of a circular economy has roots in various schools of thought and disciplines, including industrial ecology, regenerative design and cradle-to-cradle principles. It began to gain prominence in the late 20th century, with the publication of several influential works. An important one was *Cradle to Cradle: Remaking the way we make things* (McDonough and Braungart, 2002). The authors advocated for designing products and systems that eliminate waste and create closed-loop cycles.

The Ellen MacArthur Foundation has played a significant role in popularizing the concept and highlighting its economic and environmental potential.

The UK inventor and entrepreneur Arthur Kay provides a good example of the idea of the circular economy being put into action, through his company Bio-Bean. Kay invented a process for turning waste coffee grounds into flammable material that can be used for generating electricity, powering public transport, and heating homes. By finding a use for the material that would otherwise be thrown away, Kay has found a way to generate value while simultaneously reducing waste to landfill and preventing CO_2 emissions.

Everyday items like clothing, furniture and electronics are all eminently suited to a circular form of usage, and a wide range of initiatives are already innovating to this end.

The circular economy has gained increasing attention from governments, businesses and academia as a promising approach to address resource scarcity, environmental degradation and climate change while promoting innovation, economic growth and job creation.

The EU has embraced the concept of circularity as a positive contributor to sustainability. As we have seen above, Europe is not afraid of taking strategies and plans into the regulatory realm. Along this same path, the circular economy has gained a place within the European Green Deal.

The EU Circular Economy Action Plan (EU CEAP) is a framework intended to reduce the usage and waste of raw materials by prolonging the lifespan of products, increasing the rate at which they are reused and recycled, and reducing rates of consumption and disposal. First proposed in 2015, a renewed CEAP was issued in 2020 that proposes mandatory circularity requirements for public procurement, and mandatory product labels for energy products.

Attention has also been devoted to creating technical standards to make products more durable, reusable and recyclable. This supports the circular economy ethos. The European Commission working through European standardization organizations has developed standards and eco-design laws. Self-regulation remains central to these plans. The current model for the eco-design law focuses on voluntary actions, self-regulation, and businesses' direct involvement in the process. Manufacturers are part of an advisory forum that has a significant role in defining product categories and creating eco-design standards, and voluntary tools like the Eco-Management and Audit Scheme (EMAS) and ecolabelling are recommended.

For you as a business leader, the CEAP and its evolution should be on your radar, particularly if you are a product company. No longer is your job finished when the product ships out to your customer. The EU regulation will expect you to take some responsibility for the entire life cycle of the products you produce in order to minimize their negative impacts on the planet and people. This can require a big shift in an organization's thinking, and can impact everything from manufacturing to procurement to packaging to pricing and to product design.

In many ways, CEAP and similar regulations promoting the circular economy are a force pushing companies up the sustainability awareness curve. This sort of regulation requires integrated thinking on impacts of sustainability across the organization. As a leader you are central to considering the ramifications this has on your business – both inside and outside the EU.

As with other areas considered in this chapter, the shift from the 2015 to the 2020 iterations of the CEAP demonstrates a move towards making standards mandatory. As these whole of life cycle regulations continue to evolve, additional data will be required by the organization to ensure there is compliance with existing requirements and the ability to track against future requirements.

As a business leader, finding metrics to track the circularity of your business will create unique challenges, especially where your product is unique or difficult to reuse or recycle. Planning what ESG data points are needed to measure circularity should be part of what you challenge your management team to get in place now.

There is more evidence of this trend to come! An element of the European Green Deal that clearly demonstrates the increasing data need at the product level is the journey of the European Digital Product Passport. This work is also part of the European Commission's Circular Economy Action Plan. We will look at this shortly.

Company-level data vs product-level data

Circularity raises new questions about what data is needed and where to collect it if you are considering product-level sustainability. If your organization produces multiple products and services in multiple places around the world with different supply chains under the same umbrella company, this distinction between company-level data and product-level data may be significantly meaningful. Figure 7.1 helps illustrate this.

The products/services listed on the right-hand side of Figure 7.1 have unique ESG data outputs and they are made in different countries (which

Figure 7.1   Data at the company and product levels

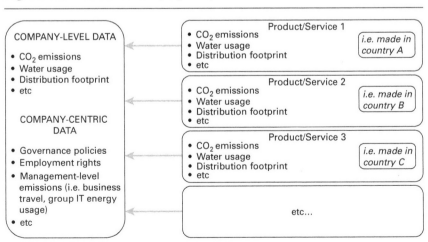

NOTE Data collected at the product/service level contributes to the company-level data, but can be used for review at the product level as well. Company data may add unique data that does not sit at the product level.

may have different regulatory disclosure requirements). Data on each product production process needs to feed into the overall company-level data in order for the company to meet its disclosure requirements as an entity.

However, it may be relevant to you as a leader to drill down to the product level in order to understand better where your impacts on climate and people are coming from. For example, if Product 1 is made in Germany and adheres to high standards of emission reduction requirements and uses only electric vehicles for delivery of its product and minimizes its waste, Product 1's contribution to the company's overall ESG disclosures may make a positive impact. On the other hand, if Product 2 is made in Kazakhstan and uses low-cost coal-fired power plants to drive its manufacturing processes and has poor water and waste management methods, it could be negatively impacting the company's overall ESG metrics. If Product 2 comprises 90 per cent of the company's outputs, the board of directors and senior management may need to consider how to make changes to address its sustainability profile, because it materially impacts the company – no matter where the company itself is headquartered.

If the organization aspires to be an ESG Proficient Producer or ESG Expert Educator looking down to the product level may be the only way for you as a leader to understand the changes the company will need to make that will matter most.

The European Digital Product Passport

Europe is also thinking about sustainability at the product level. The European Digital Product Passport aims to enhance the traceability of products and their components. The 'Passport' will require companies to make their products more sustainable by streamlining access to consistent information across supply chains, and product life cycle, allowing customers to make product comparisons more easily.

The main objective of the Digital Product Passport is to provide a digital platform that stores and shares information about products throughout their entire life cycle. It will require organizations to store various types of information related to a product, including:

- **Materials and components:** Detailed information about the materials, components, and chemicals used in the product, which can help in recycling, repairing and remanufacturing processes

- **Environmental footprint:** Information about the product's environmental impact, including data on its carbon footprint, energy consumption, and emissions generated throughout its life cycle

- **The production process:** Details about the manufacturing process, including the location of production facilities, certifications, and compliance with environmental and labour standards

- **Usage and maintenance:** Information on the optimal use and maintenance of the product to enhance its durability efficiency and overall performance

- **End-of-life management:** Guidelines on how to properly dispose, recycle or repurpose the product at the end of its useful life

At the time of writing, the EU is considering three industries for Product Passport implementation in 2026: apparel, batteries and consumer electronics. The implementation of the Passport will impose stringent requirements on organizations in terms of data collection and management.

Some attention to how your organization could implement the Passport requirements before they are mandated is likely to pay dividends in future operations. If you are a product organization, this regulation, if it continues its trajectory, will affect your business.

Do the CEAP and the Digital Product Passport affect my ESG data needs?

It may seem like the EU's far-reaching regulations are a little distant from your required ESG data needs today. In the areas of the circular economy and the efforts to trace sustainability at the product level, the granularity of information is one step removed from an organizational-level disclosure of ESG data as illustrated in Figure 7.1 above.

The value chain of data we discussed to build up your Scope 3 emissions data is also applicable within your own firm if you have multiple value chains, products or services. Product-level data rolled up into the organization can be valuable at both the product level and at the company level. There are many links between these levels to consider today – even before the product-centric regulations are in force.

Firstly, there is a very high likelihood that any company falling under European regulations (be that CBAM, CEAP, the Digital Product Passport or any other regulations Europe will dream up) will also require entity-level ESG data to be disclosed (i.e. CSRD-type disclosure data).

Secondly, getting your ESG data house in order will help to create a culture of data management that makes sustainability an important pillar in an organization's strategic priorities. If you are an ESG Data Debutant, it is possible your category distinction is driven by an immaturity in your organization's overall relationship with data. To move up in the Sustainability Data Categories, you will need to enhance your ability to collect, review and use your data – both to drive sustainability and to drive your business. This should be a win-win.

Thirdly, governance (the G in ESG) will be affected by product-level sustainability regulations and requirements. G currently includes data points covering the adequate governance of all elements of an organization's operations. Regulations that already affect or are projected to affect the business in the future will need to be included in adequate governance today. Effectively recognizing future disclosure impacts is sound governance at work.

The EU as a global leader in ESG regulation

The EU is a tour de force of sustainability regulation. The above overview, accurate at the time this book was published, demonstrates Europe's dedication to sustainability and its knock-on effects on your organization's need for ESG data.

The development of regulations pertaining to ESG governance in the EU clearly demonstrates a steady increase in the scope, granularity and complexity of the requirements they impose. At the beginning, regulatory guidance was voluntary, and organizations had extensive discretion in terms of the form and content of disclosures. Regulators have since tightened things up considerably, and changes in the coming years will impose much higher demands on ESG data for compliance.

The EU is not the only jurisdiction deeply committed to sustainability and demanding data disclosures. We'll look at the rest of the world in the next chapter to show a fuller perspective.

References

Ellen MacArthur Foundation (nd) The circular economy in detail: Deep dive, https://ellenmacarthurfoundation.org/the-circular-economy-in-detail-deep-dive (archived at https://perma.cc/DC4S-2X92)

GSIA (2018) *Global Sustainable Investment Review 2018*, www.gsi-alliance.org/wp-content/uploads/2019/03/GSIR_Review2018.3.28.pdf (archived at https://perma.cc/Q9E5-3DQZ)

McDonough, W and Braungart, M (2002) *Cradle to Cradle: Remaking the way we make things*, New York, North Point Press

PwC (2022) *Asset and Wealth Management Revolution 2022*, www.pwc.com/gx/en/financial-services/assets/pdf/pwc-awm-revolution-2022.pdf (archived at https://perma.cc/UHT5-R92H)

International sustainability data trends

8

REFLECTIVE QUESTIONS

- What trends in regulation, standards and taxonomies are going on worldwide?
- This is fast-moving stuff – how do I keep up?
- What do I need to consider as a multinational company?

We spent some time in Chapter 7 reviewing sustainability regulations in Europe and how they affect the need for ESG data. In this chapter we'll expand our scope to look at other global jurisdictions. We will start by reviewing the state of play on ESG data disclosure standards. We'll then look at various countries' regulations and policies. We'll have a look at capital markets and the disclosure rules for public companies before we give a roundup of global ETSs and carbon credits.

As was the case in the last chapter, there may be some acronyms in the pages to come. Use Table 8.1 as reference for what they all refer to when you need it.

If we are going to look at global trends, we should first discuss which countries in the world are the largest emitters of greenhouse gases (GHGs). These countries are in the spotlight and arguably need to take the most urgent action.

Table 8.1 Acronym buster 2

Acronym	Full name	What is it?
AIM	AIM (previously Alternative Investment Market)	A sub-market of the London Stock Exchange, designed for smaller, growing companies seeking access to public funding.
ASIC	Australian Securities and Investments Commission	An independent Australian government body that enforces laws relating to corporations, financial services and market integrity.
ASX	Australian Securities Exchange	An Australian public company that operates Australia's primary securities exchange.
BRR	Business Responsibility Reporting	A framework that requires companies to report on their social, environmental and economic impacts and their efforts to address them.
CBAM	Carbon Border Adjustment Mechanism	A policy proposal by the European Union to tax carbon emissions embedded in imports from countries that lack equivalent carbon pricing.
CDP	CDP (previously Carbon Disclosure Project)	A not-for-profit charity that runs the global sustainable data disclosure system for investors, companies, cities, states and regions.
CEAP	EU Circular Economy Action Plan	A plan to promote sustainable resource use and waste reduction within the European Union.
CSA	Canadian Securities Administrators	An umbrella organization of provincial and territorial securities regulators in Canada, responsible for harmonizing and coordinating securities regulation across the country.
CSR	Corporate Social Responsibility	A company's commitment to ethical, social and environmental responsibilities in its business practices.
CSRC	China Securities Regulatory Commission	The main securities regulator in China, responsible for overseeing the country's securities markets and protecting the interests of investors.

(continued)

Table 8.1 (Continued)

Acronym	Full name	What is it?
CSRD	Corporate Sustainability Reporting Directive	A proposed directive by the European Commission to revise and strengthen the Non-Financial Reporting Directive, which requires certain large companies to report on their sustainability impacts.
EFRAG	European Financial Reporting Advisory Group	An organization that provides advice on accounting standards to the European Union.
EMAS	Eco-Management and Audit Scheme	A voluntary environmental management system that enables organizations to assess, manage and improve their environmental performance.
ESRS	European Sustainability Reporting Standards	A set of ztandards for the disclosure of sustainability information by companies operating in the European Union.
ETS	Emissions trading system	A market-based mechanism that allows companies to buy and sell permits to emit greenhouse gases, with the aim of reducing emissions at the lowest possible cost.
GGFI	Global Green Finance Index	An index that ranks the depth and quality of green financial products and services in different countries and cities.
GRI	Global Reporting Initiative	A non-profit organization that provides a framework for sustainability reporting, including guidelines for companies to report on their ESG impacts.
GSIA	Global Sustainable Investment Alliance	A collaboration of membership organizations around the world that promote sustainable investment practices and the integration of ESG factors into investment decision-making.

(continued)

Table 8.1 (Continued)

Acronym	Full name	What is it?
IASB	International Accounting Standards Board	An independent organization that develops and sets accounting standards used in many countries around the world.
IFRS	International Financial Reporting Standards	A set of accounting standards developed and published by the International Accounting Standards Board, which are used in many countries around the world.
ISSB	International Sustainability Standards Board	A board of the International Financial Reporting Standards Foundation that aims to develop a set of sustainability reporting standards that are globally accepted.
MAS	Monetary Authority of Singapore	Singapore's central bank and financial regulatory authority.
NDRC	National Development and Reform Commission	A macro-economic management agency in China that oversees economic planning, energy policy and environmental protection.
NFRD	Non-Financial Reporting Directive	A European Union directive that requires certain large companies to report on their social and environmental impacts, as well as their diversity policies.
PAI	Principal Adverse Impact	An impact that has, or may have, a negative effect on sustainability factors, such as the environment, society or human rights.
PBOC	People's Bank of China	The central bank of China, responsible for monetary policy and financial regulation.
QCA	Quoted Companies Alliance	An independent membership organization that represents the interests of small- and mid-sized quoted companies in the UK.
SASAC	State-owned Assets Supervision and Administration Commission	The main agency that oversees China's state-owned enterprises, responsible for managing and supervising the assets of these companies.

(continued)

Table 8.1   (Continued)

Acronym	Full name	What is it?
SASB	Sustainability Accounting Standards Board	A non-profit organization that develops and publishes industry-specific sustainability accounting standards to help companies report on their sustainability performance.
SEBI	Securities and Exchange Board of India	The regulator of the securities market in India, responsible for protecting the interests of investors and promoting the development of the securities market.
SFDR	Sustainable Finance Disclosure Regulation	A European Union regulation that requires financial market participants to disclose how they integrate sustainability risks into their investment decisions.
SOE	State-owned enterprises	Companies that are owned by the government or state, typically established to carry out strategic or public policy objectives.
SSEI	Sustainable Stock Exchanges Initiative	A global platform that promotes sustainable investment and encourages exchanges to integrate sustainability into their operations.
SZSE	Shenzhen Stock Exchange	One of two main stock exchanges operating independently in mainland China, based in Shenzhen.
TBL	Triple bottom line	A framework that measures a company's performance based on its social, environmental and economic impacts, also known as the three Ps: people, planet and profit.
TCFD	Task Force on Climate-related Financial Disclosures	An international initiative that aims to develop a framework for companies to disclose climate-related financial risks and opportunities.
WFE	World Federation of Stock Exchanges	A global association of exchanges and clearing houses that promotes the development of fair, transparent and efficient capital markets.

The world's top 10 emitters of GHGs: a ranking and analysis

Understanding the countries responsible for the highest levels of GHG emissions is crucial in formulating effective climate policies. Below, we will review the top 10 emitters, as ranked by the World Resources Institute (WRI) and based on the most recent data available, from the year 2021. Additionally, we will explore the primary sources of GHG emissions for the top three countries on the list.

Ranking of top 10 emitters:

1 **China:** As the world's most populous country and a major industrial powerhouse, China's total emissions in 2021 surpassed those of any other nation. The country's rapid economic growth and urbanization have led to significant energy consumption, mainly derived from coal. China's heavy reliance on coal-fired power plants for electricity generation contributes substantially to its carbon dioxide emissions. Moreover, its vast manufacturing sector, which supplies goods for the global market, also plays a significant role in its emissions profile.

2 United States: The United States, a long-time major emitter, ranks second on the list of global emitters. While it has made progress in reducing its emissions over the years, it remains a substantial contributor to global GHG levels. In 2021, the US continued to rely on fossil fuels, including coal, oil and natural gas, for electricity generation and transportation. The transportation sector, with its extensive network of cars, trucks and planes, is a primary source of emissions, as is the industrial sector, which contributes to the nation's overall carbon footprint.

3 India: India, with its large population and growing economy, ranks third among the top emitters of GHGs. In recent years, India's emissions have seen significant growth due to its expanding industrial and energy sectors. Coal remains the primary source of electricity generation in India, and the country continues to invest in coal-fired power plants to meet its energy demands. Additionally, the transportation sector, along with agricultural practices that release methane, contributes significantly to India's emissions.

4 Russia: Russia ranks fourth on the list of top GHG emitters. Its emissions are predominantly driven by its abundant reserves of fossil fuels, which are utilized for both energy production and exports. The energy sector, along with industrial activities, contributes substantially to Russia's emissions profile.

5 **Japan**: Japan, a technologically advanced nation, holds the fifth position among the world's top emitters. The country's industrial sector, which includes electronics, automobile manufacturing and steel production, is a significant source of emissions. Additionally, Japan's reliance on fossil fuels following the Fukushima nuclear disaster has contributed to its emissions levels.

6 **Germany**: Germany ranks sixth on the list, with a notable portion of its emissions stemming from its strong industrial base. The country heavily relies on coal for energy production, although it has made significant strides in transitioning to renewable energy sources in recent years.

7 **Iran**: Iran, an oil-rich nation, holds the seventh position among the top emitters. The country's energy sector, driven by its abundant fossil fuel resources, accounts for a substantial share of its GHG emissions.

8 **South Korea**: South Korea ranks eighth on the list. The nation's emissions primarily come from industrial activities, including steel and petrochemical production, and the energy sector's reliance on fossil fuels.

9 **Saudi Arabia**: Saudi Arabia, another major oil producer, is the ninth-largest emitter of GHGs. The country's vast oil reserves drive its economy, and the energy sector, dominated by oil extraction and refining, is the main contributor to its emissions.

10 **Canada**: Canada ranks tenth on the list of top emitters. The country's emissions are primarily linked to its energy-intensive industries and the extraction and processing of oil sands, as well as transportation.

The top 10 emitters of GHGs, as listed above, play a crucial role in shaping global efforts to combat climate change. The rankings demonstrate the significant impact of industrialization, energy consumption and reliance on fossil fuels in driving emissions for these countries. Addressing the emissions from these top emitters is essential for achieving meaningful progress in mitigating climate change on a global scale.

If your organization does business in any of these countries, you may find that your stakeholders are increasing their scrutiny of your sustainability commitments. They will look for data from you to help them assess your contributions to these geographies that already top the list of global emissions sources.

Unfortunately, when it comes to embracing sustainability data disclosure regulation, the top 10 global GHG emitters are not the top 10 most active jurisdictions. We will have a look at some significant countries' efforts to introduce climate legislation below.

First, we will consider the progress of ESG data standards and how they are being embraced in various global territories.

One standard to rule them all

Some of the most vocal opponents to the collection of ESG data suggest that since there is no global standard for data disclosures, the data becomes useless for decision-making due to its lack of comparability. As we have outlined in other areas of this book, ESG data disclosure is maturing. As reporting on sustainability data points matures, the standardization of ESG data definitions that align with disclosure requirements will also continue to evolve.

As we have seen from the European example in Chapter 7, the EU is integrating ESG data disclosure standards into its work on the European Sustainability Reporting Standards (ESRS) via the work of the European Financial Reporting Advisory Group (EFRAG). EFRAG's work is delivering one type of ESG data standard. There are others.

Two of the most commonly used ESG reporting standards are Sustainability Accounting Standards Board (SASB) and the Global Reporting Initiative (GRI), which we reviewed in previous chapters. There is a desire by many players to create a single ESG data-reporting standard to drive comparability and consistency globally. One important initiative is that of the International Sustainability Standards Board (ISSB), which is aiming to create a global standard for reporting ESG data.

The reason ISSB should be called out is its growing supporter base, which includes other standards-centric groups. In fact, in 2022, SASB integrated itself into the ISSB and aligned to supporting the outputs of the ISSB standards. CDP also announced at COP27 in Egypt that it will align its questionnaire to the ISSB standards when launched. As mentioned before, the Task Force on Climate-related Financial Disclosures (TCFD) is also folding into the work of the ISSB.

The *ISSB* is the ESG-dedicated body of the International Financial Reporting Standards (IFRS) – which also houses the International Accounting Standards Board (IASB). IFRS frameworks for financial statements have been a globally accepted standard for over three decades, enhancing comparability, transparency and efficiency between and among organizations and financial markets. The ISSB aims to do the same for ESG reporting.

The ISSB released two standards frameworks in June 2023: IFRS S1 General Requirements for Disclosure of Sustainability-related Financial Information; and IFRS S2 Climate-related Disclosures.

Let's jump into discussing the environment-centric disclosures in ISSB's S2 framework first.

IFRS S2 Climate-related Disclosures overlaps extensively with the reporting recommendations of the TCFD, but takes things a step further. S2 imposes extra, and more granular, reporting requirements in the areas of strategy, and metrics and targets. Table 8.2 gives a side-by-side comparison of TCFD and S2.

Table 8.2   TCFD vs IFRS S2

Disclosure	TCFD guidance	ISSB framework
Climate risks and opportunities	Recommended	Recommended
Risk management and resilience	Recommended	Recommended
Climate targets and progress	Recommended	Recommended
Corporate governance	Recommended	Recommended
Scopes 1 and 2 emissions	Recommended	Recommended
Scope 3 emissions	Encouraged	Required
Capital/financing	Recommended	Recommended
Financial performance/cash flow	Recommended	Recommended
Use of carbon offsets	Recommended	Recommended
1.5°C transition-compatible	Not required	Based on developments in international agreements
Strategy implementation	Not required	Recommended
Information on intangibles	Not required	See IFRS S1
Capacity to adjust and adapt	Not required	Recommended
Stakeholder consideration	Not required	Not required
Double materiality	Not required	Not required

Adapted from Gagnon, 2022

The S2 framework has other differences from TCFD. A very practical one is that the ISSB requires sustainability data disclosures to be released at the same time as an organization's financial statement disclosures. This alignment is designed to mitigate the confusion that can come from temporal differences in data available in the market about the same data point. It promotes ease in comparability year on year and across peer groups.

ISSB's S1 is intended to provide the basis for industry-specific sustainability reporting frameworks in the future. This is based on a recognition that different sectors and organizations have different needs and responsibilities, and reporting requirements need to be sufficiently flexible to accommodate these.

For example, a poultry-packing and -distribution organization might need to disclose data on climate-related risks related to food safety, or the health and safety of its employees. A telecommunications company would need to factor in SASB standards relating to privacy and competitive behaviour. If an organization were to identify water-related risk as an item of material interest to investors, it could refer to ISSB S1 for guidance on how to report data on governance, strategy, risk management, and the relevant metrics and targets associated with them.

We referenced the work that EFRAG was doing to put detail behind the ESRS regulations of the EU earlier. Thankfully, the ISSB's work is not happening in a bubble or without discussion with the European thinkers working with EFRAG. The governance and methodology differs between the two organizations, but there is substantial discussion between the two.

Figure 8.1 captures well the process each group has used to come up with their initial work (and after the publication of this book, these systems will likely stay in place for future iterations produced by ISSB and EFRAG).

Looking at the two standards side-by-side can be helpful. At the time of writing, this can be summarized as follows:

Notably, ISSB has significantly more companies impacted and a singular focus on climate. As a leader doing business in Europe, your organization should keep an eye on both of these significant standards stakeholders as they develop further guidance and detail.

ISSB's goal to create a global standard seems to be getting traction. A *Wall Street Journal* article in June 2023 noted that major countries that have indicated they are considering using the ISSB standards include Australia, Canada, Japan, Hong Kong, Malaysia, New Zealand, Nigeria, Singapore and the UK (Toplensky, 2023).

Figure 8.1 How do the ISSB and ESRS compare?

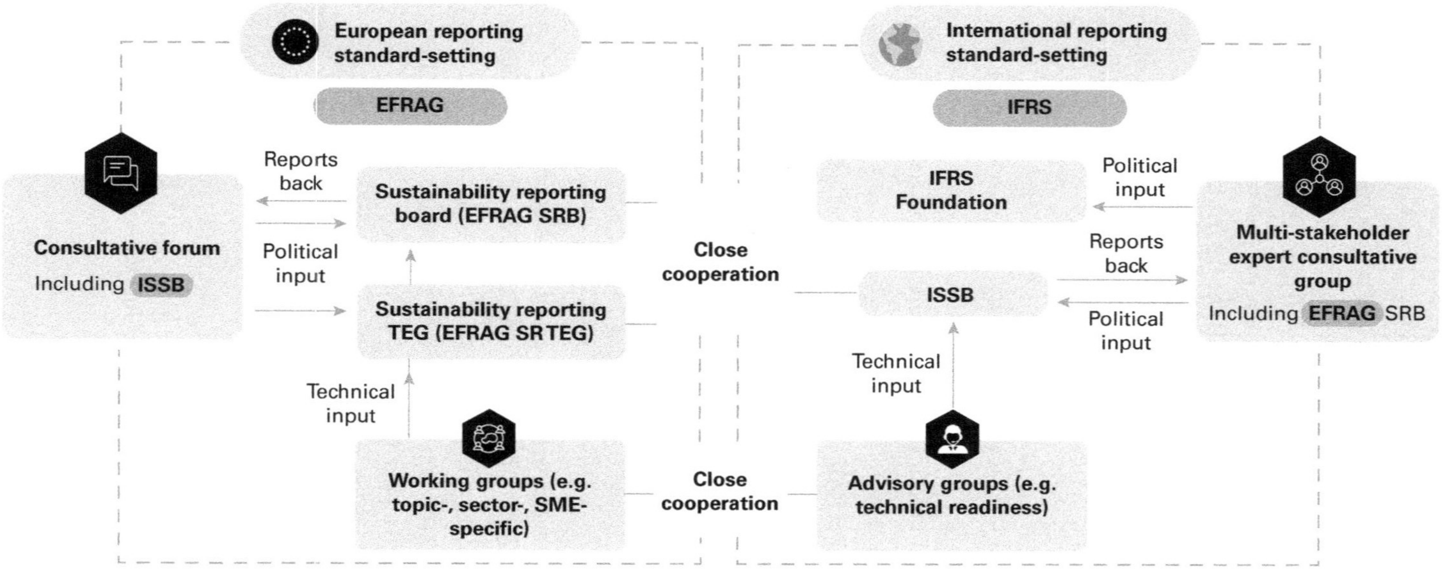
European reporting standard-setting
EFRAG
Consultative forum
Including ISSB
Reports back
Political input
Sustainability reporting board (EFRAG SRB)
Sustainability reporting TEG (EFRAG SR TEG)
Technical input
Working groups (e.g. topic-, sector-, SME-specific)
Close cooperation
Close cooperation
International reporting standard-setting
IFRS
IFRS Foundation
Political input
ISSB
Reports back
Political input
Multi-stakeholder expert consultative group
Including EFRAG SRB
Technical input
Advisory groups (e.g. technical readiness)

Reproduced with permission of ESGBook

Figure 8.2   ESRS and ISSB side by side

Double	Materiality	Financial
Cross-cutting E, S and G	Focus	Climate
Cross-cutting with industry-specific guidance	Industry Scope	Industry-specific standards for 77 SASB industries
50,000+	Companies impacted	130,000+
2025	First reports due	Depending on jurisdiction

Reproduced with permission of ESGBook

It is fair to say that understanding the similarities and differences of ISSB and ESRS can be confusing, especially when they have landed in detail in the market nearly simultaneously. Figures 8.1 and 8.2 can hopefully give you a bit more information on how they compare. It may be that 2023 will have proven to be a tipping point in the creation of a global sustainability data disclosure standard. At the time of writing, it was still too early to tell.

Global views on ESG data regulations

Let's now consider what the situation is on the ground in various jurisdictions around the world, and what this means for your organization. We'll start with the UK.

Looking across the Channel from the EU at the UK

The UK has drawn on the TCFD recommendations extensively. The UK used the TCFD to be a world leader in formulating recommendations for voluntary disclosures for listed companies. In the lead-up to the 2021 COP26 conference in Glasgow, the UK government announced that these recommendations would gradually be made mandatory – first for large, listed firms, but then encompassing an increasingly wider remit in the years to follow. This is an example of how the UK used hosting COP26 to focus on domestic sustainability data policy advancements.

Changes and alignment with TCFD go further in the UK. From 6 April 2022, any UK retailer employing more than 500 employees, or with £500 million or more in turnover, has been obliged to comply with TCFD disclosure requirements. Smaller businesses will need to start doing this kind of reporting from 2025.

Many suppliers will face pressure to start making environmental and emissions data available before that deadline. Large retail customers, for example, will need to know what's happening in their smaller suppliers' processes, as this information is required in their own compliance data. This is the power vested in Scope 3 emissions disclosures that we reviewed in Chapter 3. This means that even smaller firms will begin to see the need to start implementing ESG auditing and reporting, to stay competitive in the UK.

What's happening in Asia and the Pacific

Singapore

The shift from voluntary to mandatory reporting on ESG data is also evident in the case of Singapore. In 2016, Singapore Exchange introduced mandatory sustainability reporting for all listed companies. The requirement aligns Singapore's regulatory system with international reporting standards like GRI and SASB.

Singapore's central bank, the Monetary Authority of Singapore (MAS), has also introduced new rules for funds focusing on ESG issues similar to the EU's SFDR, which we reviewed in the previous chapter. These guidelines took effect on 1 January 2023, and require ESG funds to share information regularly and keep investors informed about their progress towards their ESG goals every year.

Funds must share details about their focus areas, how they choose investments, their investment strategies, the way they spread their money across different assets, and any risks or challenges tied to their strategies. To qualify as an ESG fund, they must use at least two-thirds of their net assets for investments that align with their sustainability strategies. In addition, the funds must choose names that accurately represent their focus on ESG issues. If they use words like 'sustainable' in their name, it should be clear that their investments genuinely reflect this commitment.

As financiers need to demonstrate their own ESG credentials, they will need the organizations they finance to do so too. Singapore is an example of the access to capital use case at work.

In addition, the Singapore government promulgated the Green Finance Action Plan in 2019, which includes initiatives such as green bonds, sustainability-linked loans and green insurance products. The government has also established the Singapore Green Plan 2030, which stipulates the country's ESG goals for the year in question. These include increasing the transition to renewable energy, reducing GHG emissions, improving waste management and enhancing biodiversity.

China

China is often perceived as a villain in the sustainability space. Its status as the world's largest GHG emitter is widely publicized (usually without the much more flattering – and reasonable – per capita equivalents being considered). The nation is also often accused of lagging in genuine attempts to address sustainability.

But China's stock exchange has made a significant push to include sustainability considerations. In fact, the country's Green Bond Catalogue predated the EU Taxonomy. In recent years, China has emerged as the largest green bond market globally, reflecting its commitment to promoting sustainable development and addressing environmental challenges. In 2022, China issued the largest value of green bonds of any nation in the world, at a total of $76.25 billion. Deloitte analysts forecast that the figure for 2023 may reach $100 billion (S&P Global Market Intelligence, 2023).

China's Green Bond Catalogue, officially known as the 'Green Bond Endorsed Project Catalogue', is a set of guidelines that outline the types of projects eligible for green bond financing. It was first introduced in 2015 by the People's Bank of China (PBOC), the National Development and Reform Commission (NDRC), and the China Securities Regulatory Commission (CSRC) to promote the development of the green bond market and support China's transition to a low-carbon and sustainable economy.

It categorizes eligible projects into six main sectors: energy conservation and efficiency improvement; pollution prevention and control; resource conservation and recycling; clean transportation; clean energy; and ecological protection and climate change adaptation.

The Green Bond Catalogue is thus an essential tool in China's green finance landscape, helping to standardize green bond issuances and providing clarity for market participants. It is also an evolving document, with revisions and updates being made periodically to reflect new developments and best practices in the green bond market, both domestically and internationally.

In 2020, the CSRC and the Ministry of Ecology and Environment released the updated 'Guidelines for Environmental Information Disclosure of Listed Companies', which requires listed companies to disclose environmental information in their annual and interim reports. The Guidelines apply to all listed companies on China's stock exchanges, regardless of their size or industry.

However, companies in industries with significant environmental impacts or those that have experienced impactful environmental incidents may face higher expectations and scrutiny regarding their environmental disclosures.

Under the Guidelines, companies are required to disclose information on their environmental impact, environmental management system, and environmental goals, among other aspects. The Guidelines provide a general framework for companies to disclose their environmental information, but do not specify a strict format or template for the disclosures. However, listed companies in China are still required to follow certain standards and requirements set by the CSRC, the Shanghai Stock Exchange and the Shenzhen Stock Exchange.

Companies in industries with significant environmental impacts, such as mining, steel and electricity generation, face more stringent requirements regarding environmental performance disclosure. These requirements are imposed and monitored by the Ministry of Ecology and Environment and other industry-specific regulatory authorities.

The requirements vary across industries, but some common aspects include increased frequency of reporting, more comprehensive information on their emissions, real-time monitoring data, and comprehensive environmental impact assessments.

Finally, China has a set of requirements pertaining to the reporting requirements of state-owned organizations. The State-owned Assets Supervision and Administration Commission (SASAC) is the regulatory body responsible for overseeing and managing China's state-owned enterprises (SOEs). Over the years, the SASAC has issued several guidelines to promote and improve ESG disclosure and performance among SOEs.

The most recent of these was 'Guiding Opinions on Strengthening the Work of Central Enterprises in Fulfilling Social Responsibilities in the New Era', issued in 2021. This guidance document covers a wide range of ESG issues, including environmental protection, resource conservation, employee rights, supply chain management and community engagement. The document also urges central SOEs to enhance the transparency and quality of their ESG disclosures.

While the SASAC's guidelines mainly apply to central SOEs under its direct supervision, the principles and requirements can also provide a reference for local SOEs managed by provincial or municipal SASACs. The guidelines and requirements emphasize the importance of comprehensive, transparent and high-quality ESG disclosures to help drive improvements in the overall ESG performance of China's state-owned enterprises.

New Zealand

The New Zealand government made climate-related financial disclosures mandatory for banks, insurers, investment managers and publicly listed companies from 1 January 2023. In practice, this legislation will affect about 200 organizations in the country to begin with.

For other organizations, the pre-existing recommendation of voluntary reporting remains in place, and it can be expected that wider swathes of the market will come under mandatory reporting requirements sooner rather than later. New Zealand's reporting requirements are based on the TCFD framework.

Australia

Australia has been notoriously behind in its overall sustainability policies. In 2020, the Australian Securities and Investments Commission (ASIC) revised its guidelines on climate risk disclosure, encouraging companies to adopt the TCFD recommendations. Certain ESG disclosures are mandated under the terms of pre-existing legislation, such as the Climate Change Act of 2022 and the Modern Slavery Act of 2018.

The ISSB standardized set of ESG reporting requirements is expected to be implemented by Australia on a mandatory basis when it is issued.

India

In FY 2021–22, the Indian financial authorities implemented a voluntary ESG reporting regime in which large organizations were encouraged to disclose relevant data. However, when only 175 organizations made such disclosures, a mandatory reporting framework was imposed starting from 2023.

Requirements for these reports will be derived from the Securities and Exchange Board of India's (SEBI) Business Responsibility Reporting (BRR) criteria, and will apply to the 1,000 largest organizations in the country, by market capitalization. The BRR format contains various sections addressing each of the nine principles observed and requires companies to provide both qualitative and quantitative information related to their ESG practices and performance.

The financial regulator has floated the idea of a ratings system based on these disclosures, to enhance the consistency and reliability of ESG information provided to the market. From FY 2024–25, the 250 largest locally listed organizations will also be required to provide data from their value chains, in line with equivalent developments in the EU and elsewhere. There are also proposals pertaining to ESG investing, intended to make the requirements in this area more watertight.

While India may be lagging behind other jurisdictions in some respects, it has devoted more attention to the S of ESG than most others. For example, India's Companies Act requires at least one female director on the board of every listed company, as well as every other public company with a paid-up share capital of $13.4 million or more, or turnover of $40.3 million or more. Additionally, the 2,000 largest listed companies (by market capitalization) are required to have at least one independent female director on their board.

Japan

Japan tightened up its ESG reporting regulations in 2022. The Japan Financial Services Agency has proposed an amendment to the relevant legal provisions that will mandate the reporting of a range of ESG data for all listed companies in Japan from 31 March 2023. Organizations will need to add the relevant reporting to their securities registration statement and incorporate an ESG section in their annual securities report. The new disclosure requirements include subsections pertaining to governance, risk management, strategy, and index and target.

They will also need to provide information on the number of women in management, the number of male employees taking paternity leave, and differences in remuneration between male and female employees. It has been hinted that the currently voluntary 'sustainability' component will soon be made mandatory.

Such sustainability disclosures are based on the Code of Conduct for ESG Evaluation and Data Providers, which was finalized on 15 December 2022. The code implements a 'comply or explain' approach, and is intended to ensure transparency and a level playing field between potentially varying standards adopted by ESG evaluation and data providers; to address potential conflicts of interest, such as ESG evaluation and data providers also providing consulting services to the company under evaluation; and to ensure robust and high-quality evaluations.

Across the pond: the Americas

USA

The USA has been a lot slower than places like the EU and the UK to move towards mandatory disclosure, but even there, some requirements are now beginning to be implemented. The SEC has long required organizations to disclose ESG data that may be 'material' to investors, without applying any specific framework for this. In practice, this has therefore left much to the discretion of the discloser. In 2022, however, the regulator issued a raft of proposals to systematize such reporting.

The SEC's climate disclosure rule proposal of 21 March 2022 moves towards the broadest corporate ESG data disclosure requirement ever proposed in the USA. Aiming to improve the consistency, quality and comparability of company-reported climate-related risks, the rule will mandate reporting on GHG emissions and a range of climate-related financial data and qualitative disclosures. In some cases, GHG emissions data will need to cover Scope 1, 2 and 3, along with other relevant aspects.

For 'large accelerated filer' organizations, the proposal is for all data except that pertaining to Scope 3 GHG emissions to be required from FY 2023 (to be reported in 2024), and Scope 3 GHG emissions data to be required from FY 2024. For accelerated and non-accelerated filers, the timeframe shifts back one year for each requirement. Smaller reporting companies (those with <$250 million in public float) would be required to report the same data one year after these in turn – although it is proposed that smaller reporting companies be exempted from Scope 3 disclosures.

This systematic onboarding will allow for companies to get prepared, but the timeline is still tight. Firms with US-based operations, capital market listings or supply chain elements in the country need to get prepared now for future disclosures. And, of course, in any multiparty democracy, things can change from administration to administration. Under the Trump administration, ESG requirements were rolled back significantly, while Joe Biden's has moved to make them more binding, along with broad legislative interventions such as the Inflation Reduction Act (IRA). Much depends on which party is in power.

Canada

The Canadian Securities Administrators (CSA) have been working on improving ESG disclosure requirements for companies listed on Canadian stock exchanges. From 2024, banks, insurance companies and federally regulated financial institutions will be required to provide specific ESG reporting and climate disclosures. As has occurred in other countries, these requirements can be expected to be rolled out to other sectors soon after.

As evidenced by the action in multiple jurisdictions, there's a distinct global trend of voluntary measures being made mandatory, first for larger organizations, but trickling down to smaller ones a few years later. These developments demonstrate the value of alignment with what are currently voluntary but recommended best practices.

Staying abreast of developments in the area will have a wide range of benefits for organizations. By keeping an eye on recommended best practices, organizations will be able to anticipate upcoming changes in the regulatory and legislative frameworks that will govern their operations. This will give them more time to adjust their own processes, and to identify opportunities presented by the changes. All such factors indicate the value in being proactive in addressing ESG issues, not just at the mandatory level, but also in terms of what is currently only recommended.

Latin America

Latin America has been slower to adopt sustainable finance regulation compared to other regions, but there have been some positive developments in recent years. Brazil has introduced the Green Finance Programme, which provides incentives for banks and other financial institutions to invest in sustainable projects.

Mexico has also introduced the Sustainable Stock Exchange Initiative, which aims to promote sustainability reporting and the integration of ESG factors into investment decisions.

Africa

In Africa, the level of regulations and guidelines regarding ESG reporting varies more than elsewhere. So, while some countries have established regulations and guidelines for ESG reporting, others have yet to implement formal reporting requirements.

In South Africa, for instance, the Johannesburg Stock Exchange has set up a Socially Responsible Investment (SRI) index and the Ghana Stock Exchange with its Sustainability and Social Responsibility (SSR) index has something similar. The Nigerian Stock Exchange has its ESG reporting framework, while Kenya's Capital Markets Authority and Egypt's Financial Supervisory Authority both issue guidelines encouraging listed companies to disclose information about their environmental and social performance in their annual reports.

However, there are still significant challenges in promoting sustainable finance in Africa, including a lack of reliable data on ESG risks and opportunities, limited availability of sustainable financial products, and the need for greater awareness and education on sustainable finance among investors and other stakeholders.

Stock markets and financial centres

Global capital markets provide us with a good reference point for sustainable finance regulations. The need for ESG data disclosures is at the heart of most disclosures being promoted by financial centres.

The UN-backed Sustainable Stock Exchanges Initiative (SSEI) was launched in 2015, with the goal of getting every stock exchange in the world to develop tools, methods and requirements for the reporting of ESG data on the part of listed companies. To this end, the SSEI has developed a 'Model Guidance' template that exchanges can use in developing a set of ESG reporting requirements suited for their own purposes.

An influential adoption of the SSEI's Model Guidance has been that of the World Federation of Stock Exchanges (WFE). The WFE's ESG Guidance and Metrics are intended as a reference for exchanges that want to introduce, enhance or mandate ESG reporting on their markets. The significant developments in the 2018 version include the following:

- Recognizing intervening sustainability developments, such as the UN Sustainable Development Goals (SDGs) and the TCFD recommendations.

- Incorporating feedback received from investor groups on the initial WFE Guidance and Metrics document.

- Adjusting the metrics based on implementation experience in certain markets. There are now 30 baseline metrics (33 in 2015) that form the revised guidance, covering indicators across a range of ESG categories, such as: emissions intensity; climate risk mitigation; gender pay ratio; human rights; ethics and anti-corruption; and disclosure practices.

- Specifying that investors are the target audience for listed company ESG disclosures. Exchanges should therefore focus on ensuring the availability of investor-relevant, decision-useful information.

- Providing greater guidance around ESG report preparation, across four key areas:

  o Governance/responsibility and oversight: Reporting issuers could include a board statement outlining how the company determines ESG issues; how they are embedded in the firm's strategic direction; and how progress is reviewed and measured.

  o Clarity of purpose/clear link to business value: Issuers should articulate how the ESG issues they have identified link back to value creation/destruction.

  o Materiality: Issuers should provide investors with information about their materiality determination process.

o Quality/frequency of reporting: Issuers should ensure reporting is accurate; aligns to one of the internationally recognized reporting standards; and is timely (WFE Research Team, 2018).

More than 35 exchanges globally have issued or announced plans to issue ESG reporting guidance for listed companies. Worldwide distribution is varied, however, with some regions performing better than others – and there are some nifty novel metrics with which to assess this.

Another lens to consider global engagement in sustainability data disclosures is through looking at global financial centres. Z/Yen has created the Global Green Finance Index (GGFI), the eleventh edition of which was published in April 2023. One of the primary aims of the index is to address the problems of the complexity and cost of ESG reporting, its liability to greenwashing, and its low impact on carbon emissions.

The GGFI 10 raised the likelihood of the increased centrality of carbon pricing in sustainability regulation in coming decades, and the eleventh edition confirms this, finding that carbon markets are now listed as one of the top factors with an impact on climate change. It also emphasizes the importance of system-wide intervention, considering the economy as a whole, and the importance of the availability of relevant skills in the workforce.

The GGFI 11 evaluates the green finance offerings of 86 major global financial hubs, providing rankings for the various centres:

- London retained its first position in the index, with New York moving up one place to take second place.

- Washington moved into the top 10, replacing Sydney.

- Western European centres take six of the top 10 places, with US centres taking the other four top 10 places.

- The margins separating centres at the top of the index continues to be tight in GGFI 11. Among the top 10 centres the spread of ratings is 31 out of 1,000, compared to 42 out of 1,000 in GGFI 10.

- Confidence in green finance appears to be strong, with all centres improving their rating in GFCI 11, and the average rating up just over 10 per cent compared with GGFI 10 (Z/Yen Group Ltd, 2023a).

Figure 8.3 illustrates the GGFI 11's evaluation of regional progress in ESG reporting. As can be seen here, the Middle East and Africa region demonstrated the most significant improvements between the ninth and tenth iterations of the index, demonstrating the global penetration of green financing and the data requirements associated with it. This is further underscored by the sharp global uptick in the last six months.

Figure 8.3 Regional performance in ESG finance reporting, GGFI 11

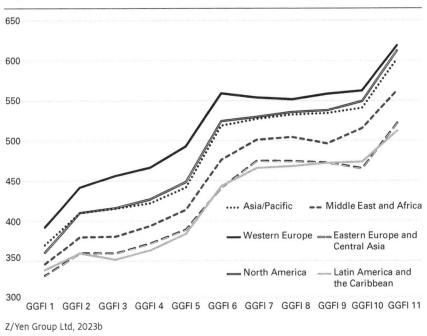

Z/Yen Group Ltd, 2023b

The GGFI 11 notes that Policy and Regulatory Frameworks and International Initiatives were rated equally as the most important drivers of green finance, with Risk Management Frameworks being rated the third most important (Z/Yen Group Ltd, 2023b). The all-round competitiveness of green funds in all jurisdictions also indicates that these forces will continue to provide strong impetus.

This is certainly not a passing fad. The GGFI takes a very long-term perspective, and in this view, ESG trends up and up.

Junior boards and sustainability data

Several national stock markets have dedicated junior boards or alternative markets for smaller companies, which typically have less stringent listing requirements and provide an easier access to capital for start-ups and smaller organizations. For example, the Australian Securities Exchange (ASX) operates the ASX Emerging Companies Index, which focuses on small-cap companies; and in China, the ChiNext Market, a part of the Shenzhen Stock Exchange (SZSE), is designed for innovative, fast-growing SMEs.

The less onerous disclosure and listing requirements on 'junior' exchange boards also include less onerous and prescriptive ESG data disclosure regulations. As noted in the previous section, overall, the more stringent reporting requirements are being applied to larger organizations first in all jurisdictions, with much of this remaining voluntary for smaller ones. But this does not mean there are no ESG reporting guidelines for junior boards. Some markets geared towards smaller companies are already putting in place some requirements important for companies interested in accessing these markets to be aware of.

Let's look at London's 'junior' market.

The AIM market, operated by the London Stock Exchange, is a sub-market designed for smaller, growing companies that may not meet the listing requirements of the main market. There is no minimum market capitalization requirement, and in 2021 the largest listed firm was worth around £4 billion. They do, however, tend to have high growth potential, with the purpose of the AIM being to help them access the capital they need to fund this growth.

Under the AIM Rules for Companies, companies listed on the AIM market must maintain a website containing specific information, including details about their corporate governance. While there is no explicit requirement for ESG disclosure, the London Stock Exchange encourages AIM companies to follow best practices in corporate governance, which often include addressing ESG issues.

AIM-listed companies are not required to comply with the UK Corporate Governance Code, which applies to premium-listed companies on the main market. However, AIM-listed companies must disclose which recognized corporate governance code they have chosen to apply and explain any non-compliance. Many of these codes, such as the Quoted Companies Alliance Corporate Governance Code, include recommendations related to ESG matters.

For the moment, the mandatory TCFD-aligned disclosure requirements announced by the UK government primarily apply to premium-listed companies (as noted previously). The TCFD disclosure requirement will nevertheless become mandatory in 2025, and large listed firms will increasingly need their suppliers, partners and customers to provide relatively detailed data on ESG factors, for the compliance of the former with what are already mandatory requirements.

Similarly, as ESG factors become increasingly important to investors, AIM-listed companies may face growing pressure to disclose ESG information, even in the absence of explicit regulatory requirements. Demonstrating a commitment to ESG principles will improve an organization's reputation, attract investment and reduce risk exposure.

Other junior boards show equivalent trends. In China, for example, the SZSE's junior board ChiNext imposes the same requirements as for firms listed on the main board – with the CSRC's 2019 guidelines applying to all listed companies. Insofar as these firms are smaller than their main board-listed counterparts, however, the special provisions imposed in China for high-impact organizations will generally not apply.

While NASDAQ's and Australia's Emerging Companies Index reporting recommendations remain voluntary (somewhat emphatically so, in the case of the former), they are being systematized and standardized, and broader trends suggest that it is only a matter of time before a wide range of information becomes mandatory. NASDAQ's ESG Reporting Guide of 2018 is based on frameworks such as the GRI, SASB and TCFD recommendations. Australia's ASIC recommends that all listed companies follow TCFD guidelines and adopt ISSB standards as these are published.

Global rules and standards – a continuing journey

As this chapter has shown, global rules and regulations relating to ESG disclosure demonstrate steady development. These developments include the creation of standards. While we know from the journey taken by financial data standards that the end result may never be a single global agreed standard for ESG data disclosures, progress to codifying the definitions of datasets helps to make disclosures interoperable.

With organizations such as the ISSB, EFRAG and the SEC producing tools, standards and expectations in the area are becoming clearer around the world. In practice, requiring enhanced data reporting from the high impact organizations forces other upstream and downstream organizations to start collecting and providing similar information. A general trend is for initially voluntary requirements to become mandatory – sooner rather than later, and with increasing speed, as legislative momentum builds.

All such factors underscore the value of understanding and implementing acknowledged best practices pertaining to ESG data collection and disclosure, even for organizations that are not currently mandated to do so. ESG data is going to be central to competitiveness for a long time to come. Make sure you're not left behind.

Where in the world are ETSs currently operative?

We reviewed ETSs and carbon markets and how they can be effective in a number of the ABCs of sustainability data use cases in Chapter 5. The first framework for a carbon credit market originated with the 1997 Kyoto Protocol, an international treaty between 192 parties. The Kyoto Protocol envisaged a global carbon market acting at an international level, with nations committing to emissions allowances, and under-emitters selling their offsets to over-emitters without borders.

This has yet to be achieved on the global stage, but there are many examples of ETSs at work in various countries and regions. We will outline a number of these below so you can better understand how your organization can consider their use or be aware of their requirements if you are in scope of their carbon emission limits.

International

The United Nations

The framework established by the Kyoto Protocol has since been superseded by the Paris Agreement of 2015, but the latter includes provisions for continuity between the two. Under the International Emissions Trading (IET) system, countries can buy and sell carbon credits to make up for any gaps in meeting their emission targets. Countries that have cut more emissions than required can sell their extra credits to countries that are falling short.

The system is administered and monitored by the United Nations Framework Convention on Climate Change (UNFCCC) secretariat (usually called UN Climate Change). The jurisdiction is international, encompassing all national signatories to the treaty, and administered according to the terms of the Marrakesh Accords (UNFCCC, 2017).

These treaties also make provisions for infrastructure and development projects focused on clean energy and GHG emissions reductions, such as the Clean Development Mechanism (CDM) and Joint Implementation (JI). Via the CDM, a country can earn certified emission reduction (CER) credits, each equivalent to one tonne of CO_2, by funding emission reduction projects in developing countries, which can be used to meet part of their emission reduction targets. JIs do the same, but via shared planning, development and construction between the partner countries, rather than just investment.

These mechanisms are intended to promote investment and sharing of expertise and resources between developed and developing countries, and help transform the economies of the latter. Basically, this system allows country-level players to interact with the carbon markets.

Private organizations get involved in such initiatives, and large organizations are in a position to influence national policy and how the country goes about meeting its obligations under the treaty. But the primary parties to the framework thus established are the nations themselves. Nations have established targets, which they seek to meet by managing the emissions of the organizations operating within their jurisdiction. The frameworks by which they do so then become the national-level ETS instruments that govern organizational emissions.

The European Union

The European Union's ETS is the oldest in the world, and the largest in terms of trading volume and value. Initiated in 2005, it has completed three phases, with the fourth having begun in 2021 and being scheduled to run until 2030. The terms of the ETS vary by sector. The strongest emphasis is on the energy-intensive sites termed 'stationary installations': carbon-intensive plants for the production of energy, metals, minerals and paper. Full details on the sites that fall under this category are listed in Annex I of the EU ETS Directive, 2003/87/EC (European Commission, 2003).

For these installations, a fixed EU-wide cap on emissions is established, and this is reduced by 2.2 per cent every year. In practice, this brings allowances down by 43 million tonnes annually (out of around 2 billion tonnes).

The third phase faced numerous challenges, demonstrating some of the difficulties facing large-scale ETSs. For example, the third phase saw an oversupply of allowances, which led to a decrease in the price of carbon. The oversupply resulted from a range of factors, including economic downturn that reduced activity; excessive free allowances; and the impact of related initiatives to promote clean energy.

This price volatility not only undermined the incentive for firms to reduce their emissions in the short term, but also potentially the effectiveness of the ETS as a tool for encouraging long-term investment in low-carbon technologies. The third phase of the EU's ETS therefore illustrated a number of unforeseen challenges and limitations of the mechanism as a means of using the market to shape organizations' carbon profiles. In response, the Market Stability Reserve (MSR) decreased the auction allowance by close to 40 per cent in 2021, the first year of the fourth phase.

Allowances are allocated through a combination of benchmark-based free allocation and auction. Income from the selling of allowances goes to member states, with the requirement that at least 50 per cent of these be used for energy- and climate-related targets. In Phase 4, the EU ETS will not permit the trading of offsets and credits. The EU ETS is linked with the Swiss version (discussed below), and allowances can be traded interchangeably between the two.

In Phase 4, the power sector is to operate on a 100 per cent auction basis. This does, however, include some scope for lower-income member states to grant free allocation to energy providers to promote modernization and industry diversification. For industry, benchmarks will be based on previous phases, adjusted in line with annual reductions. Benchmarks may also be updated in line with new technologies or changes in production patterns.

Non-compliance is penalized with fines of €100 per excess tCO_2, and a 'name and shame' system that makes such organizations' non-compliance public.

National

China

China's national ETS was launched in 2021 and is already the world's largest in terms of covered allocations (ICAP, 2022a). For the present, it includes power plants that produce more than 26,000 tonnes of CO_2 a year (including those that are part of other industries). The system covers over 4 billion tonnes of CO_2, which is more than 40 per cent of the country's total carbon emissions.

Organizations are allocated an allowance on the basis of benchmarking. There are four distinct benchmarks according to type and size of the plant. Allocations are adjusted to reflect actual generation. China Certified Emissions Reductions (CCERs) are provided for offsets and can be used against up to 5 per cent of an organization's verified emissions. At present, only compliance-required organizations can participate in the carbon credit market.

South Korea

Launched on 1 January 2015, the South Korean Emissions Trading Scheme (KETS) was initiated as part of South Korea's pledge at the Copenhagen Accord of 2009 to reduce GHG emissions by 30 per cent by 2020. The KETS applies to over 525 companies, which are accountable for approximately

68 per cent of the nation's GHG output (International Emissions Trading Association, 2016).

The KETS covers 684 of the country's largest emitters in various sectors, including power, industry, buildings, waste, transport and domestic aviation (ICAP, 2023). Credits are allocated through free allocation and auctioning. At least 10 per cent of allowances must be auctioned, while free allocation is provided for energy-intensive trade-exposed sectors based on production cost and trade intensity benchmarks.

The scheme also awards more free allowances to the top 10 per cent most efficient covered entities per sector and those that implement new energy efficiency measures. In the first phase of the KETS (2015 to 2017), the government allocated 1.69 billion Korean Allowance Unit (KAU) emission permits to 525 companies. The second phase (2018 to 2020) saw permits for 1.8 billion KAU, and the third phase allocates 2.7 billion KAU (Korean Joongan Daily, 2021).

The KETS has encountered similar difficulties to those seen in the EU, with the government being forced to enforce a temporary price floor in 2021 in response to plunging demand. This was in addition to a reserve price that is a constant aspect of the market, and which is based on the average price over various points during the previous three months.

Non-compliance with the KETS incurs a penalty set to three times the average market price, with a cap of ₩100,000 (about $86) per tonne of CO_2 equivalent (Kim and Yu, 2018).

The UK

The UK ETS went live on 1 January 2021, taking the place that before Brexit was filled by the EU ETS (GOV.UK, 2022). It is based on the fourth phase of the EU ETS, with requirements and provisions having largely been carried over seamlessly – partly in the anticipation of a future interoperability agreement, partly out of convenience (the UK having played a big role in developing the EU ETS anyway).

For example, the scope is the same (mandatory participation for the power sector, energy-intensive industries and aviation), the cap level has been transposed from the UK's calculated portion in the EU ETS (less 5 per cent, because of UKIP), and monitoring, reporting and verification requirements are the same.

About 40 million allowances are provided for free to carbon-intensive stationary installations for which the cost would otherwise be a big enough competitive disadvantage to incentivize them to relocate operations. Additional allowances are traded via an auction-based pricing mechanism.

The final price is determined by the price at which the total number of allowances demanded matches or goes above the total number of allowances being sold, to ensure that cost is being calibrated according to supply and demand. However, if this price is much lower than what allowances are being traded for in other markets, then the final price in the auction is raised. In this case, the price becomes that of the lowest bid that is not significantly lower than the current market price. There is also an auction reserve price of £22 (which is likely to be raised in coming years).

Bids that do not meet the price established are unsuccessful, which means that not all available allowances will be sold at every auction. For example, the auction of 6 October 2021 put about 5 million allowances up for sale. The pricing mechanism produced a unit price of £60, and about a million allowances received a bid below this threshold. The bids were therefore unsuccessful, and the allowances were not sold.

Auctions are held every two weeks, allowing organizations to assess their needs and responsibilities on an ongoing basis, and to make adjustments as necessary. The total number of allowances available for purchase in 2023 is about 79 million. A carbon credit futures market has also been established in connection with the UK ETS, called the UK Allowance Futures Contract.

Switzerland

The Swiss ETS was established in 2008. Initially a voluntary system, in 2013 participation was made mandatory for large, energy-intensive companies. Switzerland and the EU linked their ETS systems in 2020, allowing participants in the Swiss system to use allowances from the EU system for compliance, and vice versa.

The interoperability between the EU and Swiss markets requires that the regulations and requirements of the markets align. For example, the same entities and sectors are covered: electricity generation, emissions-intensive industrial entities (mainly the cement, chemicals, pharmaceuticals, paper, refining and steel sectors), and aviation. On this basis, about 60 Swiss entities were subject to the requirements in 2022.

Credits are allocated on the same basis as the EU (benchmarking and auction), and non-compliance penalized in the same way, with fines of €100 per excess tCO_2, as well as naming and shaming.

Notable sub-nationals

California

We called out California's ETS in Chapter 7. California's cap-and-trade programme, launched in 2013, is the fourth largest in the world. The system is linked with Quebec's cap-and-trade programme, allowing businesses in one jurisdiction to use emission allowances issued by the other.

The California Air Resources Board implements and enforces the programme, which first applied to entities emitting 25,000 tCO_2e per year or more. The programme's GHG emission cap declined by 3 per cent annually from 2015 through to 2020, and it is planned to decrease an additional 5 per cent annually from 2021 to 2030. Emission allowances are distributed by a mix of free allocation and quarterly auctions. The majority of allowances are sold at auction, generating significant revenue for the state (Center for Climate and Energy Solutions, nd).

Impressively, the compliance rate for the cap-and-trade programme has been near 100 per cent at each compliance event.

Quebec

The Quebec cap-and-trade system started its operations in 2013, formally linking its system with California's in 2014. The system was implemented in phases over several years, each with a different compliance period. The first compliance period started in 2013 and lasted for two years, followed by several three-year periods.

The cap on emissions began at 23.2 million tCO_2e in 2013, then rose to 65.3 million tCO_2e in 2015 as the system expanded to include fuel distribution. Over time, the cap has been gradually reduced at an average rate of between 2.2 per cent and 3.5 per cent per year (ICAP, 2022b).

The system covers fuel combustion emissions in the power, buildings, transport and industrial sectors, as well as industrial process emissions, accounting for approximately 80 per cent of Quebec's GHG emissions. Participation is mandatory for organizations that emit 25,000 tCO_2e or more per year, or fuel distributors that distribute 200 litres or more of fuel.

Most allowances are auctioned, but some are freely allocated to emissions-intensive, trade-exposed sectors and to electricity producers with fixed-price sales contracts concluded before the announcement of the system. Quebec also maintains an allowance reserve account to adjust levels of free allocation and sell to entities that do not have enough allowances to cover their obligations.

The cap for 2023 is set at 52.8 million tCO_2e. As of 2022, the average auction price was CAD 36.29, with total revenue since the beginning of the programme reaching CAD 7 billion (ICAP, 2022b).

Quebec is planning to reduce the level of free allocation for the 2024–30 period based on the cap decline factor, an extra expected effort based on the carbon leakage risk, and the proportion of fixed process emissions. A trajectory modulation factor will also be introduced, which will reduce the rate of reduction in the initial years and increase it in the later ones. A portion of the allowances resulting from the reduction in the level of free allocation will be put up for auction on behalf of businesses. The proceeds from the sale of these allowances will be set aside on behalf of each business to finance projects related to the climate transition.

It is anticipated that this new approach will result in a reduction of 2.9 million tCO_2e free allowances between 2024 and 2030.

As we can see from the above systems, ETSs and carbon markets are spreading around the world, with more and more entities seeing their value as a means of advancing sustainability goals. However, as previous chapters have outlined, they are not without their critics. The SBTi argues that they can promote complacency and distract from the more fundamental changes that are needed to head off global warming. It does nevertheless appear likely that ETSs will play an increasingly prevalent role in business and industry for a good few decades to come. You'd therefore do well to familiarize yourself with the current provisions in your jurisdiction and keep an eye on forthcoming developments. Doing so will enable you to capitalize on the opportunities they present to the greatest possible extent.

This chapter's tour of various global jurisdictions should leave you with the clear message that sustainability data disclosures are not a topic limited to a few countries. It is a global discussion and a global effort. Regulations, standards, tools and trading markets are all focused on improving transparency for the global ecosystem to make decisions to allocate all kinds of resources to sustainability-positive organizations.

But – what is a sustainability-positive organization? And how can you be sure you're properly representing the organization you are associated with?

In the next chapter, we consider this within the next topic for a deep dive: greenwashing.

References

Center for Climate and Energy Solutions (nd) California cap and trade, www.c2es. org/content/california-cap-and-trade/ (archived at https://perma.cc/4VQC-ZX5B)

European Commission (2003) Directive 2003/87/EC establishing a scheme for greenhouse gas emission allowance trading within the Community and amending Council Directive 96/61/EC, https://eur-lex.europa.eu/legal-content/EN/TXT/PDF/?uri=CELEX:32003L0087 (archived at https://perma.cc/9C7Q-6D9W)

Gagnon, S (2022) Frameworks explained: What is the ISSB?, Sustain.Life, www.sustain.life/blog/frameworks-explained-issb (archived at https://perma.cc/Y9EG-8KTV)

GOV.UK (2022) Policy paper: UK Emissions Trading Scheme markets, www.gov.uk/government/publications/uk-emissions-trading-scheme-markets/uk-emissions-trading-scheme-markets (archived at https://perma.cc/TZ95-LZMM)

ICAP (2022a) *Emissions Trading Worldwide: Status Report 2022*, https://icapcarbonaction.com/system/files/document/220408_icap_report_rz_web.pdf (archived at https://perma.cc/6SJ8-HLAS)

ICAP (2022b) Canada – Quebec cap-and-trade system, https://icapcarbonaction.com/system/files/ets_pdfs/icap-etsmap-factsheet-73.pdf (archived at https://perma.cc/R4X2-T9G8)

ICAP (2023) Korea Emissions Trading Scheme, https://icapcarbonaction.com/en/ets/korea-emissions-trading-scheme (archived at https://perma.cc/LB29-LZKU)

International Emissions Trading Association (2016) *Republic of Korea: An emissions case study*, www.ieta.org/resources/2016%20Case%20Studies/Korean_Case_Study_2016.pdf (archived at https://perma.cc/9VSY-R56X)

Kim, W and Yu, J (2018) The effect of the penalty system on market prices in the Korea ETS, *Carbon Management*, 9 (2) pp 145–54

Korean Joongan Daily (2021) Carbon trading, at six years old, still has teething problems, https://koreajoongangdaily.joins.com/2021/06/05/business/industry/emissions-permits-emissions-trading-carbon-emissions/20210605070100841.html (archived at https://perma.cc/L4DY-GNAL)

S&P Global Market Intelligence (2023) China to keep lead in green bond market amid alignment with global standards, www.spglobal.com/marketintelligence/en/news-insights/latest-news-headlines/china-to-keep-lead-in-green-bond-market-amid-alignment-with-global-standards-74039783# (archived at https://perma.cc/6UHN-P4UA)

Toplensky, R (2023) Pro take: Forget the SEC, international climate reporting standards could become the global baseline, *Wall Street Journal*, www.wsj.com/articles/pro-take-forget-the-sec-international-climate-reporting-standards-could-become-the-global-baseline-ea01d05a (archived at https://perma.cc/FK95-JND5)

UNFCCC (2017) Greenhouse gas inventories and additional information submitted by Parties included in Annex I Reporting, accounting and review requirements relating to the second commitment period of the Kyoto Protocol, https://unfccc.int/files/ghg_data/kp_data_unfccc/compilation_and_accounting_data/application/pdf/compilation_cmp_decisions_for_2nd_commitment_period_v01.06_with_convention_6_july17.pdf (archived at https://perma.cc/8SXW-XKA8)

WFE Research Team (2018) The WFE publishes revised ESG guidance and metrics, https://focus.world-exchanges.org/articles/wfe-publishes-revised-esg-guidance-metrics (archived at https://perma.cc/M3Q7-SLGK)

Z/Yen Group Ltd (2023a) The Global Green Finance Index 11 Supplement: The carbon transition, Long Finance, www.longfinance.net/publications/long-finance-reports/the-global-green-finance-index-11-supplement-the-carbon-transition/ (archived at https://perma.cc/7F54-ZK9N)

Z/Yen Group Ltd (2023b) The Global Green Finance Index 11, Long Finance, www.longfinance.net/media/documents/GGFI_11_Report_2022.04.20_v1.1.pub.pdf (archived at https://perma.cc/UDN3-R7W3)

Identifying greenwashing

9

REFLECTIVE QUESTIONS

- What is greenwashing?
- How can I de-risk my organization from the dangers of greenwashing?
- What can we learn from existing examples of greenwashing?

What is greenwashing?

Greenwashing refers to the practice of organizations making false or misleading claims about their environmental performance to appear more environmentally friendly than they actually are. Greenwashing is a growing problem, as organizations seek to respond to increasing public awareness of the need to address the climate crisis and associated social harms. At its most extreme, it's a form of fraud.

There are, however, numerous degrees of greenwashing that, while not representing outright criminality, are nevertheless a serious organizational liability. One good example is provided by the oil giant Shell, which asked its followers on Twitter, 'What are you willing to change to help reduce emissions?'

The seemingly innocuous question inspired a tsunami of criticism. Thousands piled in to point out the hypocrisy. Shell has systematically sought to downplay the role of its own product in climate change, and to prevent legislative and other changes to address it. People accordingly interpreted the question as an attempt to shift responsibility. Responses to the tweet pushed back against this, drawing significant attention to precisely the issues Shell appeared to be trying to minimize.

What are the risks to an organization?

Greenwashing presents numerous risks to an organization. The potential reputational damage is significant. If stakeholders become aware of the false claims, the measures taken will have outcomes diametrically opposite to those intended.

Stakeholders will perceive the organization as cynical, untrustworthy, and destructively self-interested. Direct consequences of these perceptions include consumers not purchasing the organization's products or services, and investors being reluctant to finance the organization. The indirect consequences include lasting damage to trust in the organization, which would undermine subsequent PR and marketing efforts. Both these direct and indirect outcomes entail significant risk of financial cost.

Greenwashing can also lead to legal consequences, as regulators may take action against companies that make false or misleading claims about their environmental performance. Increasingly commonly, investors, consumers or businesses are filing legal claims against businesses that they accuse of greenwashing.

CASE STUDY   Danimer Scientific Inc

In 2021, a group of investors brought a class-action suit against Danimer Scientific Inc, a bioplastics company. Danimer's primary market offering is a plastic substitute called Nodax, which the company states is 100 per cent biodegradable.

These claims, however, came under scrutiny, with some accusing Danimer of exaggerating the biodegradability of its product. The company's stock price dropped, and investors brought legal action against Danimer for making materially false and misleading statements regarding the green credentials of its product. While Danimer disputes the allegations, the damage to the stock price has already occurred – and further penalties may still be forthcoming.

The increasing prevalence of ESG-focused investment offerings, and of litigation focused on them, has led the US Securities and Exchange Commission (SEC) to begin formulating measures to regulate activity in this area. SEC

Commissioner Allison Herren Lee spoke about ESG in 2022. She recognized the explosive growth in investor interest and demand around (ESG) investments, and the need to protect investors by promoting transparency and accountability for investment decision-making.

Commissioner Lee suggested that market players offering ESG-related investments must fully and fairly disclose what they are selling, and act consistently with those disclosures. She was specific, and called for investors to 'say what you mean and mean what you say.'

When I met Commissioner Lee in 2019, she already held these views and was very practical and vocal about her support for measuring and managing risks of greenwashing by companies publicly listed in the USA. It took some time for the American administration to be amenable to these suggestions – further evidence of the ties between ESG disclosure directives and politics.

One means by which the SEC has sought to meet these needs is by establishing a Climate and ESG Enforcement Task Force, charged with identifying 'material gaps or misstatements in issuers' disclosure of climate risks under existing rules'. The Task Force got off to an eager start. In May 2022, it charged the investment firm BNY Mellon with material inaccuracies and omissions in ESG-related statements, leading to a $1.5 million fine and the implementation of measures to address such problems, and numerous other similar cases have been engaged.

This formalization of regulatory structures – and the authority of institutional recognition of the phenomena in question – is likely to make litigation more common in future. And once precedents have been established, it will become easier still. The case studies at the end of this section suggest that this kind of momentum has already passed a tipping point.

The EU has taken the issue of greenwashing into the world of regulatory directives. In March 2023, the European Commission published its proposed Directive on Green Claims. The proposal is the latest EU initiative to take aim at the practice of greenwashing. The EU's work is based on research. According to a study carried out by the EU on ESG claims, 53.3 per cent of claims were vague or misleading, and 40 per cent of claims were unsubstantiated (European Commission, 2020). Claims of net zero and carbon neutrality were included in areas called out as misleading (European Commission, 2023).

Greenwashing is an issue the sustainable finance world has been aware of for some time. The advent of green and sustainable taxonomies (see Chapter 5) is a direct result of worries about greenwashing in the absence of clear definitions and benchmarks for the area. And given such indeterminacy and ambiguity, definitions of what can be offered as a genuinely sustainable claim will benefit from detail, clarity and precision.

However, creating these definitions and cross-referencing their applicability and accuracy against multiple industries and use cases is a lot of work – and work that is still ongoing. In the meantime, business leaders fear being called out for greenwashing. This has spawned an unusual counter-term: greenhushing.

Greenhushing refers to the increasingly prevalent practice of organizations choosing not to provide any disclosures on their green initiatives, even when these initiatives are in good faith and achieving positive outcomes. Greenhushing is a response to the risks posed by accusations of greenwashing: in the absence of unambiguous criteria for green activities – and given the enormity of the challenges society faces in this regard – organizations can perceive a residual risk in any disclosure of green activity, insofar as any measures can be criticized for being insufficient.

Some organizations therefore opt to avoid the risks posed by greenwashing by doing without saying. Of course, this is seen by some leaders as a missed opportunity for both external and internal stakeholders to take pride in an organization's activities that are supporting a positive sustainability agenda.

As an organization's board gets familiar and comfortable with sustainability more widely, inevitably the balance between the risks of greenwashing and the missed opportunity of greenhushing must be determined. This will predominantly be governed by the organization's confidence in the claims and the data that back them up, paired with the overall risk culture of the group. Such factors vary from organization to organization and can be aided by capacity building at the level of the board of directors and C-suite on understanding the sustainability priority for their business, clients, employees and market.

Data as a solution

As the example of Shell's disastrous attempt at Twitter PR influencing shows, stakeholders are becoming better and better informed about the substantive facts of ESG – and increasingly critical of substance-less platitudes. In such a context, it's vital to substantiate your ESG disclosures with data. By collecting and making use of ESG data, your organization can ensure that it avoids the risks associated with greenwashing. Basing ESG disclosures on substantive data will ensure that any claims can be backed up, and that the organization can demonstrate genuine commitment to these goals.

CASE STUDY   Volkswagen's emissions cheating

In 2015, Volkswagen was accused of greenwashing after it was revealed that the company had installed software in its diesel cars that allowed them to cheat emissions tests. The scandal originally blew up in the USA, when it was noticed that on-road performances were not aligning with the results being reported in the official tests. This brought to light the 'defeat device' that kicked in during emissions tests, and which enabled VW to systematically misrepresent its cars' performance.

The United States Environmental Protection Agency (EPA) found that Volkswagen had intentionally programmed its cars to activate emissions controls only during laboratory emissions testing. So, while the vehicles' NOx output met US standards during regulatory testing, it increased by up to 40 times in real-world driving. The fact that this occurred in conjunction with a massive push on the company's part to sell diesel cars in the States, driven by a marketing campaign that trumpeted their low emissions, made the situation appear especially cynical.

VW's share price dropped by more than 40 per cent in three days following the first news of the scandal. The company came under legal scrutiny by regulators in countries around the world, and it was forced to recall 11 million cars. The total cost to VW of the event is estimated to have been about $30 billion.

Very few forms of greenwashing are likely to be as intentional and cynical as Volkswagen's cheating of emissions tests. Nevertheless, in a large modern organization, operations are distributed widely, and the collection and reporting of data occur across a range of independent sectors and individuals. In such circumstances, it's very easy for distorted images of the situation on the ground to be transmitted – especially in a context in which people feel pressured or incentivized to paint a green picture of things.

The road to hell is paved with good intentions, as they say, and greenwashing can arise even from a genuine commitment to ESG goals. This is why reliable data, and systematic management and handling of that data, are so important.

Transparency about the data behind the data and its handling may be even more important. ESG reporting is still a nascent and rapidly developing field, and it is widely recognized that there is huge scope for inconsistency in organizations' disclosures. Extensive work is being done to establish how this can be overcome, and how such disclosures can be standardized as outlined elsewhere in this book.

In the meantime, organizations need to work out their own approach. Legal requirements provide a basic outline, but wide discretion remains. In such a context, transparency on the data behind the data being disclosed provides a valuable means of forestalling many risks of greenwashing. By being explicit and transparent about the data on which ESG disclosures are based, your organization can ensure that it avoids any risk of accusations of greenwashing, and the various consequences of this.

Transparency of data and disclosures is not risk-free in and of itself. Most organizations operate in a competitive environment where they hold their unique selling features dear. This extends further into the public markets, where there are explicit rules to ensure that data disclosed cannot be reverse-engineered ahead of the reporting period to create advantages to investors who access this data outside the official reporting channels.

In both these contexts, an organization's leadership needs to consider the materiality of the data to competitors, the wider ecosystem (i.e. clients considering entering into contracts) and the financial community. For example, data about an organization's plans to shift to more sustainable production processes may have a bearing on its market competitiveness, and disclosing this could benefit competitors or harm investors.

The upshot of this is that transparency requires a careful balancing of competing demands and priorities. An organization needs to consider what investors and other stakeholders need to know, and what the organization needs to keep secret, and navigate a course between these two to find the balance that is best for its unique purposes.

Data limitations you need to be aware of

Limitations that should be considered include:

- How old is the data?
- Is the data still relevant?
- How are you managing misaligned data updates?
- Is the data granular enough to reflect what you are claiming? (E.g. data points from the question 'Does your business have a diversity policy? Yes or no' would not reflect the quality of that policy; it may not be fit for purpose.)

Overall, investors and stakeholders like transparency, and transparency in the sustainable data disclosed by organizations is no different. What do we mean by transparency in this context?

For example, it's crucial to be transparent about how old the data in question is, and the implications of this age. Data collection and reporting need to fit in with the operations of the organization, which means these functions usually occur at established intervals; and the time required to process, verify and double-check data interposes a further delay. Disclosed data is therefore always data about the past.

By being clear and transparent about what time period the data refers to, an organization can ensure that any disclosures take appropriate cognizance of the implications of this lag. For example, if the delay includes a significant change in operating context that affects the applicability of the data to the current situation, being clear about the impact of this will safeguard the integrity of your disclosures.

Even more fundamentally, being clear about when the data point for a quantitative data disclosure was extracted is essential for external stakeholders, including investors, to be able to compare that data to others' disclosures. For example, the disclosure of water usage at a shoe manufacturing plant dated end of 2020 may not be comparable to data of water usage at a competitor's shoe manufacturing plant dated February 2020. Both these data points are from 2020 and may reflect 12 months of usage. However, anyone who lived through the Covid-19 pandemic would know that these numbers cannot be used to derive meaningful water conservation comparisons between the firms.

Granularity of data is also important. It's one thing to claim to have a diversity policy in place, but if this was created in 1992, and hasn't been updated since, it's unlikely to have kept pace with recent developments. Even from a strictly legal perspective, laws have been passed in the interim that a diversity policy would need to account for.

Often, data mined from organizations' disclosures supply binary answers to more complicated questions. For example, a firm may have a disclosed data point related to the G (governance) area of ESG answering the question 'Do you have a waste management policy?' The data collected in this instance would be a clear 'yes' or 'no'. This gives the investor or reader no information on whether that policy is fit for purpose, or if it ranks as best practice versus other organizations in a similar field.

As this example illustrates, simply checking the relevant boxes will not suffice. As an organization's leader you need to demonstrate an engagement with the substance of the issues, and – again – this can best be done by adopting a principle of both internal and external transparency as a guiding orientation. 'Internal transparency' means being clear within the organization about how you're performing on these metrics and acknowledging where work may be required. External transparency means being straight with stakeholders about such issues.

The importance of reliable data cannot be overstated. ESG investors base their analyses on the pictures provided by the data. If the data is wrong, the picture is wrong, and everything that follows will be erroneous. Decisions based on poor raw data build up to irrelevant ESG scores, ESG benchmarks and incorrect portfolio disclosures to regulators, among other problems. This is why the quality of the raw data matters to investors.

As noted above, it is becoming increasingly common for investors to seek legal remedies when they feel they have been misled in respect of ESG data, so it is incumbent upon the organization to make every effort to ensure that the data it's using is reliable and fit for purpose.

A story from Chinese history illustrates the risks of cumulative data errors very clearly. In the early days of the People's Republic, there was great enthusiasm for national rejuvenation. Agricultural communes were given quotas to fill and were encouraged to exceed them. In their eagerness to show that the nation was succeeding, people exaggerated their crop yields slightly. From the very lowest level, all the way up through the bureaucracy, people inflated the data a tiny bit, to make the picture that little bit better.

On the basis of a single commune, this isn't a big deal. But when it occurred throughout the system, these slight errors contributed to massive misrepresentations of the situation in the silos. From 1957, the central government accordingly began to report huge super-abundances of grain – 50 billion pounds of grain, when the reality was about 12 billion pounds. Of course, decisions based on this misrepresentation were wildly out of step with reality.

The results were catastrophic, leading to the Great Famine of 1959–61, considered the worst famine in human history, and one of the worst human-made disasters ever. The event demonstrates the importance of reliable data collection, synthesis and management protocols, and indicates how easily things can go wrong.

Transparency should be seen as the superordinate virtue in the organization's approach to data-based ESG disclosures. Estimation, extrapolation and a given margin of error are not always terrible data points for the market. As noted previously, the legal and institutional frameworks for these kinds of disclosures are still developing, which means that organizations need to do a lot of their own work in deciding what to include, and how to include it. All such factors contribute to a certain fuzziness, which can easily give rise to conflicting interpretations.

The most reliable way to forestall misunderstandings is by being transparent about the kinds of parameters discussed earlier in this section. The organization needs to provide transparency by basing ESG disclosures on data, but also be transparent about what this data demonstrates, and what it does not. In doing so, the organization can be sure that its ESG disclosures represent a good faith attempt to engage substantively with the issues driving the concerns and reduce the risk of being accused of a cynical attempt to manipulate perceptions.

The following section provides four case studies of high-profile accusations of greenwashing against organizations. The first two, H&M and Enviva, represent cases of organizations being accused of misleading stakeholders about the green credentials of their products. The third, the French oil firm TotalEnergies, represents an accusation of greenwashing on the basis of company strategy and the explicit commitments entailed by it. Finally, the mining company Vale S.A. was accused of misleading investors through false disclosures about its investments and risks related to ESG factors.

The case studies illustrate the different forms such accusations can take, and the different aspects of organizational operations they can focus on: product or service; strategy and commitments; or disclosures of investments and risks. There are lessons for the organizational leader in all of them.

Case studies

CASE STUDY   H&M

In 2022, a class-action lawsuit was launched against the apparel company H&M for misleading and false sustainability marketing. The lawsuit focuses on H&M's 'Conscious Choice' range, which targets consumers who are willing to pay more for green clothing. H&M claim that each Conscious Choice product contains at least 50 per cent or more sustainable materials.

The lawsuit alleges that these figures are false. An article in *Quartz* magazine showed that H&M had allegedly exaggerated its clothing's green credentials, and in some cases may have used data that was demonstrably erroneous (Shendruk, 2022). A primary bone of contention has to do with whether shirts made from polyester created from recycled plastic bottles can be considered 'green'. As the lawsuit states:

> Basing sustainability strategies on the idea that consumers can continue to consume disposable plastic goods (because they can be recycled into more products) is highly problematic. This method of 'green' marketing does not address the fundamental issue of perpetuating disposable solutions and over-consumption of natural resources. Indeed, these strategies encourage consumers to buy more clothes or throw away garments sooner, in the belief they can be recycled in some magic machine.

This framing of the problem demonstrates the increasing levels of precision and transparency that are required in ESG disclosures. Stakeholders are becoming more and more critical of platitudes in this realm and demanding higher standards and accountability from organizations. As the SEC has noted, many organizations appear to have regarded ESG concerns primarily as a licence to print money, by making unsupported claims and using empty verbiage to exploit increasing public interest in sustainability.

H&M is one of a spate of recent lawsuits, however, that indicates that regulators, consumers and investors are becoming savvier, and that organizations may accordingly need to recalibrate their expectations in this regard.

The dangers of exaggerating green credentials are similarly demonstrated by a securities class-action lawsuit brought by a shareholder against a company called Enviva.

CASE STUDY   Enviva

Enviva builds and operates plants that produce wood products intended to substitute for coal in power generation. It presents itself as a 'growth-oriented' ESG company, on the basis of its activity in this area associated with pressing environmental concerns. In 2022, however, short-seller Blue Orca Capital published a scathing report of the company, stating: 'Ultimately, we think that any legitimate ESG investor or allocator should be embarrassed to own this stock' (Blue Orca Capital, 2022).

Enviva claims to be a pure-play ESG company. A particularly striking aspect of Blue Orca's analysis is that the greenwashing is taken to represent a liability in and of itself. The argument is not that greenwashing may be instrumental in generating negative outcomes through reputational damage, for example. Blue Orca's analysis instead shows that the presence of such greenwashing indicates a fundamental and systemic shortcoming in the conception and structure of the business itself.

Enviva's share price dropped more than 19 per cent following the report, and, soon after, a securities class-action lawsuit was filed against the company and certain directors and officers (Boughedda, 2022). The complaint alleges that the defendants made false and misleading statements regarding the company's business, operations and compliance policies – basically, that they engaged in greenwashing, as Blue Orca alleged. It must be emphasized that Enviva denies any wrongdoing, and that the legal ramifications are still being played out.

It is, however, notable that Enviva's own data played a crucial role in Blue Orca's assessment of the reliability of the company's claims:

> Hidden GPS data embedded in Enviva's Track and Trace disclosures allowed us to geolocate the Company's harvests. Satellite imagery indicates that contrary to the Company's claims, in many instances Enviva is procuring wood from the widely condemned practice of clear-cutting. (Blue Orca Capital, 2022)

This demonstrates, again, the importance of transparency, and reliable management of data and the disclosures based on it. It also highlights the growing sophistication of data sources and their application to a company's business. While this example from Enviva is a cautionary tale, the fact that geolocation data was used in assessing the company's claims shows the power of data if it is accurate and transparent. That same geolocation data could be an essential verification tool for positive action.

The examples of Enviva and H&M both show how product attributes can be greenwashed. But greenwashing can also occur in respect of organizational strategy and the commitments associated with it, as is shown by the case of France's largest energy company, TotalEnergies.

CASE STUDY   TotalEnergies

TotalEnergies was sued in March 2022 by a group of environmental organizations (Greenpeace France, Friends of the Earth France, Notre Affaire à Tous and ClientEarth). The plaintiffs allege that the company misled customers through its explicit commitment to meet net zero emissions by 2050, while simultaneously developing plans to produce more fossil fuel.

The action was brought under the terms of the European Unfair Consumer Practices Directive, which proscribes misleading advertising and statements intended to deceive consumers and other stakeholders. The environmental organizations bringing the action explained their reasoning thus:

> We are taking TotalEnergies to court today because it is using sly propaganda to try to convince us of the impossible: that carbon neutrality can be reached while producing and selling ever more fossil fuels when, in reality, our dependence on fossil fuels is driving up bills, wrecking our climate and funding war. Just as tobacco manufacturers misled people about the link between cigarettes and health, TotalEnergies's advertising acts as a smokescreen for the harm it is causing to the planet and the people. We need to protect consumers from disinformation PR strategies that leave them trying to tell fact from fiction and delay the urgent climate action we need.
> (Les Amis de la Terre, 2022)

The lawsuit was prompted by an extensive promotional campaign in which TotalEnergies emphasized its commitment to net zero. Notably, it occurred at the same time as executives from Exxon, Shell, BP and Chevron were called to testify to US Congress on their firms' campaigns to spread misinformation about fossil fuel-driven climate change.

Given that their stock in trade is probably the number one cause of climate change, it's not surprising that oil companies feature prominently in the list of organizations that have had adverse brushes with accusations of greenwashing. This appears to be driving increasingly desperate PR and marketing efforts, as the case of TotalEnergies demonstrates. But unfounded ESG claims can be more of a liability than the actions they're seeking to disguise, as a number of organizations discussed in this section demonstrate.

A third type of greenwashing allegation focuses on organizations' disclosures about their investments and risks related to ESG factors. The case of VW's emissions scandal falls into this category, as does that of the Brazilian mining company Vale S.A.

CASE STUDY   Vale S.A.

In April 2022, the SEC charged Vale S.A. with securities fraud, on the basis of the company's materially false and misleading statements regarding its 'commitment to sustainability', among other factors. The focus of the action was the collapse of a dam operated by the company in January 2019. The event caused the deaths of 270 people, and the release of 12 million cubic tonnes of toxic waste into the local water supply.

The SEC claimed that Vale knew about the risks of the dam but hid the information from safety auditors. Vale was also accused of misleading investors about the dam's safety (United States District Court, Eastern District of New York, 2022).

While Vale disputes the allegations, the events have already caused a $4 billion loss in market capitalization for the company, with many headaches still to come, as the legal proceedings begin to rake through the sensitive details of the firm's operations.

In conclusion, you need to watch out for greenwashing. Data can help, as long as you can stand by its veracity. In fact, data can be the proof you need to combat any greenwashing charges that come your organization's way. However, it is better to avoid any greenwashing charges at all rather than spend time and resources on justifying your organization's credibility.

You can do this by being mindful of the statements you make, and careful of the claims you put out into the public domain. This does not mean shying away from talking about the sustainability credentials of your business or your products and services. It does mean taking care not to overreach on your sustainability qualifications. No one likes a boaster. In terms of sustainability, boasting may become very costly.

References

Blue Orca Capital (2022) Report on Enviva Inc., SquareSpace, https://static1. squarespace.com/static/5a81b554be42d6b09e19fc09/t/6346b1258ad5f2402cf 6ad66/1665577256589/Blue+Orca+Short+Enviva+Inc+%28NYSE+EVA%29.pdf (archived at https://perma.cc/CT24-WTUC)

Boughedda, S (2022) Enviva Partners 'greenwashing its wood procurement' claims Blue Orca Capital, Investing.com, www.investing.com/news/stock-market-news/enviva-partners-greenwashing-its-wood-procurement-claims-blue-orca-capital-432SI-2910815 (archived at https://perma.cc/AZ4L-VH3T)

European Commission (2020) 2020 – sweep on misleading sustainability claims, https://commission.europa.eu/live-work-travel-eu/consumer-rights-and-complaints/enforcement-consumer-protection/sweeps_en#ref-2020--sweep-on-misleading-sustainability-claims (archived at https://perma.cc/9GF7-VL7D)

European Commission (2023) Proposal for a Directive of the European Parliament and of the Council on substantiation and communication of explicit environmental claims, https://eur-lex.europa.eu/legal-content/EN/TXT/?uri=COM%3A2023%3A0166%3AFIN (archived at https://perma.cc/65VR-6CDZ)

Les Amis de la Terre (2022) Environmental groups sue TotalEnergies for misleading the public over net zero, www.amisdelaterre.org/communique-presse/environmental-groups-sue-totalenergies-for-misleading-the-public-over-net-zero/ (archived at https://perma.cc/JQJ3-DHMP)

Shendruk, A (2022) *Quartz* investigation: H&M showed bogus environmental scores for its clothing, *Quartz*, https://qz.com/2180075/hm-showed-bogus-environmental-higg-index-scores-for-its-clothing (archived at https://perma.cc/2X5D-MJ3S)

United States District Court, Eastern District of New York (2022) Complaint, SEC v. Vale S.A. (No. 22-cv-2405), www.sec.gov/litigation/complaints/2022/comp-pr2022-72.pdf (archived at https://perma.cc/9HUU-KRF5)

Sustainability data in the modern board: KPIs and engagement

10

REFLECTIVE QUESTIONS

- What is the role of the board of directors in an organization's sustainability agenda?
- How do I contribute around the board or management table on ESG data topics?
- How do we set organizational key performance indicators (KPIs) for ESG data?
- What are the challenges and opportunities for a company to engage in ESG disclosures?

This book is focused on sustainability data. Data is increasingly a tool and a requirement for operating in the 21st century. It can be powerful for decision making. It can be expensive to collect and create. ESG data is both a friend and foe of the modern leadership team and board of directors.

In this chapter we will explore how you can engage with ESG data no matter what Sustainability Data Category you have assessed your organization to be today. ESG data can give you the opportunity to shape the external environment in which you work. Policy and standards do not spring magically from thin air. They are formed through active cooperation of organizational leaders such as yourself, often as they gather under umbrella associations, coalitions or working groups. We will explore some of these structures and how you can choose to participate later in this chapter.

As we have said throughout this book, data on sustainability topics is still developing. It is on a journey, and in your role as a business leader you have the chance to shape the path that sustainability data takes.

As we cover the board's role, KPI development and shaping the external environment, hopefully it will inspire you to take actions based on reliable data.

What's the role of the board of directors?

The board of directors holds a crucial responsibility in setting a company's strategic direction, and sustainability should be an integral part of that vision. By embracing sustainability, boards can create long-term value, mitigate risks, enhance reputation, and align their businesses with stakeholder expectations.

It is clearly in the board's purview to request decision-useful ESG data. To make informed decisions about sustainability targets, the board of directors should actively request and use ESG data from the business. This data includes information on environmental impacts, employee welfare, community engagement, diversity, and other relevant factors indicated by the sustainability use cases the organization prioritizes.

By obtaining comprehensive ESG data, boards can assess the company's current sustainability performance, identify areas for improvement, and set ambitious yet realistic targets.

According to Paul Polman, former CEO of Unilever, boards need to focus on long-term value creation in their companies, and to do so they should request the right ESG data in order to understand risks and opportunities (Polman and Winston, 2021). This highlights the importance of data-driven decision-making and the role of the board in obtaining accurate and relevant ESG information.

The need for boards to request decision-useful ESG data goes straight to the heart of the board of directors' purpose. Boards have a critical role in safeguarding strong governance and championing transparency. Robust governance structures and processes need to include sustainability topics – this has been abundantly proven in earlier chapters based on the ABCs of sustainability data use cases.

To do this effectively, boards need to ensure directors with relevant sustainability expertise are appointed to join the board. Establishing board committees dedicated to sustainability and regularly reviewing sustainability performance is also good stewardship of sustainability oversight.

Catherine Howarth, CEO of ShareAction, emphasizes the need for transparency and accountability. She has said that boards should make ESG considerations integral to their governance frameworks, ensuring transparency and accountability to shareholders. This underscores the role of the board in fostering a culture of transparency and actively engaging shareholders in sustainability matters.

The board plays a role in setting the organization's net zero targets and other pledges and commitments on sustainability. As we reviewed in Chapter 6, target-setting is a critical part of an organization's sustainability ambitions. As the world seeks to combat climate change, achieving net zero emissions has become a critical target for many companies. The board of directors plays a crucial role in agreeing to and overseeing the implementation of net zero targets. Even if your organization has chosen not to set targets yet, the board should be actively monitoring the market and the pros and cons of establishing realistic targets on a rolling basis.

Board commitments are critical in setting bold targets, including net zero emissions. Equally as critical is that boards hold management accountable for achieving these bold targets. The board is responsible for ensuring that sustainability targets align with the company's overall strategy and are supported by actionable plans and adequate resources.

The board of directors plays a role externally for the organization as well. The board members should be engaging with stakeholders to gain insights and ensure the alignment of sustainability targets with broader societal expectations. As we have stated many times in this book, this is a rapidly moving space. Ignorance is no defence, and board directors should be alive to the sustainability demands of external stakeholders. Stakeholder engagement helps boards identify key issues, build trust, and drive meaningful change.

According to Peter Bakker, President and CEO of the World Business Council for Sustainable Development, boards should actively engage stakeholders to better understand the sustainability context and enhance decision-making (Balch, 2023). Looking beyond the boardroom doors is essential.

Management and leaders

Organizational leaders are responsible for setting strategic vision and direction, even if they do not sit on the board of directors. Integrating sustainability into their vision is crucial. Incorporating sustainability into the organization needs to be based firmly in reality. The elements of this book should help to keep leaders grounded by understanding their current Sustainability Data Category, priority use cases and ambitions.

The desire to be a sustainable organization must be firmly rooted in the reality of where the organization is today on its ESG data journey. Leaders must champion sustainability as a core value and align it with the overall business strategy for sustainable outcomes (measured by ESG data) to be successful. By establishing sustainability targets, leaders provide a clear direction for the organization and inspire employees to embrace sustainable practices.

To facilitate informed decision-making on sustainability targets, leaders must ensure the availability and accessibility of ESG data to decision-makers, including the board of directors. This is an example of leaders managing up – and requesting the same from the managers and employees in their teams.

By establishing robust mechanisms to collect, aggregate and report ESG data, leaders can enable a whole-of-organization approach to achieving sustainability – whatever that means for their unique priority use cases. This can be achieved through regular monitoring, measurement and verification of sustainability metrics. The data should be accurate, reliable and comprehensive to enable effective analysis and decision-making. Leaders can instil this philosophy throughout the organization to promote success.

As we learned in Chapter 3, ESG data does not come from a single source within a business. Leaders should foster collaboration between departments within the organization to collect and report ESG data effectively. By involving key stakeholders and subject matter experts, leaders can ensure the accuracy and relevance of the information provided.

Not all data comes from within the organization, either. Leaders may also seek external expertise and partnerships to enhance their understanding of sustainability issues and best practices and to attain macro data to help make business decisions. They can collaborate with sustainability consultants, industry associations, NGOs and other external stakeholders to gain insights, benchmark performance and refine sustainability targets. Leveraging external expertise helps leaders stay informed about emerging trends, regulatory changes and stakeholder expectations.

Leaders should also integrate sustainability considerations into the organization's governance structure and decision-making processes. By establishing dedicated sustainability committees or task forces, leaders can facilitate the review and analysis of ESG data, enabling decision-makers to make informed choices aligned with sustainability goals.

Leaders should be ready to adopt recognized frameworks and standards for reporting ESG data, such as the International Sustainability Standards Board (ISSB), Global Reporting Initiative (GRI) or other regional- or industry-specific standards as they develop. There may be specific standards associated with regulatory or compliance requirements. It is the job of the organizational leader to be well aware of these requirements and mobilize resources as needed.

The data collected and reported against standards can and should be used for multiple purposes. Once you have robust, comparable, verifiable ESG data, it is the leader's role to see if it can help build efficiencies or promote the business positively. This is just good practice: write once, read many.

Sustainability monitoring and progress towards targets is not a static activity. It requires continuous improvement. Leaders must ensure that the ESG data provided to decision-makers evolves over time. Establishing a feedback loop that enables the identification of emerging sustainability risks and opportunities helps to plan for what additional data may be needed to make sound organizational decisions. By continuously monitoring and reporting on ESG performance, leaders can drive improvement and adjustment of sustainability targets as needed.

As we have seen in our deep dive on greenwashing, if an organization's leaders are not monitoring sustainability progress, statements and claims, other stakeholders may do it for them – and call out irregularities to the organization's potential detriment.

Setting ESG KPIs

As businesses increasingly recognize the importance of sustainability, setting clear and measurable key performance indicators (KPIs) becomes crucial. KPIs enable organizations to track their progress, identify areas for improvement, and align their efforts with ESG goals.

KPIs also bring back into focus what type of business you are. You may be a Competent Commentator in the Sustainability Data Category ranking, but that doesn't reflect what your underlying business does. The Sustainability Data Category only reflects your organization's ESG data maturity. It is the work you have done in Chapters 4, 5 and 6 that integrates your specific organization's priorities, which will be in part based on the industry and sector you are in.

For instance, a manufacturing company may prioritize reducing greenhouse gas (GHG) emissions (squarely an E metric), while a technology company may focus on data privacy and ethical sourcing (a decidedly S metric). The KPIs you set should be aligned with your business so that they are embraced by everyone in the organization. This helps make KPIs reviewed by the board everyone's priority because it makes sense to everyone in the organization as to why they are needed.

Turning back to specific ESG KPIs, here are some useful suggestions on measurable areas to consider.

Environmental KPIs

Environmental KPIs focus on reducing the company's impact on the planet and address its relationship to climate change. Examples of environmental KPIs include:

- **GHG emissions:** Frankly, it is impossible *not* to include GHG emissions in suggested KPIs. GHG emissions disclosures are the foundations of many of the pledges and agreements making up the global actions to tackle climate change. Tracking and reducing carbon emissions is crucial. KPIs can include Scope 1 (direct emissions), Scope 2 (indirect emissions from purchased energy) and Scope 3 (indirect emissions from the value chain) emissions. For example, setting a target to reduce Scope 1 emissions by 30 per cent within five years would need to be supported by ongoing updates on the GHG emissions KPI to your organization's leadership teams.

- **Energy consumption:** Monitoring energy usage and setting targets for renewable energy adoption and energy efficiency improvements can be game-changing for an organization as transition plans and targets gain momentum. For instance, aiming to source 50 per cent of energy from renewable sources by a specific year can reflect year-on-year progress to decrease carbon emissions.

- **Waste management:** Setting targets for waste reduction, recycling rates and promoting circular economy practices. A KPI could be to achieve zero waste to landfill by implementing effective recycling and waste management systems by a target date.

- **Water usage:** Tracking water consumption and setting targets to reduce water usage, implement water-saving technologies or improve water stewardship practices. Water is a scarce resource. This scarcity has impacts on climate and on biodiversity and nature. These impacts need to be measured and managed, and this topic is gaining in importance at the time of writing.

An example of a company implementing environmental KPIs is Unilever, a global consumer goods company. Unilever has set ambitious environmental targets, including achieving net zero emissions from its products by 2039, using 100 per cent renewable energy by 2030, and halving its environmental footprint by 2030.

Another example is Microsoft, a technology company, which has set KPIs including commitments to remove its historical carbon emissions and become carbon negative by 2030. The company also aims to be water positive by 2030, meaning it will replenish more water than it consumes in its operations.

Social KPIs

Social KPIs focus on promoting social equity, inclusivity, and positive impacts on communities and stakeholders. Examples of social KPIs include:

- **Employee wellbeing:** Measuring and improving employee satisfaction, diversity and inclusion, health and safety, and professional development opportunities. A related KPI could be to increase employee satisfaction scores by 15 per cent over a specific timeframe.

- **Community engagement:** Tracking and reporting on community investment, philanthropy, volunteer hours and initiatives that benefit local communities fall into this category. A KPI might involve investing a percentage of annual profits in community development projects.

- **Supply chain ethics:** Ensuring responsible sourcing, fair labour practices and supplier diversity. A KPI could involve increasing the percentage of suppliers adhering to sustainability standards or achieving specific certifications.

- **Human rights:** Monitoring and addressing human rights risks and impacts throughout the value chain, aiming to align with international human rights frameworks. Often this area is mandated by law and regulation, but it can also be set as a KPI to go above and beyond the minimum requirements, including providing education and training to other organizations in geographies where your business operates to raise standards worldwide.

How do I set a diversity and inclusion KPI?

Step one: Set targets for increasing diversity at all levels of the organization, including gender, ethnicity and age. These should be quantitative targets and can include qualitative attributes to make clear the intended goal. (E.g. 'We target 30 per cent representation of women in leadership positions by 2030.')

Step two: Monitor representation in leadership positions, aiming for proportional representation of underrepresented groups. Continually ensure your targets are the right ones for your organization.

Step three: Collect and calculate data on your KPI. Conduct regular diversity audits to identify any disparities or barriers and develop strategies to address them. In the example above regularly track the number of women in leadership positions in your organization. Make this data collection at least annual, but you may wish to share data quarterly or monthly depending on your targets and business size and shape.

Step four: Establish employee resource groups and mentorship programmes to support the development and advancement of underrepresented employees. Set up procedures to foster a fair and diverse hiring process. In the example above, this may be requirements on the proportion of women taken through the stages of a hiring process from longlists of candidates through to final stage interviews.

Step five: Assess your progress on your KPI regularly. Be prepared to course-correct if you are not seeing progress towards your goals. Celebrate success when it is achieved and continue to monitor the KPI to ensure it remains at the level the organization strives for.

Governance KPIs

Governance KPIs focus on transparency, accountability and ethical practices within the company. Examples of governance KPIs include:

- **Board diversity:** Tracking the diversity of the board of directors and setting targets for gender, ethnic and cultural diversity representation. A KPI might involve achieving a specified percentage of board members from diverse backgrounds within a certain timeframe.

- **Ethical business conduct:** Implementing robust anti-corruption policies, whistleblower mechanisms and codes of conduct. A KPI could be to achieve a specific score on ethical compliance audits.

- **Data privacy and cybersecurity:** Setting targets for data protection and cybersecurity measures, and ensuring compliance with privacy regulations.

- **Stakeholder engagement:** Developing processes to engage with stakeholders, such as shareholders, employees, customers and local communities. A KPI might involve conducting regular stakeholder satisfaction surveys and addressing identified concerns.

Setting KPIs for your organization sends a clear message that these metrics will be prioritized and tracked. Be sure to set deadlines for your goals so that you can monitor progress towards them and make changes to the actions you are taking as an organization to realign or accelerate where necessary.

KPIs can be internal metrics monitored by the leadership teams and board of directors. KPIs can also be made public or shared with specific external audiences. It is up to you as leaders what KPI goals, data and tracking remain internal and what you make public.

We have already reviewed in Chapter 6 some options for public KPIs – the setting of sustainability-related targets including net zero, carbon neutrality and alignment to the SDGs. These are big, meaty pledges that will register with your stakeholders. That does not mean that more specific, subtle or near-term KPIs are not valuable. They can be very valuable to external stakeholders to showcase your organization's priorities and the governance of them.

When and how should you get your ESG data verified?

As ESG considerations gain prominence in the business world, organizations are increasingly recognizing the importance of external verification of their ESG data. External verification provides stakeholders with assurance that an organization's ESG data is accurate, reliable, and in line with established standards and frameworks.

Organizations should consider seeking external verification of their ESG data in the following situations:

- **Materiality:** When ESG issues are deemed material to the organization's operations and have a significant impact on financial performance, reputation or stakeholder expectations, external verification helps ensure the accuracy and credibility of reported data.

- **Regulatory compliance:** If regulatory frameworks or reporting guidelines require or encourage external verification, organizations should adhere to these requirements to demonstrate compliance and enhance transparency. Note that the ISSB's standards encourage external assurances on data.

- **Stakeholder demand:** When stakeholders, including investors, customers and NGOs, demand independent assurance on an organization's ESG performance, seeking external verification can foster trust and confidence.

- **Benchmarking and comparisons:** Organizations aiming to benchmark their ESG performance against peers or industry standards may choose external verification to ensure consistency and comparability of reported data.

What verifications are required?

Different types of verification are available depending on the specific needs and objectives of the organization. The commonly sought verifications include:

- **Independent verification:** This process involves an independent assessment of an organization's ESG data, ensuring that it aligns with specified standards, frameworks or reporting guidelines. Verification typically focuses on accuracy, completeness, relevance, and reliability of the reported data.

- **Assurance:** Assurance engagements go beyond verification by also evaluating the processes, systems and controls in place to collect, manage and report ESG data. Assurance provides a higher level of confidence in the reliability and robustness of the organization's ESG data.

- **Audit:** An ESG audit is a comprehensive review of an organization's ESG performance and reporting, examining the accuracy, consistency and compliance of data. It involves an in-depth examination of systems, processes and evidence to support the reported ESG information.

The terminology used may vary across jurisdictions and contexts, but these terms are generally accepted and used interchangeably to describe the work conducted.

Who conducts verifications?

External verifications are conducted by independent third-party organizations that possess the necessary expertise and qualifications. These entities include:

- **Accounting firms:** Established accounting firms often have specialized sustainability and ESG services teams that conduct external verifications. These firms leverage their expertise in financial audits to perform ESG verifications.

- **Sustainability consultancies:** Specialized sustainability consultancies offer verification services as part of their broader sustainability and ESG consulting offerings. They bring sector-specific knowledge and experience in assessing ESG performance.

- **Certification bodies:** Certain certification bodies specialize in verifying and certifying specific sustainability standards or labels, such as ISO 14001 (environmental management) or B Corp certification. These organizations conduct verifications based on specific frameworks or standards.

- **Non-profit organizations:** Some non-profit organizations provide external verification services to validate ESG data against their own frameworks or standards. These organizations often focus on specific sustainability issues or sectors.

Several well-established companies offer external verification services globally. These include the 'Big Four' accounting firms, some specialists such as ERM (Environmental Resources Management) and other players that focus on a single or multiple territories. These companies have extensive experience in conducting audits, verifications and assurance engagements across various industries and sectors.

External verification of ESG data is a practice that enhances the credibility, reliability and transparency of an organization's sustainability reporting. Seeking external verification provides assurance to stakeholders, validates compliance with reporting standards, and enables benchmarking against industry peers. Organizations should consider engaging independent verification entities to conduct the verifications.

The terminology used for this work includes 'verification', 'assurance' and 'audit', the meanings of which vary based on the specific engagement.

By embracing external verification, organizations can demonstrate their commitment to robust ESG practices and strengthen stakeholder trust in their sustainability performance.

What about the costs?

The average costs of verification, assurance and audit of ESG data can vary significantly depending on several factors, including the scope and complexity of the engagement, the size and industry of the organization, the geographical location, and the chosen verification entity. It is important to note that these costs are subject to market dynamics, competition, and the specific requirements of each engagement. Consequently, it is challenging to provide precise average costs. However, the following estimates can serve as general guidelines.

Verification costs

The costs of ESG data verification typically range from $10,000 to $50,000 or more, depending on the organization's size and complexity. Smaller organizations with less extensive ESG reporting requirements might fall on the lower end of the range, while larger organizations with complex operations and extensive reporting might face higher costs.

Additionally, engaging a reputable accounting firm or specialized sustainability consultancy might result in higher costs compared to other verification entities.

Assurance costs

The costs of ESG data assurance engagements are generally higher than for verification due to the broader scope of work involved. Assurance costs can range from \$30,000 to \$100,000 or more, depending on the organization's size, complexity, and the level of assurance required. The costs can also vary based on the thoroughness of the assurance process, the depth of data and process evaluation and the expertise of the assurance provider.

Audit costs

ESG data audits typically involve the most comprehensive and in-depth assessment, covering both the accuracy of the reported data and the underlying processes and controls. As a result, audit costs tend to be higher than verification and assurance. Audit costs can range from \$50,000 to several hundred thousand dollars, depending on the scale, complexity and geographic presence of the organization. Factors such as the number of sites, subsidiaries and reporting boundaries may impact the final cost of the audit.

It is essential for organizations to engage in discussions with potential verification, assurance or audit providers to obtain detailed cost estimates tailored to their specific requirements. The costs can vary significantly based on individual circumstances, and it is advisable to consider the value and benefits derived from the engagement rather than focusing solely on the cost.

Your organization's role in sustainability forums

We have discussed the role of sustainability in your organization from the perspective of your organization as a supplier of ESG data. You have a base of knowledge on where to find data from your operations and how to disclose it internally and externally.

Now we can flip that thinking on its head: how does your organization fit into the sustainability agenda more widely? I like to consider this question through three different intersecting lenses: CSR, product and policy.

Corporate social responsibility (CSR) is a phrase I have tried to avoid using in this book. The reality is that sustainability and ESG data influences the core activities of an organization and the use cases for ESG data go to the heart of a business's priorities. Often CSR matters are considered to be optional. I hope the ABCs of sustainability data use cases have compelled you as a leader to agree that sustainability is a necessity, and not a nice to have.

Figure 10.1   How your organization can fit into the sustainability agenda

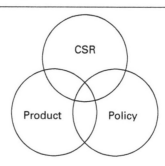

With that being said, CSR through the lens of how your organization can influence the outside world can be compelling. If you think about how your industry or sector impacts the environment and society it is working in, you would certainly prefer that impact to be positive. In which case, how can your actions as an organizational leader inspire other organizations and individuals in your industry, sector or geography to want to make a positive impact too?

By walking the walk on best practices in sustainable topics such as environmental protection, social welfare, human rights, transparency in business practices, etc, you can influence those around you. This can not only yield positive societal results by lifting standards for everyone, but it can positively influence the image of your organization. You may be seen as a leader, as a group that sets a high bar for engagement or that is genuinely interested in the market and environment it works in. This can build goodwill – from external and internal stakeholders.

The product circle in Figure 10.1 refers to how your product and output can influence the environment you work in. We have talked a lot about ESG data and disclosures at the corporate level, but there exists the opportunity to reflect sustainability priorities at the product level. We touched on this in Chapter 7 through a regulatory lens.

Your organization could be leading the way in recycling or waste management of the product you produce throughout its life cycle. It could be ensuring the services you offer are accessible by all through a robust design and policy regime taking into account all of society with the full range of abilities. It could be very technical – embracing product-level environmental metric tracking to allow for accurate ecolabelling and comparison of products on a sustainability scale.

All of these efforts help you as an organization influence the world around you. These actions can showcase your team and business as a leader and inspire others in the market to raise their standards.

Engaging in the formation and evolution of policy is another way that your organization can influence the market and economy you work in. The 'policy' circle in Figure 10.1 is very active at the time of writing. You heard a lot about this in Chapters 7 and 8. It is definitely a route to your organization making an impact on the wider world should you get involved in shaping that policymaking.

No matter where you are on the ESG Data Maturity Journey, you can find opportunities to influence the policy being developed, the detail for your industry, or how policies are implemented as they roll out. A particular opportunity if you are an Expert Educator is to push the boundaries of sustainability data policy and explore areas that would benefit from inclusion in ESG data collection and review in the future. One such area may be data that can measure and manage an organization's influence on biodiversity and nature.

How can my organization get involved in influencing sustainability policy?

By actively participating in shaping regulatory frameworks, engaging with policymakers, and offering their own experiences through case studies, organizations can contribute to the development of robust and effective sustainability data policies. Here are some effective strategies for companies to exert influence:

1 **Advocacy and lobbying:** Companies can engage in advocacy efforts by actively voicing their opinions and recommendations to policymakers and regulatory bodies. This can involve participating in public consultations, attending hearings and meeting with policymakers to discuss specific issues and propose sustainable finance policies aligned with their business interests and sustainability goals. Lobbying efforts can include sharing research, data and economic analysis that support the adoption of specific policies.

2 **Participation in industry associations and alliances:** Companies can join industry associations and alliances that focus on sustainable finance to collectively advocate for policy changes. By aligning with like-minded organizations, companies can amplify their influence and contribute to shaping policies that promote sustainability. These associations often have established relationships with policymakers and can provide a platform for companies to have their voices heard.

3 Collaboration and partnerships: Companies can collaborate with other stakeholders, including NGOs, academic institutions and other businesses, to influence sustainable finance policymaking. Partnerships can involve joint research projects, sharing best practices, and collectively advocating for specific policy reforms. By pooling resources and expertise, companies can present a united front and have a stronger impact on shaping policies.

4 Thought leadership and expertise sharing: Companies can establish themselves as thought leaders in sustainable finance by sharing their expertise and knowledge. This can be done through publishing research papers, contributing to industry reports, speaking at conferences and participating in panel discussions. By positioning themselves as experts, companies can influence policy discussions and shape the narrative around sustainable finance.

5 Voluntary commitments and self-regulation: Companies can take the initiative to adopt sustainable practices voluntarily and implement self-regulatory measures. By setting ambitious sustainability goals, implementing transparent reporting mechanisms and disclosing ESG data, companies can demonstrate the feasibility and benefits of sustainable finance. Such actions can influence policymakers by showcasing the effectiveness of voluntary measures, potentially leading to the adoption of similar practices as regulatory requirements.

6 Engaging with international standards and frameworks: Companies can actively engage with international standards and frameworks related to sustainable finance, such as the United Nations Sustainable Development Goals (SDGs), the GRI and the Task Force on Climate-related Financial Disclosures (TCFD). By aligning their practices with recognized global standards, companies can demonstrate their commitment to sustainability and encourage policymakers to integrate these standards into regulations.

7 Investor engagement: Companies can leverage their relationships with investors to influence sustainable finance policymaking. Institutional investors are increasingly considering ESG factors in their investment decisions, and companies can engage with these investors to advocate for stronger sustainability regulations. By providing investors with transparent and reliable ESG data, companies can drive demand for more robust regulations and standards.

8 Piloting and case studies: Companies can undertake pilot projects and share case studies that demonstrate the positive outcomes of sustainable finance practices. By showcasing the economic and environmental benefits achieved through these initiatives, companies can influence policymakers by providing real-world examples of the effectiveness of sustainable finance policies.

You may not have considered influencing sustainability data policy or the sustainability agenda for your industry before. Hopefully, you now have the inspiration to consider where you can contribute. The byproduct of offering your viewpoints is that you will learn from others around you. This is knowledge you can bring back to your own organization to improve everyone's understanding of the ESG agenda.

Some associations, organizations and NGOs to consider engaging with to influence sustainable finance policy globally:

- United Nations Environment Programme Finance Initiative (UNEP FI)
- Global Reporting Initiative (GRI)
- Principles for Responsible Investment (PRI)
- Sustainability Accounting Standards Board (SASB)
- International Integrated Reporting Council (IIRC)
- CDP (Carbon Disclosure Project)
- Climate Bonds Initiative (CBI)
- Climate Action 100+
- Sustainable Markets Initiative
- GFANZ (Glasgow Financial Alliance for Net Zero)
- Task Force on Climate-related Financial Disclosures (TCFD)
- European Sustainable Investment Forum (Eurosif)
- Asian Sustainable Investment Network (ASIN)
- Sustainable Finance Network Asia (SFNA)
- Ceres
- Social Venture Network (SVN)
- World Economic Forum (WEF)

- We Mean Business Coalition
- Global Impact Investing Network (GIIN)
- Responsible Investment Association Australasia (RIAA)
- Sustainable Finance Geneva (SFG)
- UK Sustainable Investment and Finance Association (UKSIF)
- Interfaith Center on Corporate Responsibility (ICCR)
- United Nations Race to Zero campaign
- American Sustainable Business Council (ASBC)

Some associations and groups are industry agnostic, some are geared to drill down on specific sectors or areas of the economy. Some are global, and some are regional or local. You have endless choices to get more involved as a leader, as a management team or as an organization.

What could I offer more widely to the market? Your organization as a case study

Organizations can bolster their influence by offering case studies that highlight their journey towards collecting and disclosing ESG data. These case studies provide real-world examples of how organizations have implemented sustainability practices, tackled challenges and improved their ESG performance.

Sharing such experiences not only enhances transparency but also provides valuable insights for policymakers and regulators when formulating data policies. By demonstrating the benefits and impacts of ESG data disclosure, organizations can contribute to the wider adoption and refinement of sustainable finance policies.

The modern board of directors and leadership have a duty to include sustainability considerations in the management and governance of their organizations. Your role as a leader is to clearly and transparently decide what the organization needs to measure and what data needs to be collected, so that decisions can be made taking sustainability into account. As we have learned in this chapter, the data can be used internally and externally. KPIs are a useful tool to align your whole organization with your sustainability goals.

The decisions you make will be influenced by your ESG data maturity as captured by your Sustainability Data Category developed in Chapter 4. Decisions you take will also logically be influenced by your corporate ambitions for engaging in the sustainability agenda – an element you reviewed in Chapter 6.

Pulling all this knowledge together should help you to not only scope what data you need to make decisions, but how you decide to verify and audit that data to build robust transparency and build positive momentum on the three Cs of good data and mitigate the three Es of bad data that we learned about in Chapter 3. You can also choose to take steps to influence the wider market through external engagements.

You are now well placed to implement your knowledge to raise the bar for measuring and managing your organization's sustainability risks and opportunities. The learning you are doing about ESG data will set you up well as this topic continues to grow and evolve in the years to come.

References

Balch, O (2023) Meet the sustainability champion who converts fellow CEOs to the cause, Raconteur, www.raconteur.net/climate-crisis/meet-the-sustainability-champion-who-converts-fellow-ceos-to-the-cause (archived at https://perma.cc/ARC9-SU27)

Polman, P and Winston, A (2021) Net Positive: How courageous companies thrive by giving more than they take, Boston, MA: Harvard Business Review Press

Conclusion
Future-proofing with sustainability data

REFLECTIVE QUESTIONS

- What actions should I prioritize for my organization's sustainability data journey?
- How do I embed the value of ESG within my organization to match our priority use cases?
- What are my next steps?

We launched the Future of Sustainable Data Alliance (FoSDA) in 2020 at the World Economic Forum meetings in Davos. This annual jamboree of the world's business and political leaders was talking only about the challenges of climate change that year. However, discussions about *data* needed to measure and manage the crisis were few and far between. The ESG data 'industry' was still in its infancy. Since then, the number of data points that can fall under the Sustainability Data Category have proliferated. In 2023, at the time of writing, sustainability data disclosures are top of the agenda.

One of the first goals of FoSDA was to promote the importance of ESG data in sustainable finance policymaking and investment decision-making. At the time FoSDA was founded, there was a huge amount of great work being done on frameworks and principles for the financial community to align with global sustainability goals such as the Paris Agreement and net zero pledges.

However, there was less activity in the more granular step below these frameworks and principles to identify the specific datasets required to uphold the good work being done at the higher level.

As data for sustainable finance has become more mainstream, so too have the number of specific datasets linked to E, S and G. It has become a data tsunami with different players in the value chain requiring and defining different datasets. Like the Nespresso coffee pod inventor who had some regrets following the success of his invention due to the negative environmental footprint the used pods have on our planet, I sometimes worry that sustainability data has been too prolific. Or perhaps it has become a central topic too quickly.

Success in raising the profile of data has put it higher on the agenda, but still without the specificity needed to harness the power of that data easily and effectively. More data is never a bad thing in my opinion, but ensuring there is a focus on the data that really matters to a sustainable future is important.

Building up the density in datasets that lead to impact should be the most important goal for sustainable reporting. And that is where you come in. As a leader, you have the influence to embed ESG data into the DNA of your organization. Hopefully from the evidence in this book you will agree that ESG data is not only for measuring and mapping doing good for people and planet. Perhaps that is the highest-level benefit, but sometimes we need a reason to act that is closer to home.

The reasons to make ESG data a priority for your organization rest in the ABCs of sustainability data use cases. No matter if you prioritize access to capital, business growth and efficiencies or compliance and regulation – or all three! – these use cases live at the core of your business's success.

It is pointless for you to advocate for your organization to become prolific at publicly reporting ESG data if you are starting from a position where your data collection today is minimal. That's why our work in mapping your organization to the ESG Data Maturity Journey and determining your Sustainability Data Category is foundational work for you and your organization.

Your standing today as an ESG Data Debutant, ESG Competent Commentator, ESG Proficient Producer, ESG Skilful Services or ESG Expert Educator gives you a snapshot of your reality today. All the categories give you opportunity to build on what you have. It may be that you are exactly where you want to be. There is no wrong answer – only one that reflects your organization's ambitions. Your category needs to be fit for purpose for your unique organization in the geographies where you work, and with the stakeholders that influence your success.

It may be useful to make a list of activities for you as a leader to progress through as you continue your journey with ESG data for your organization. Personally, I am a big fan of lists. In my opinion, the best list is one that once you have completed writing it you can cross something off immediately (I regularly make lists with the first item being 'make a list').

Here's a list for your organization's journey with ESG data:

1 Assess your current sustainability data maturity, data use case priorities and ambitions for the future: You have already done this by working through the MUD process in Chapters 4, 5, 6 and 7.

2 Commit to setting science-based targets that align with limiting global warming to well below 2°C above pre-industrial levels. These targets should cover both direct and indirect emissions associated with the organization's activities.

3 Ensure you are aware of the regulatory requirements you face today and tomorrow: In collaboration with your colleagues, you may need to assess the current state of play for your voluntary and mandated sustainability data disclosures. Do some horizon scanning to assess where you may be in scope in the years to come.

4 Analyse the organization's long-term strategy and assess its alignment with climate goals. This may involve developing scenarios to understand different climate-related futures and how they may impact the organization.

5 Integrate climate considerations into the organization's governance structures and decision-making processes. Build KPIs into your objectives around your top tables. This may involve creating a dedicated sustainability committee or assigning climate-related responsibilities to existing committees.

6 Enhance ESG data collection and reporting, and develop a robust framework for tracking and reporting climate-related metrics. These may include GHG emissions, energy consumption, water usage and other relevant indicators that support your targets, strategy and key performance indicators (KPIs).

7 Collaborate with supply chain partners to assess and address climate risks collectively. Encourage suppliers to adopt sustainable practices and disclose relevant climate-related information.

8 Involve employees in climate-related initiatives and provide training to increase awareness and understanding of climate risks and opportunities. Be clear about the data that needed to make sustainability-aligned decisions at all levels of the organization.

9 Explore opportunities for innovation and investment in sustainable technologies and practices. Embrace renewable energy sources and explore circular economy models. Be curious about carbon credits and offsets and their responsible use in transition.

10 Get involved in shaping the future. Use your knowledge – at all levels – to be externally engaged to help shape policy and data disclosure requirements on ESG topics including new areas such as nature and biodiversity, impact, adaptation and resilience.

Hopefully this list helps you on your path forward in embracing sustainability data for your organization. Without data, we have little guidance on how we as people and entities are doing against our plans. This is an obvious statement to any leader. But it is worth making again with reference to ESG data.

As stated up-front, data disclosures from entities to the public on their sustainability metrics is work in progress. We don't have all the data we need or want – as leaders, as employees, as investors, as regulators, as humans. But we are getting there, and your attention to improving data density and quality helps the journey.

It may sound geeky, but I truly believe data is an essential part of the solution to climate change. It seems obvious to me that we need to make changes to our behaviours at all levels of the economy to limit global warming and transition to a world that uses less fossil fuels in favour of renewable energy sources.

This is why collecting, calculating and disclosing your organization's GHG emissions is so essential. This single metric can help us guide our actions globally. It also helps to make the link between our day-to-day lives and businesses and the total carbon emissions that are affecting the atmosphere.

We all sometimes feel like a tiny cog in an enormous wheel. It may be that this feeling leads us to ignore the little actions we can take to minimize the carbon footprint we have control over – be that personal or at the organizational level. This is all very normal and human. It is also costing us precious time.

By embracing the numbers – the data – that show that all the little emissions every one of our organizations produce are the building blocks that make up the global whole, we can hopefully accept the part we play in both the problem and the solution. Data helps us navigate this.

Let's call out a truth about ESG data: it can be depressing. The Intergovernmental Panel on Climate Change data is difficult reading at the most macro level. We may discover uncomfortable data from our organization's collection of data points – be they environmental, social or governance related.

Depressing as it may be, there is also the opportunity for the data to pleasantly surprise us. It may turn out your organization is top of its class in certain sustainability categories. It may be that even a few years ago your data was not something to be proud of, but through implementing strategic transition plans, your data is showing improvement. The trend in the data itself is worth celebrating. It may be exactly the message your team – and future top talent – needs to see.

Don't be afraid of sharing your sustainability data today, even if it is not painting the picture you would like to show yet. So long as you have a plan for improvement and you contextualize the data in your industry, sector, product category or geography, your data is valuable. At the very least, sharing your ESG data builds transparency. The value of transparency as we all work towards a climate solution is invaluable.

There is no doubt that sustainability data will continue to be an important part of organizational leadership for many years to come. Hopefully after reading this book you feel better equipped to navigate ESG data for your organization and to use it at the core of your business priorities. It can set your organization up for success. And it helps to support our common goal of working to mitigate the effects of climate change.

Sustainability data is your tool to future-proof your organization. Use it well.

INDEX

The index is filed in alphabetical, word-by-word order. Numbers in main headings are filed as spelt out in full; excepting COP sessions and numbers for Article funds, Global Green Finance Index, Scope emissions and SDGs, which are filed in chronological order. Acronyms and 'Mc' are filed as presented. Page locators in *italics* denote information contained within a Table or Figure.

Looking for another book?

Explore our award-winning
books from global business
experts in Business Strategy

Scan the code to browse

www.koganpage.com/business-
strategy

Printed in the USA
CPSIA information can be obtained
at www.ICGtesting.com
JSHW071029210124
55669JS00016B/30

9 781398 612242